Public Attitudes toward Immigration in the United States, France, and Germany

Public Attitudes toward Immigration in the United States, France, and Germany explores the causes of public opposition to immigration and support for anti-immigrant political movements in the three industrialized Western countries. Combining sophisticated modeling of recent public-opinion data with analysis of the past 110 years of these nations' immigration history, the book evaluates the effects of cultural marginality, economic self-interest, and contact with immigrants. Though analysis partly confirms a role for each of these three explanations for opposition to immigrants, the author concludes that being a cultural outsider usually drives immigration-related attitudes more than economics or contact does.

Professor Joel S. Fetzer teaches West European politics and international relations at Central Michigan University. Professor Fetzer's research has been funded by the MacArthur Foundation, the Friedrich Ebert Foundation, the U.S. Institute of Peace, and the Yale Center for International and Area Studies. His main areas of investigation are comparative immigration politics, and religion and political behavior, and he has published articles on these topics in various journals and edited volumes.

Public Attitudes toward Immigration in the United States, France, and Germany

WITHDRAWN

JOEL S. FETZER
Central Michigan University

CAMBRIDGE
UNIVERSITY PRESS

PUBLISHED BY THE PRESS SYNDICATE OF THE UNIVERSITY OF CAMBRIDGE
The Pitt Building, Trumpington Street, Cambridge, United Kingdom

CAMBRIDGE UNIVERSITY PRESS
The Edinburgh Building, Cambridge CB2 2RU, UK   http://www.cup.cam.ac.uk
40 West 20th Street, New York, NY 10011-4211, USA   http://www.cup.org
10 Stamford Road, Oakleigh, Melbourne 3166, Australia
Ruiz de Alarcón 13, 28014 Madrid, Spain

© Joel S. Fetzer 2000

First published 2000

Printed in the United States of America

Typeface Janson Text Roman 10.25/13 pt.   *System* QuarkXPress [BTS]

A catalog record for this book is available from the British Library.

Library of Congress Cataloging in Publication data

Fetzer, Joel S.
  Public attitudes toward immigration in the United States, France, and Germany /
Joel S. Fetzer.
      p.   cm.
  Includes bibliographical references and index.
  ISBN 0-521-78149-3 (hb) – ISBN 0-521-78679-7 (pb)
      1. United States – Emigration and immigration – Public opinion.   2. France –
  Emigration and immigration – Public opinion.   3. Germany – Emigration and
  immigration – Public opinion.   4. Public opinion – United States.   5. Public
  opinion – France.   6. Public opinion – Germany.   I. Title.
  JV6455 .F47   2000
  325′.1 – dc21
                                                                99-059173

ISBN 0 521 78149 3   hardback
ISBN 0 521 78679 7   paperback

Dedicated with love and gratitude to my parents,
Joan Gloria Foreman Fetzer and Carl Frederick Fetzer,
and in memory of my "new immigrant" great-grandfather,
Фёодор Александрович Симов (Feodor Aleksandrovich Simov)

Contents

Figures and Tables

Figures

Tables

Acknowledgments

This study had its origins in a 1996 dissertation in political science at Yale University. For making this book what it is I owe my greatest debt of gratitude to my chair, Martin Gilens. Very sincere thanks also go to the other members of my committee, David Cameron, Donald P. Green, and Bruce Russett, for reading numerous drafts and performing such other "advisory" chores as writing countless letters of recommendation. Several other members of the Yale faculty, especially William Foltz, David Lumsdaine, and Rogers Smith, gave me valuable advice at the theory-building stage and/or during revisions, and former graduate-student colleagues Deborah Guber, Soo Yeon Kim, and Eric Schickler helped me out of various methodological and/or computer jams.

Although he might not share all of my views on immigration, I am very much intellectually indebted to Jeremy Rabkin of Cornell University. Professor Rabkin taught me to think of politics as a struggle between good and evil in which what is good is often unpopular. By advising me not to "yield to [the] temptation" of pursuing a life of crime in the law, he also steered me (correctly) toward an academic career.

The extensive travel and analysis needed for this book would never have been possible without substantial financial help from several sources. A Jacob Javits Fellowship from the U.S. Department of Education funded the preliminary planning of this research. A Foreign Languages and Area Studies Fellowship from this same source also paid for a summer of language study and research in Germany. Two MacArthur Foundation Fellowships in International Security Studies funded a pair of research trips to France. The Yale Center for International and Area Studies granted me a dissertation fellowship for field work in Europe. The Friedrich Ebert Foundation of Bonn, Germany, allowed me to conduct research for five months in Mannheim and to participate in several policy seminars in Bonn. A Peace Scholar Fellowship from the U.S. Institute of Peace permitted me to finish writing the dissertation. Yale Graduate School awarded me a dissertation-year fellowship which also greatly aided me during the last year of dissertation writing. The Center for International Studies at the University of Southern California financed an additional year of revisions. Responsibility for the analysis and interpretations in this book, however, rests solely with the author.

Several institutes proved gracious hosts during my field work abroad. The Zentrum für Umfragen, Methoden und Analysen (ZUMA) in Mannheim provided me with an office and computer facilities for the winter semester of 1995. All of my *Mitarbeiter* there went out of their way to make this *Ausländer* feel at home in *Deutschland*. But I owe a special *herzlichen Dank* to my advisor at ZUMA, Rolf Porst, for arranging the logistics of my stay and showing me around the German survey-research scene. On the other side of the Rhine, Jacqueline Hecht and her colleagues at the Institut national d'études démographiques (INED) in Paris guided me to the right French libraries (the most important of which was INED's) and archives and put me in touch with many historians and social scientists specializing in French immigration. Finally, Klaus J. Bade of the Institut für Migrationsforschung und Interkulturelle Studien (IMIS) at the Universität Osnabrück allowed me to present an early version of Chapter 4 to participants in his research seminar on German migration history. The comments I received from him and his students proved invaluable.

Transforming the rather unpolished and unwieldy dissertation into a book manuscript largely occurred during a year as Visiting Scholar at the Center for International Studies at the University of Southern California. I would particularly like to thank the center's director, Laurie Brand, for being exceptionally helpful and advising me at critical stages of my academic career. I also greatly benefited from the academic and technical expertise of Mara Bird, Michaela Dabringhausen, Amy Gurowitz, Jeff Knopf, Abraham Lowenthal, Marisela Schaffer, Claude Williams, and Geoffrey Wiseman.

The research in this book is very data-intensive and would never have been possible without the assistance of data archives and archivists in all three countries. In New Haven, JoAnn Dionne, formerly of Yale's Social Science Data Archive, tracked down and ordered a seemingly endless number of American and European surveys on immigration for me. Horst Weinen of the Zentralarchiv für Empirische Sozialforschung at the Universität zu Köln provided me with an equivalent quantity of German immigration polls during my two visits to Cologne and even tolerated my offenses against *die schöne deutsche Sprache*. Finally, Bruno Cautrès, Daniel Masson, and Danielle Hermitan of the Banque de Données Socio-Politiques at the Institut d'Études Politiques de Grenoble generously supplied me with relevant French data during my visit to Grenoble and afterward.

Besides the scholars already mentioned, several researchers reviewed drafts of parts of this book and gave me valuable suggestions for improvement. In particular, I would like to thank Roger Daniels, Jürgen Falter, Ulrich Herbert, Nonna Mayer, and Patrick Weil. Yvan Gastault, Amy Gurowitz, Jürgen H. P. Hoffmeyer-Zlotnik, and Catherine Wihtol de Wenden also provided crucial insights into their areas of expertise.

At Pepperdine University and later Central Michigan University, my chairs and colleagues have proved wonderfully collegial and tolerant. Special thanks go to Joyce Baugh, Dan Caldwell, Stephen Monsma, and Chris Soper for helping keep me employed, well funded, and saner than might otherwise have been the case. At CMU, furthermore, Gretchen Carnes, Bernd Sprenzel, Ana Aguilar, Sara Spencer, and Heather Venzke greatly helped with final copyediting and cite-checking.

Alex Holzman of Cambridge University Press deserves special thanks for guiding me through the production process and deciding to take on this rather bulky manuscript in the first place. I am also grateful to his assistant, Alissa Morris, for helping out with various publication-related details, to Cambridge's two anonymous reviewers for very useful suggestions for revision, and to Brian R. MacDonald for exemplary copyediting.

Portions of this book have appeared elsewhere previously and are used with permission. Parts of Chapters 6, 7, and 8 formed the basis for the articles "Religious Minorities and Support for Immigrant Rights in the United States, France, and Germany" in the *Journal for the Scientific Study of Religion* (© 1998 by *JSSR*) and "Economic Self-

Interest or Cultural Marginality? Anti-Immigration Sentiment and Nativist Political Movements in France, Germany and the USA" in the *Journal of Ethnic and Migration Studies* (© 2000 by Taylor & Francis Ltd.). Some data in Tables A1.2 and A1.5 were likewise originally published in Pierre Villa's *Une analyse macroéconomique de la France au XXe siècle* (© 1993 by CNRS éditions of Paris, France), SOFRES's *L'état de l'opinion: Clés pour 1989* (© 1989 by *Éditions du Seuil*), and in various issues of *Le Figaro Magazine* (© 1988–1998 by *Le Figaro Magazine*).

At a more personal level, various relatives, friends, and communities of faith have supported me with their concern, prayers, and encouragement during the past eight years. My parents unfailingly displayed their love at all stages of my research and didn't mind flying over to Europe every now and then to make sure I was still OK. My friends from Yale Graduate Christian Fellowship and the Yale Baptist Student Union, in particular David Lumsdaine, Dale Peterson, and William Vance, were constantly encouraging me and lifting me up in prayer as I drifted from one crisis to another. Stan Moore, Roberto Jiménez, and their families kept me from feeling like an East Coast exile during my two years in Los Angeles. Finally, I am very grateful for the love and support shown by *mis hermanos y hermanas* at Iglesia Evangélica Bethel and Fiesta de Alabanza and by the Mennonite communities of Ludwigshafen, Châtenay-Malabry, Northern Virginia, and Saginaw.

ואהבת את יהוה אלהיך בכל־לבבך

1

Marginality, Economic Self-Interest, and Contact

In this society, will the present majority peaceably hand over its political power to a group that is simply more fertile? Can *homo contraceptivus* compete with *homo progenitivo* if our borders aren't controlled? . . . Perhaps this is the first instance in which those with their pants up are going to get caught by those with their pants down. As whites see their power and control over their lives declining, will they simply go quietly into the night? Or will there be an explosion?

       U.S. English cofounder John Tanton, in Daniels (1990:399)

The French have had enough of watching the dregs of North Africa invade the country, of watching herds of Algerians roam the large cities just looking to commit a crime. The French have had enough of encountering vermin, vice, and syphilis.

       French reader of the *Nouvel Observateur*, in Gastault (1993)

Udo to me (Ali): How many Turks will fit in a VW?
Me (Ali): Don't know.
Udo: Twenty thousand. Don't believe it?
Me (Ali): Whatever you say.
Udo: You wanna know, anyhow?
Me (Ali): I'd rather not.
Udo: Very simple. Two in the front, two in the back, the others in
   the ashtray.

       German industrial worker, in Wallraff (1985:111)

Over the past two decades, immigration has come to dominate the internal politics of western Europe and, to a lesser extent, the United

States. Explicitly anti-immigrant political parties such as the French Front national have attracted alarmingly large proportions of the European electorate, while in the United States such arguably nativist movements as those espousing Official English and Proposition 187 have won resounding victories in many state referenda. Public debates over the "multiculturalism" brought on by the increasing migration from Latin America, Asia, and Africa rage on both sides of the Atlantic. And in the streets of Rostock, Marseilles, and Los Angeles, xenophobes have vented their frustrations, using firebombs and clubs.

Such nativism threatens not only to destabilize domestic society but also to jeopardize relations between host and sending countries. Neo-Nazi violence against Turkish nationals in Germany (Bundesministerium des Innern 1993:66–78) continues to hinder good rapport between Turkey and the Federal Republic, major trading partners and NATO allies. The racist murder of several Algerians in Marseilles in the 1970s convinced Algeria to cut off for a time the flow of migrant workers to France (Wihtol de Wenden 1988:162), and discrimination against Maghrebis in France seems to have largely motivated Kheled Kelkal's wave of deadly anti-French terrorism in the *métropole* in 1995 (Loch 1995). On the American continent, the Mexican government viewed the passage of Proposition 187 as an enormous affront to its dignity and to the human rights of its nationals (Fineman 1994). Ordinary Mexicans, meanwhile, expressed their outrage by vandalizing a U.S.-affiliated business in Mexico City (*Los Angeles Times* Wire Service 1994). Yet maintaining the goodwill of this Latin American country's government and people has become even more vital to American commercial and political interests with the signing of the North American Free Trade Agreement, or NAFTA (Lee 1994; *Los Angeles Times* Staff 1994).

Not only is nativism a problem for international peace, prosperity, and security now, but it promises to continue to trouble us for decades to come. As Paul Kennedy (1993:44) argues in *Preparing for the Twenty-First Century*, the reaction of the industrialized world to the overwhelming demographic pressures from developing nations may well be one of the most vexing problems of the next hundred years:

Given the political and social tensions that the *relatively limited* transnational migration has recently provoked, there is reason to be concerned should a massive surge in population occur from one country to another. [Yet, i]n view of the imbalances in demographic trends between "have" and "have-not" societies, it seems unlikely that there will not be great waves of migrations [to the developed nations] in the twenty-first century. (emphasis in original)

If anything, then, the potential for public backlash against immigration threatens to increase in the decades ahead.

Theories of Public Attitudes toward Immigration

This study cannot hope to solve the problem of global economic inequality, which largely drives immigration to the United States, France, and Germany (see Ravenstein 1889). But by isolating the principal causes of mass attitudes toward foreigners,[1] this investigation can help find ways to reduce public hatred of immigrants. In particular, the work will examine the strength of three major explanations of opposition to immigrants: marginality (especially cultural forms, but also economic, gender-based, etc.); economic self-interest (both labor-market and use-of-services versions); and contact (both individual-level and aggregate). The book not only investigates the overall persuasiveness of each interpretation but also looks for any special circumstances that increase or decrease each theory's explanatory power.

Examples from the Literature on Immigration Attitudes

Each of these perspectives has its advocates in the literature on attitudes toward immigrants and immigration. Espenshade and Calhoun (1993; see also Betz 1994:100–101; Martínez-Ebers and Deng 1996; Soule 1997), for example, seem to hold to something approximating cultural-marginality theory. In their view, "cultural affinity" is one of the most important determinants of immigration-related public opinion: "Cultural and ethnic ties to immigrants promote pro-immigrant attitudes and support for a more open immigration policy."[2]

More economic interpretations seem to dominate not only popular explanations of anti-immigrant sentiments but also many scholarly studies of public attitudes. One of the principal proponents of the economic self-interest school, Harwood (1986) first appears to cast doubt on the culturally based theories: "[T]he public opinion data do not support the hypothesis that neorestrictionism is motivated by racial or ethnic prejudice." Instead, "[e]conomic concerns appear to be the main reason for the increase in opposition to both legal and illegal immigrants" (Harwood 1983). Simon (1987; see also Simon and Alexander 1993:29–47) seems to endorse a similar hypothesis focusing on labor-market competition:

> Immigrants represent a greater threat to the livelihoods and living standards of lower-status respondents than they do to persons with higher education and more skills. So, the poorer the person, the greater the fear that more immigrants will mean fewer jobs, lower rates of pay, fewer opportunities for mobility, and more competition for housing, schools, and social services. Illegal immigrants are feared most because they are viewed as the strongest contenders for lower-status jobs and benefits.

Ultimately, according to these theorists, opposition to immigration arises from economic deprivation and the fear of further financial decline.[3]

Finally, contact analysis by Perrineau (1985) of support for the anti-immigrant Front national (FN) party represents one form of the third major theory. Showing the lack of correlation between the vote for the Front national in 1984 and the percentage of immigrants in a given city precinct (*commune*), Perrineau first dismisses the hypothesis that close, personal contact causes xenophobia (see also Charbit and Lamy 1975; Mayer 1987; Loch 1990:90–94). The high correlation between the vote for Le Pen's FN and the proportion of foreigners in the much larger *département*,[4] however, remains high (Perrineau 1985; Le Bras 1986:64–66, 214–221). Perrineau's explanation (1985) of these paradoxical results reminds one of the "casual contact" thesis to be examined later in this chapter:

> [T]he zones where the extreme right achieves its best results are often regions where the more or less distant outlying areas have heavy concentrations of immigrants. Thus, the fears, repulsions, or worries that feed voting for the National Front sometimes seem to arise more from fantasy than from the actual perception of objective, lived difficulties or dangers. It is the unknown person who is disturbing, the stranger with whom one doesn't live but whom one senses at the city limits. . . . The modern [European] town seems to

revive the fears of the medieval town for whom the edges of the city were the realm of crime, marginality, and destitution.[5]

In France, contrary to the situation in the United States, the suburbs contain society's disadvantaged. Upper- and middle-class French city dwellers would therefore experience little or no close personal contact with immigrants. According to contact theory, natives might increasingly become aware of the rising foreign population in the suburbs via such superficial or "casual" contacts as riding the Métro with immigrants, passing the ubiquitous North African sanitation worker on the street, or even watching a television news program on "crime in the suburbs." Such interactions, scholars such as Perrineau would probably argue, can only breed suspicion and exacerbate hostility.

Marginality

Classic Statement of Theory

Though not necessarily focusing on immigration-related attitudes, several social-science classics have set out elements of each of the three major theories. Parts of the first main explanation (marginality theory) have already been adumbrated, especially by theorists of "status politics." These various strands, however, have apparently never yet been synthesized to yield an equally generalizable theory of public opinion. A major task of this book is thus to elaborate and test this potentially powerful explanation.

In its most universal form, marginality theory states that the experience of being oneself marginalized, oppressed, or outside the "mainstream" breeds sympathy with marginalized or oppressed people in general, even if they do not belong to one's own group.[6] In particular, having a marginality-producing characteristic would, *all else being equal*, create greater support for the welfare and rights of other marginalized groups. A particular characteristic produces marginality if, relative to the "mainstream" or "dominant" trait, it subjects one to the threat of or actual discrimination, persecution, or widespread public hostility or ridicule.[7] In the United States, for example, the "mainstream" ethnicity is (northwest) European American, while being African American would be a marginality-producing characteristic. One's solidarity with other marginalized groups will increase, moreover, to the extent that one is oneself marginalized.[8] It should also increase to the extent that the marginalization (at least of the other marginalized group) approximates brutal persecution of clearly defined, clearly innocent victims.[9]

Although someone might instead restate these principles using the terms "the weak" or "the powerless," the foregoing formulation seems to include these latter ones as special cases of the general rule. The connotations of "weak" or "powerless," moreover, might not apply to all persons with marginality-producing characteristics. This book treats American Jews and French Protestants, for instance, as relatively marginalized, yet neither group is "weak." American Jews are instead cultural outsiders in a country with a Protestant Christian majority, and French Protestants constitute a religious minority in the predominantly Catholic France.

A second proviso relates to the first. Protestants in France do not at first strike us as "powerless" or even particularly "marginalized" because on criteria other than religious affiliation (e.g., education, income, occupational status) these French citizens seem relatively advantaged. Marginalized persons sympathize more with other marginalized groups, then, *all else being equal*. Where ethnicity correlates strongly with education, for example, we cannot expect all members of an ethnic minority to support immigrant rights more strongly than all members of the ethnic majority. In statistical terms, we must think *multivariately* instead of *bivariately*. After controlling for education, income, gender, and the like, we assume that ethnic minorities should support pro-immigrant policies more strongly than the ethnic majority.[10]

Thinking multivariately also implies cross-cutting cleavages. All French-born, ethnic North Africans in France will not necessarily hold identical views. Rather, this ethnic minority itself contains other "minorities" (in power or status, if not always in number) of gender, religion, income, occupation, and native language. Each trait might also influence attitudes toward immigration.

The marginality thesis developed and examined in this book originates in several schools of thought. Hints of the general form of this hypothesis appear in classic works by Marx and Engels (Tucker 1978), Myrdal (1944), and Allport (1979). Studies of Holocaust era rescuers have also set out a more context-dependent form (London 1970; Tec 1986:152–154; but see Oliner and Oliner 1988:176, 306).

Though concentrating on economic marginality, Marx and Engels see industrialization forcing all relatively disadvantaged individuals more and more into the proletariat (Tucker 1978:474, 479–480):

> Our epoch, the epoch of the bourgeoisie, possesses, however, this distinctive feature: it has simplified the class antagonisms: Society as a whole is more and more splitting up into two great hostile camps, into two great classes directly facing each other: Bourgeoisie and Proletariat. . . . The lower strata of the middle class – the small tradespeople, shopkeepers, and retired tradesmen generally, the handicraftsmen and peasants – all these sink gradually into the proletariat. . . . Thus the proletariat is recruited from all classes of the population.

Although this Marxist analysis ultimately reduces almost all differences to economic ones, the general idea of all relatively powerless people uniting against the "ruling class" bears similarities to marginality theory.[11] The marginalized may well be economically disadvantaged, but I would include disadvantages correlated with race, ethnicity, religion, language, and gender[12] as well. The crucial insight from Marx is that all of society's disadvantaged may come together to oppose the dominant group.

Though also a socialist, Myrdal refuses to view all inequality as ultimately economic. In his classic work *An American Dilemma*, he lists a multiplicity of disadvantaged people (1944:67; see also 1073–1078): "To these other disadvantaged groups in America belong not only the groups recognized as minorities, but all economically weak classes in the nation, the bulk of the Southern people, women, and others. This country [the United States] is a 'white man's country,' but, in addition, it is a country belonging primarily to the elderly, male, upper class, Protestant Northerner." In the America of 1944, he did not see an effective coalition among all such oppressed groups. Rather, he wrote that "[e]very vertical split within the lower class aggregate will stand as an obstacle to the feeling of solidarity" (1944:68). Yet he does not rule out this possibility for the future. The general increases in education and economic and social security in the United States, Myrdal hypothesizes, may eventually "work for increased solidarity between the lower class groups." Such "liberal ideological forces" as the "American Creed" also "tend to create a tie between the problems of all disadvantaged groups in society and . . . work for solidarity between these groups" (1944:72; see also Stonequist 1961:160–161). He even looks to mass attitudes for evidence (1944:72–73):

> A study of opinions in the Negro problem will reveal, we believe, that persons who are inclined to favor measures to help the under-dog generally, are also, and as a part of this attitude, usually inclined to give the Negro a lift. . . . If this correlation [on different issues] is represented by a composite scale running from radicalism, through liberalism and conservatism, to reactionism, it is suggested that it will be found that all subordinate groups – Negroes, women, minorities in general, poor people, prisoners, and so forth – will find their interests more favored in political opinion as we move toward the left of the scale.

Thus, although Myrdal found little empirical evidence of marginality effects in 1944, he described well the various groups of marginalized persons and suggested the possibility of such solidarity in the future.

Positing a similar model, Allport (1979:154–155) found more evidence for marginality theory. Although first noting that victimization can lead to greater hostility toward other "out-groups," he also recognizes that "in the case of many victims of prejudice . . . [j]ust the reverse happens" (1979:153–154; see also Bogardus 1928:87–88; Williams 1947:61). The middle option, according to Allport (1979:155), seems all but impossible:

> [Those] who feel that they have been victims of discrimination are usually either very high in prejudice . . . or else very low in preju-dice. They are seldom "average." In short, being a victim oneself disposes one either to develop aggression toward *or* sympathy with other out-groups. . . . With insight [the victim of prejudice] will say, "These people are victims exactly as I am a victim. Better stand with them, not against them."

Which path a victim follows seems to depend on his or her basic per-sonality (Allport 1979:160–161). Though also admitting an opposite outcome, Allport thus goes beyond Myrdal in contending that a solidarity of the marginalized not only is possible in theory but also occurs in fact.

Holocaust Era Rescuers

While focusing on a very specific case, a few studies of Holocaust era "rescuers" (i.e., those who risked their own lives to save the lives of Jews and other groups persecuted by the Nazis) suggest a similar marginality theory.[13] London's interviews (1970) with twenty-seven rescuers led him to hypothesize that "the experience of social marginality gave people the impetus and endurance to continue their rescue activities." One Dutch rescuer belonged to the Seventh-Day Adventists, a "very socially marginal" religious group "not always treated kindly in Holland"; the respondent's father, himself also a rescuer, had apparently even been jailed for his faith. A German rescuer reported "always [having] felt friendless" as a child, mainly because he stuttered and spoke the "wrong" dialect of German at home. In her more extensive study of rescuers, Tec confirms London's hypothesis, noting that many "show[ed] an inability to blend into their environment" (1986:152–154) and hence felt "unconstrained" by their society's norms (1997a).[14]

Political Behavior of American Jews

While Myrdal, Allport, and studies of Holocaust era rescuers set out the broad structures for a theory of marginality, the literature on the political attitudes of American Jews focuses on how the psychological mechanism works in practice. An early study by Allinsmith and Allinsmith (1948) suggests that Jews' strong liberalism stems from their relatively marginalized status in American society:

> [P]erhaps being only partially accepted by the latter [other middle-class groups] forces [Jews] to associate with others in a like position, with the result that they are exposed to anti–status quo values. They might develop in this way a tendency to identify with outgroups, or to side with low status groups in general. It seems very likely that they saw in [Franklin] Roosevelt a champion of minority rights and supported him heavily for that reason.

The Allinsmiths thus point to the pro-underdog norms that outsiders rejected by the dominant status group socially learn from each other. By refusing to associate with outsiders, the dominant group restricts who will be socialized into its norms and so breeds the seeds of outsider opposition.

Ebersole (1960) and Wald (1992) posit a more purely psychological model. Ebersole (1960) argues that "religious intolerance" and "ethnic discrimination" lead "in varying degrees to Catholic and Jewish minority feelings." Such feelings in turn cause increased voting for FDR's Democratic Party, which Catholics and Jews view as "the party ... of hope for minorities" (Ebersole 1960; see also Berelson, Lazarsfeld, and McPhee 1954:61–86; Campbell et al. 1960:159–160; Jelen and Wilcox 1998). Wald (1992:322; see also Fuchs 1956:175–177; Fein 1988) elaborates further:

> Scholars generally attribute Jewish political preferences to the community's sense of itself as a potential target of hostility from the non-Jewish majority. Despite attaining objective levels of prominence undreamed of by earlier generations, American Jews still feel vulnerable to persecution and anti-Semitism. Why should a sense of social marginality attract American Jews to the left side of the political spectrum? From history, Jews learned that the left historically favored the cause of minorities, and liberalism is still seen as more sympathetic to minority groups than the political alternatives. Even if they do not benefit directly from the social programs sponsored by liberals, Jews regard such programs as a safeguard against the social tensions that breed religious bigotry.

Outsider status and the continued threat of persecution, then, maintain strong Jewish support for other minorities and for liberal social policies in general (but see Levey 1996).[15]

Although most Jews in the United States still strongly back liberalism and the Democratic Party (Wald 1992:326), the recent rise of a few "dissenting" Jewish neoconservatives such as Irving Kristol (1995) might also confirm marginality theory. For if anti-Semitism has declined somewhat since the earlier parts of the twentieth century, we would expect at least a few American Jews to feel less marginalized today and hence to loosen their ties to liberalism and the Democrats.

Churches versus Sects

Lest one think marginality theory applies only to such historically persecuted groups as Jews, a parallel historical literature reaches similar conclusions about Christians. In his exhaustive survey of Christian social teaching, Troeltsch divides groups of believers into "churches" and "sects" (1960:331). Whereas a church is "dependent upon the upper classes" and "an integral part of the existing social order," a sect is "connected with the lower classes, or at least with those elements in Society which are opposed to the State and to Society." Or, in our terms, churches are composed of mainstream insiders, but sects are made up of marginalized outsiders. Not surprisingly, only sects show "their affinity with all the oppressed and idealistic groups within the lower classes" (1960:337). The church, in contrast, shows much more tolerance of "secular political and economic inequalities and cruelty" (1960:330). "[I]n this sinful world," the church holds, the Gospel law of "universal brotherhood and equality . . . could not be obeyed" (1960:343).

Yale theologian H. Richard Niebuhr draws a similar picture. His "churches of the disinherited" are composed in the Reformation era of such outsiders as "the peasants, the poorer handicraftsmen, and the journeymen of the towns" (1957:38). Such marginalized believers contrast with their "fortunate and cultured" coreligionists in the "churches of the middle class" (1957:31, 77). Again, only the first group really appreciates "the radical character of the ethics of the gospel" or "seeks and sets forth . . . the salvation of the socially disinherited" (1957:30–31). The churches of the middle class have instead "allied [themselves] . . . with those ruling classes whose superior manner of life is too obviously purchased at the expense of the poor" (1957:30).

Status Politics

Finally, the theory of status politics and its relatives also explains the mechanism of solidarity among the culturally marginalized, if from the perspective of cultural insiders.[16] Gusfield (1963:14) defines social status as "prestige" or "social honor." In other words, how much "approval, respect, admiration, or deference" can a "person or group . . . command by virtue of his [or her] imputed qualities or performance"? (Gusfield 1963:14, citing Johnson 1960:469). Within the "status order," different groups tend to have different amounts of prestige based on their "characteristic ways of life" (Gusfield 1963:14–15). The distribution of prestige does not remain static, however. Rather, "[w]hen divergent styles of life claim equal or superior prestige," status politics or conflict results when "the bearers of these styles . . . clash to establish prestige dominance and subordination"

(Gusfield 1963:18). Because "political action can [influence] and often has influenced the distribution of prestige" (Gusfield 1963:19), the various combatant groups aim to have the government take actions that will symbolically endorse their life-style or cultural values over against those of their competitors (Gusfield 1963:21; see also Allport 1979:239; Luker 1984). In terms of marginality theory, the cultural insiders will seek political "blessing" of their values as opposed to those of the culturally marginalized "interlopers."

In the American debate over immigration, for instance, the dominant white, Anglo-Saxon, Anglophone Protestants will seek public approval of their cultural characteristics at the expense of such immigrants as mestizo, Spanish-speaking Catholics. At stake is whether it will remain relatively prestigious in the United States to originate in the British Isles or at least northwest Europe, speak English as one's native language, and practice or at least nominally associate oneself with Protestant Christianity. Feeling culturally threatened by rising "multiculturalism" and increasing non-European immigration, the WASPs react by fighting for such a symbolic endorsement of their culture as having English declared the "official language" of the state or country.

The Clash of Civilizations

One also finds this emphasis on cultural conflict and threat in Huntington's "clash of civilizations" theory (1993). According to Huntington, the "fundamental source of conflict" in the post–Cold War world "will not be primarily ideological or primarily economic." The "dominating source of conflict" will rather be "cultural," especially at the "fault lines between civilizations."[17] The eight major "civilizations" Huntington identifies include "Western, Confucian, Japanese, Islamic, Hindu, Slavic-Orthodox, Latin American and possibly African." Although his theory applies most readily to relations among states, he also notes that within a given state, "[d]ifferences in culture and religion create differences over [such a] policy issu[e as] . . . immigration." Culturally divergent "North African immigration to France," for example, "generates hostility among Frenchmen and at the same time increased receptivity to immigration by [culturally] 'good' European Catholic Poles." Where immigrants originate from a different "civilization," then, natives' opposition should be "more frequent ... [and] more sustained" than where the migrants come from the same civilization. One would also presume that the native-born who themselves have ties to a minority civilization (e.g., second-generation Chicanos in the United States) would be more likely to welcome immigrants from a divergent civilization (e.g., Salvadorans or even Chinese arriving in the United States).

Economic Self-Interest

Classic Statement of Theory

In contrast to the marginality thesis, theories of "class politics" or "economic self-interest" point to immigration's supposed threat to natives' economic well-being. The class politics explanation defines a "class" as "a sociological group in the sense that its members, by virtue of their common placement in the economic structure, share common interests" (Gusfield 1963:14). Class politics occurs when the "material goals and aspirations of different social groups" conflict and produce cleavages "such as is found in the traditional right and left" (Gusfield 1963:17). Actual or threatened harm to one's economic position, then, causes political attitudes in favor of preventing or alleviating such harm. Campbell et al. (1960:383) suggest, for example, that high levels of unemployment increase support for governmental programs to ensure full employment. Blue-collar workers also seem more open to such programs than white-collar employees, presumably because unemployment threatens the former group more (Schlozman and Verba 1979:203–207).

In perhaps the definitive statement of such economic politics, Downs (1957:36) hypothesized that "each citizen casts his vote for the party he believes will provide him with more benefits than any other." Extrapolating to political opinions in general, we might expect people to support policies which are most likely to benefit them or "yield [them] the highest utility" (Downs 1957:36). Although Downs (1957:37) believed utility maximizers might also exhibit altruism or charity, later theorists of "self-interest" usually exclude such motives. To "make the [self-interest] hypothesis falsifiable and non-trivial," Sears et al. (1980; see also Green and Shapiro 1994) argue, "we prefer to restrict the range of goals to those which bear directly on the material well-being of individuals' private lives." At bottom, this hypothesis holds that people support those policies which will benefit them personally (Sears et al. 1980; see also Gilens 1999:39–42).

Labor Market versus Use of Services

At least at the individual level, one might further divide economic self-interest theories into those based on the "labor market" or "use of services" (see Muller and Espenshade 1985:91–144). According to the former, people fear that immigrants – often willing to work for less pay and filling positions demanding fewer skills – will reduce the native-born working-class's wages or take their jobs.[18] The latter, "use-of-services" formulation instead focuses on natives' fears about paying more taxes because of immigrants' (especially *indocumentados*' and refugees') use of publicly funded services (e.g., education, health care, welfare). The predictions made by these two versions of self-interest often diverge. While the labor-market hypothesis tends to see xenophobia arising among the economically disadvantaged, the use-of-services interpretation instead expects anti-immigrant resentment primarily among the affluent.

Relative Deprivation

Gurr (1970) adds a different twist to the economic hypothesis. Instead of necessarily objective economic deprivation, "relative deprivation" can produce discontent and, presumably, anti-immigrant sentiment.[19] Relative deprivation he defines as "actors' perception of discrepancy between their value expectations and their value capabilities." "Value expectations" he describes as "the goods and conditions of life to which people believe they are rightfully entitled." And "[v]alue capabilities are the goods and conditions they think they are capable of getting and keeping" (1970:24).

This hypothesis thus may lead us to expect slightly different results than the traditional economic self-interest theory predicts. The unemployed should always be xenophobic according to Downs's self-interest explanation. Relative-deprivation theory, on the other hand, might predict nativism only if keeping one's job seems feasible. In a worldwide depression, when many people are out of work, being unemployed oneself might have little effect on attitudes toward immigrants.

Sociotropic Politics

"Sociotropic politics" provides another variation of economic theory. Here the crucial variable is not one's personal "pocketbook," but rather one's perception of the national economy as a whole (Kinder and Kiewiet 1981). Thus, Kinder and Kiewiet (1981) explain Tufte's "economic voting" models (Tufte 1978) in "sociotropic" terms: "[T]he party in power suffers at the polls during hard times because voters act on their negative assessments of the national economic conditions – quite apart from the trials and tribulations of their own economic lives." Although such voting may arise from either altruism or self-interest[20] (Kinder and Kiewiet 1981), the overriding goal is to maximize national prosperity.

Contact

Classic Statement of Theory

The third major theory of attitudes toward foreigners generally focuses on the distribution of immigrants in one's neighborhood or region and on how many and what kind of personal contacts one has with newcomers. Perhaps the most noted American scholar of such "contact theories," Gordon Allport (1979:261–262), first denies that all contact is alike: "It has sometimes been held that merely by assembling people without regard for race, color, religion, or national origin, we can thereby destroy stereotypes and develop friendly attitudes. The case is not so simple. . . . Whether or not [contact reduces prejudice] seems to depend on the *nature of the contact* that is established" (emphasis in original). Rather, Allport (1979:263–268; see also Williams 1947:71–72) distinguishes between "true acquaintance" (e.g., being entertained as a dinner guest in someone's home) and superficial or "casual contact" (e.g., passing someone on the street). While the first type of contact most often decreases prejudice, the second "seems more likely to increase it." In short, the "more [casual] contact, the more trouble" (Allport 1979:263). Such contact boosts hostility because seeing a "visible out-group member" brings "to mind a recollection of rumor, hearsay, tradition, or stereotype by which this out-group is known." At least in theory, every additional encounter with a member of this group could " 'by the law of frequency,' strengthen the adverse mental associations" that a prejudiced person already has. Prejudiced people are also "sensitized to perceive signs that will confirm [their] stereotypes" (Allport 1979:264): "From a large number of Negroes in a subway [they] may select the one who is misbehaving for [their] attention and disapproval. The dozen or more well-behaved Negroes are overlooked, simply because prejudice screens and interprets [one's] perceptions."

Casual contact, then, does not require effective, personal communication with the out-group member. Such superficial interaction instead allows one's "private obsessions" to color – sometimes completely – one's perceptions of reality (Allport 1979:167–169, 264). Living in areas with ethnically segregated housing promotes a chief form of this "bad contact," sometimes leading to enhanced "racial bitterness" (Pettigrew 1971:277; see also Massey and Denton 1993).

A few limited forms of contact can have the opposite effect, however. Such "true acquaintance," or prejudice-reducing contact, demands four specific conditions. As Allport's disciple, Thomas Pettigrew (1971:275), summarizes the core of Allport's contact theory, "prejudice is lessened when the two groups (1) possess equal status, (2) seek common goals, (3) are cooperatively dependent upon each other, and (4) interact with the positive support of authorities, laws or customs." Some examples of such "good contact" include interaction "in department stores, public housing, the armed services, and the Merchant Marine, and among government workers, the police, students, and general small-town populations."[21] Pettigrew nonetheless cautions that some findings of prejudice reduction "can be interpreted not as results of contact but as indications that more tolerant white Americans seek contact with Negro Americans" (1971:310; see also Massey and Denton 1993:109–114).

Empirical Predictions

Tables 1.1, 1.2, and 1.3 summarize the predictions for each of these three major theories (i.e., marginality, economic self-interest, and contact). Three tables are needed in order to test the various hypotheses using three different methods (historical, time-series modeling, and cross-sectional modeling). All particular applications of a given theory might not explain reality equally well, and the strengths of one

Table 1.1. *Summary of Predictions for Historical Analysis*

Variables	Marginality	Economic	**Contact**
Cultural difference between immigrants and natives of dominant ethnicity	+	0	
Wave of culturally different immigrants	+	0	
Depression/recession	–	+	
Percent foreign-born			+

Note: + = characteristic increases opposition to immigration and immigrants. – = characteristic decreases opposition to immigration and immigrants. 0 = characteristic has no significant effect on opposition to immigration or immigrants.

Table 1.2. *Summary of Predictions for Time-Series Models*

Variables	Marginality	Economic	Contact
Economic			
Real disposable income per capita		–	
Unemployment rate		+	
Contact			
Percent foreign-born			+
Immigration rate			+

Note: + = characteristic increases opposition to immigration and immigrants. – = characteristic decreases opposition to immigration and immigrants. 0 = characteristic has no significant effect on opposition to immigration or immigrants.

method may make up for the weakness of another. Historical narratives add rich texture to studying the immigration experience, but they often lack the statistical rigor of mathematical models of immigration-related attitudes.

To maximize the robustness and applicability of its conclusions, this study also tests the theories on three separate countries (the United States, France, and Germany). As will become obvious later in this

Table 1.3. *Summary of Predictions for Cross-Sectional Models*

Variables	Marginality	Economic Labor Market	Economic Use of Services	Contact
Cultural				
Perceived cultural threat	+		0	
Non-Catholic minority	−		0	
Catholic minority	−		0	
Jewish	−		0	
Other religion	−		0	
No religion	−		0	
Foreign origin	−		0	
Latino	−		0	
African American	−		0	
Asian	−		0	
Native American	−		0	
Other race	−		0	
Economic				
Perceived economic threat			+	
Poor	−	+	−	
Finances declined	−	+	−	
Unemployed	−	+	−	
Professional/manager	+	−	+	
Manual laborer	−	+	−	
Nonpaid worker	−	+	−	
Perceived decline in national economy			+	
Perceived relative economic deprivation			+	
Contact				
Proximity/region				+
Proximity/neighborhood				+
Proximity/work				−
Personal contact				−
Demographic				
Education	−		−	
Female	−		0	

Note: + = characteristic increases opposition to immigration and immigrants.
− = characteristic decreases opposition to immigration and immigrants.
0 = characteristic has no significant effect on opposition to immigration or immigrants.

study, many analyses would not even be possible if one restricted oneself to a single country. If one had looked at only the American data, for example, one might have concluded (falsely) that something about Catholic doctrine or practice produces sympathy for immigrants (see Chapter 6). Comparison with the French and German data (see Chapters 7 and 8), however, suggests that the critical variable is really whether one's religious group is a minority in a particular country and hence relatively vulnerable to discrimination.

Of course, to compare nativism across three different countries one must assume that their immigration politics are indeed comparable. This assumption may occasionally do violence to reality, but ultimately the United States, France, and Germany are all Western, highly industrialized nations experiencing substantial post–World War II immigration, largely from developing countries. The three nations may frame the immigration debate differently, but essentially natives are arguing over how many and under what conditions immigrants will be allowed to enter and to settle in the country. And if, despite national differences, a given theory is confirmed by data from all three countries, we can be all the more certain that our findings are cross-nationally generalizable.

Three Forms of Nativism

To develop the three major theories as far as possible, this book similarly examines three different forms of nativism (anti-immigrant affect, anti-immigration policy preferences, and support for anti-immigrant political movements). One cannot necessarily assume that a given theory will hold equally well for all forms of nativism. On the contrary, the major theories themselves suggest that their effect will vary across the three forms. Marginality effects, for instance, should increase to the extent that a given anti-immigrant attitude or action represents severe persecution. Overall, one might expect relatively weak marginality effects for affect, stronger ones for policy preferences, and the strongest effects for such near-persecutorial political movements as the Front national, the Republikaner, and Proposition 187 proponents. Simply hating Algerian refugees does not force them back to their dangerous, civil-war-ravaged homeland, but if enough French citizens vote for Le Pen, he may well start deporting North Africans. Economic self-interest should exhibit a similar pattern, rising from a weak influence on affect to a moderate effect on policy preferences and a strong impact on support for political movements. Merely despising undocumented immigrants would not have stopped them from using public services, but Proposition 187 might have. Contact theory provides fewer relevant hypotheses, but one might expect stronger contact effects on affect than on policy preferences or support for political movements (see Allport 1979:276).

Marginality

The three major theories make various, sometimes contradicting, predictions about attitudes toward immigrants (see Tables 1.1 to 1.3). Over time, aggregate opposition to immigration should increase (denoted by a plus sign in Table 1.1) among natives of the dominant ethnicity as a wave of culturally divergent immigrants arrives. During a given historical era, natives of the dominant ethnicity or culture should also welcome immigrants from culturally similar countries more than newcomers from culturally divergent ones. Because marginality theory is not really amenable to testing with time-series models (see Chapter 5), Table 1.2 leaves the column for marginality blank. As Table 1.3 indicates, however, marginality theory predicts that belonging to a religious minority (e.g., being Protestant in a predominantly Catholic country, being Catholic in a predominantly Protestant country, being Jewish, nonreligious, or of another religion in a predominantly Christian country); being a racial or ethnic minority (e.g., being Latino, African American, Asian, Native American, or of another "race"); being a recent immigrant or the child of recent immigrants; being unemployed, poor, or female; experiencing declining finances; or working in a low-status job should all reduce opposition to immigrants and immigration (generally indicated by a minus sign in Table 1.3).

Although poorly educated respondents are also in some sense marginalized, a substantial literature holds that increased education instead socializes students to have more liberal or pro-outsider views (Erikson, Luttbeg, and Tedin 1991:155–156; Espenshade and Calhoun 1993; see also Campbell et al. 1960:475–481; Zaller 1992:11, 98; but see Williams 1947:64–65). The cultural form of marginality theory, moreover, suggests that higher education makes people more secure in their own cultural identity and hence less likely to see immigrants as a cultural threat. On balance, then, marginality predicts that education will decrease hostility to immigration.

Economic Self-Interest

In contrast to the cultural variant of marginality, economic self-interest predicts that cultural differences between immigrants and natives of the dominant cultural or ethnic group will have no influence on the overall level of nativism (see Table 1.1). Yet xenophobia should intensify during depressions and recessions. Similarly, Table 1.2's summary of predictions for the time-series models suggests that overall levels of nativism will decline with rising income per capita and increase with higher unemployment rates. Finally, most economic explanations (including the labor-market version of self-interest) foresee no effect for the cultural variables or for being female (see Table 1.3). Being affluent, enjoying improving personal finances, working in a high-status (and hence usually economically secure) occupation, and perceiving an improvement in the national economy should decrease opposition to immigration and immigrants. On the other hand, being unemployed, perceiving that immigrants threaten the national economy or one's own prosperity, and believing that they are doing better than oneself economically should boost such opposition.

Because education brings "the potential for competing successfully in the labor market" (Hernes and Knudsen 1992; see also Simon 1987; Hernes and Knudsen 1989), economic self-interest holds that education reduces nativism. Given that most immigrants to the United States, France, and Germany lack a university degree (Bade 1994a:48–49; Tribalat 1995:137–139; Portes and Rumbaut 1996:59), higher education should decrease natives' sense of economic threat as well.

The use-of-services variant of economic self-interest would make similar predictions for the cultural variables, education, gender, and the perception of an improving national economy. It usually expects the opposite individual-level results, however, for being affluent, enjoying improving finances, being unemployed, or working in a high-status occupation. When theorizing about perceived economic threat, the use-of-services version also emphasizes the effect of immigration on the public coffers instead of on the labor market.

Contact

Lastly, Tables 1.1 to 1.3 also summarize the predictions of contact theory. Because superficial or "casual" contact seems much more frequent than "true acquaintance" in the United States, France, and Germany, an increase in the immigration rate or in the over-time proportion of foreign-born should boost natives' opposition to immigration (see Tables 1.1 and 1.2). As Table 1.3 indicates, living in a region (e.g., a state, province, or city) or perhaps even a neighborhood with many foreigners should likewise increase nativism. Secondary analysis usually does not allow us to determine if all four of Pettigrew's conditions for "true acquaintance" exist. In the workplace and in other close, possibly cooperative encounters, however, frequent contact *might* reduce hostility.

Conflicting Predictions

Although many of these predictions do not contradict, occasionally two theories are at loggerheads. Marginality seems particularly likely to conflict with the labor-market version of economic self-interest. The first theory predicts that thinking that immigrants threaten the dominant culture, being native-born or female, or belonging to the religious, ethnic, or racial majority will increase an individual's opposition to immigration (see Table 1.3). Marginality theory also predicts that the culturally dominant group's nativism will rise markedly if a given group of immigrants comes from a culture very different from the dominant one (see Table 1.1). The labor-market variant of economic self-interest, on the contrary, holds that such characteristics should have no effect on attitudes toward immigration. Instead, this form of economic theory predicts that being economically disadvantaged (i.e., unemployed, poor, in personal financial decline, or in a low-prestige occupation) will boost a person's opposition to immigration. Yet marginality predicts just the opposite effect for these economic variables, reasoning that economic marginality will produce sympathy with marginalized, immigrant "outsiders" instead of hostility toward foreign-born "competitors."

As already suggested, the labor-market and use-of-services versions of economic self-interest also conflict at the individual level (see Table 1.3). While data analysis can help us decide which of these two economic theories better matches reality, differentiating between this use-of-services interpretation and economic aspects of marginality theory may prove less tractable. At least for most individual-level economic variables, both predict the same effects (see Table 1.3). Some at-first plausible "solutions" turn out not to work after further reflection. One might propose to examine how the economic variables affect attitudes toward refugees (who use disproportionately large amounts of publicly funded services) versus nonrefugee immigrants. On second thought, however, one realizes that refugees may well be more marginalized than nonrefugee immigrants and so produce greater marginality effects as well. Another approach would be to examine attitudes on policies or initiatives that have a high chance of affecting immigrants' use of services (e.g., Proposition 187) versus those which are unlikely to influence significantly the public cost of immigration (e.g., making English the official language). Assuming the public has the same immigrant group in mind (e.g., Mexicans), one might then compare the effect of the economic variables on these two types of policy-relevant attitudes. This "remedy" would likely fail as well, however, because Proposition 187 probably would have harmed (and marginalized) immigrants more grievously than the official use of English would. In the end, this theoretical tangle can probably only be straightened out by future research using focus-groups or other forms of open-ended, intensive interviews.[22]

Outline of Study

The chapters to come try in various ways to compare these three major theories with hard data about immigration-related attitudes in the United States, France, and Germany. First, Chapters 2, 3, and 4 (see Table 1.1) test the three theories against the history of public attitudes toward immigrants in the three countries since the 1880s. In particular, this historical section examines whether cultural differences between immigrants and natives, influxes of culturally different immigrants, economic downturns, and the proportion of foreign-born in the population affected the public's tolerance of newcomers. "Data" for this section come mainly from secondary historical accounts of public views on immigration during this period. The historical analysis generally finds that at any one time, natives of the dominant cultural group reject most vehemently the most culturally different immigrants; that in the United States but not in France or Germany, such natives become especially alarmed when a wave of very culturally distinct newcomers arrives; that recessions and depressions do significantly increase overall levels of nativism in a country over time; and that fluctuations in the proportion of foreign-born over time have no effect on overall acceptance of immigrants.

Chapter 5 (see Table 1.2) represents the first rigorous quantitative analysis in the book. For France and Germany, it estimates several time-series models of the effects of real disposable income per capita (or a similar measure), the unemployment rate, the immigration rate (where available), and the percentage of foreign-born on overall support for the National Front and Republikaner, two European anti-immigrant parties. Because similar American data are not available, this chapter relies on simpler plots and correlations to analyze U.S. surveys on immigration. This over-time quantitative analysis suggests that increases in the real disposable income per capita do reduce opposition to immigration and support for nativist political parties. None of the other independent variables consistently produces any statistically significant effects.

Chapters 6, 7, and 8 (see Table 1.3) empirically test the three major theories using cross-sectional surveys from the United States, France, and Germany. Each chapter tries to explain three types of nativism: anti-immigrant affect; opposition to immigration or immigrant rights; and support for anti-immigrant political movements (California's Proposition 187, Le Pen's Front national, and the Republikaner).[23] This cross-sectional quantitative analysis usually indicates that cultural marginality (e.g., belonging to a minority linguistic group, race, ethnicity, or religion) drives sympathy for immigrant outsiders in all three countries. Contact, on the other hand, yields few consistent effects, and only a few forms of economic self-interest (e.g., working as a professional or manager, but *not* being unemployed or poor) appear to increase individual nativism.

Finally, Chapter 9 synthesizes the findings from the previous chapters and attempts to explain significant differences across countries. It also suggests ways to improve tolerance of foreigners and speculates on the future course of relations between immigrants and natives.

PART I

Historical Analysis

[The] range of reactions in terms of policy toward foreign labor in the respective host countries . . . [is] not only . . . a question of the liberalism or economic strength of these governments but quite clearly also is bound up with the traditions – evolved over generations – within these societies in dealing with foreigners more generally and with foreign workers entering the host country in search of employment in particular. Only from this vantage [point] is it possible to understand why a society such as that in the United States, for example, has apparently been far better able to come to grips – at least over the middle term – with repeated waves of immigrants than have numerous states in Europe. Such states did not view themselves traditionally as countries of immigration, and the congruence between citizenship and ethnic origin played a key role ideologically for their own identity, no matter how differentially, as a state and society.

Historian Ulrich Herbert (1990:3)

Before delving into the quantitative analysis in the second part of this book, this first part of the study attempts to test the validity of the three major explanations of attitudes toward immigration (i.e., cultural marginality, economic self-interest, and contact) using primarily qualitative historical materials on the three countries. Although this historical analysis cannot approach the statistical rigor of the time-series models in Chapter 5, for example, it makes up for this drawback in the diversity of the histories on which it is based and in the longer period of time that it examines.

Each of the three following chapters (one each for the United States, France, and Germany) is divided into several major time periods (e.g., 1880–1914, 1915–1924). The narrative for each time period, in turn, begins with a short chronology of immigration into the country during this time frame, continues with descriptions of public attitudes toward immigrants, and ends with an assessment of the state of the economy. After examining all time periods for a country, each of the three historical chapters concludes with an overall assessment of the relative validity of the three main explanations (i.e., cultural marginality or distance, economic self-interest, and contact).

These chapters are more a social-scientific analysis of historical events than a detailed chronology of exactly what happened when. The historical section of this book follows more the analytic lead of Crane Brinton's *Anatomy of Revolution* (1958), in which history is used as "data" to test or develop a social-scientific theory, than the chronological, "history-as-history" account of, say, William Shirer's *The Rise and Fall of the Third Reich* (1960). Many of the methodological concerns (e.g., "selecting on the dependent variable") and much of the theoretical terminology (e.g., "independent variable") are borrowed from quantitative, empirical social research, and the following pages lack much of the fine detail of a traditional historical narrative.

If the appropriate demographic statistics and surveys on public attitudes toward immigrants were available for this period, moreover, these data would probably be better suited to test the effect of each "independent variable," or theory, on the "dependent variable," or the mass public's attitudes toward immigrants or foreigners, than are narrative histories. As it is, however, public-opinion polling is a relatively recent phenomenon, and the historical record is generally devoid of the kinds of individual-level statistics that will be used in Chapters 6 to 8, for example.

As measures of the phenomenon to be explained (public attitudes toward immigration), the historical chapters therefore rely on such secondary historical accounts as Higham (1988) for the United States, Wihtol de Wenden (1988) for France, and Bade (1983b) for Germany. Most primary historical research, such as examination of diaries, letters to the editors, or police reports, is beyond the scope of this book, and so these historical chapters essentially assume the accuracy of the secondary sources' descriptions of public sentiment toward immigrants.

These chapters try to avoid the methodological problem of

"selection on the dependent variable," or choosing cases to study based on the outcome one is trying to explain (e.g., the public response to immigrants) rather than on the hypothesized causes of that result (e.g., culture, economics, and percentage of foreign-born). Selecting cases that exhibit only the "deviant" or "problematic" behavior that one hopes to eliminate (e.g., violence against immigrants) is perfectly valid if one is attempting to *generate* causal hypotheses (so-called exploratory analysis). For *testing* such hypotheses, however, dependent-variable-based selection can bias the eventual results of such "tests" (King, Keohane, and Verba 1994:129–137).

To the extent possible, the analysis thus includes cases covering the full spectrum of the potentially causal variables. It does not restrict itself to cases of "xenophobia" or brutality against immigrants. When examining the effects of the economy on Germans' attitudes toward foreign workers, for example, Chapter 4 looks at how public opinion during the economic hardships of the immediate post–World War II period differed from public attitudes during the economic boom period of the *Wirtschaftswunder*. The analysis does not simply confine itself to the abuses against forced laborers during World War II and against Turkish *Gastarbeiter* since the 1970s and then try to work backward to the causes of such behavior.

2

History of Attitudes toward Immigration in the United States

Colored migration is a *universal* peril, menacing every part of the white world. . . . The whole white race is exposed, immediately or ultimately, to the possibility of social sterilization and final replacement or absorption by the teeming colored races. . . . There is no immediate danger of the world being swamped by black blood. But there is a very immediate danger that the white stocks may be swamped by Asiatic blood. . . . Unless [the white] man erects and maintains artificial barriers, [he will] *finally perish*.

> Madison Grant, introduction to Lothrop Stoddard's 1920
> book *The Rising Tide of Color against White World-Supremacy*,
> in Daniels (1977:67)

The *continuous* immigration of the nineteenth and early twentieth centuries was thus central to the whole American faith. . . . [I]t infused the nation with a commitment to far horizons and new frontiers, and thereby kept the pioneer spirit of American life, the spirit of equality and of hope, always alive and strong.

> President John F. Kennedy (1964:68)

This analysis of immigration to the United States can only sketch the country's experience with immigrants since 1880. For more extensive histories of migration during this period, see Handlin (1979), Takaki (1989), Daniels (1990), and McWilliams (1990).[1] The other works referred to in this section also provide good introductions to migration during the specific periods.[2]

1880–1914

Immigration

While most previous immigrants to the United States had originated in northwest Europe (especially the British Isles) or West Africa, beginning in about 1880 many began arriving from eastern and southern Europe as well. Menaced by famine and overpopulation, many peasants from Austro-Hungary, Prussia (including what is today Poland), and Russia chose emigration to America over starvation at home. Jews from eastern Europe also fled czarist pogroms. Especially after 1900, several million displaced rural Italians crossed the Atlantic, settling predominantly in America's cities. Northwestern Europeans such as the British, Irish, Scandinavians, and western Germans continued to find a new life in the United States more attractive than the crop failures, economic dislocations, and high population density at home (Baltzell 1964:58–60; Daniels 1977:66; 1990:3–184, 188–201, 223–224; 1996; Semmingsen 1978:106–120; Handlin 1979:13–33; Bade 1983b:12–28; McCaffrey 1984:70–84; Miller 1985:358–426; Higham 1988:159; Cohen 1990:55–58, 71–73, 121–124, 182–184; Rößler 1992; Sorin 1992:12–68; Bennett 1995:160–167).

Yet not all immigrants of this era hailed from Europe. From the north, Francophone Canadians found work in the mills of New England. Mexicans either moved north across the border or had found themselves on the "American" side of the Rio Grande after the Treaty of Guadalupe Hidalgo forced Mexico to cede the Southwest to the United States in 1848. Many ethnic Africans from the West Indies began arriving in the United States (especially New York City and Miami) at the turn of the century. And Chinese[3] and Japanese immigrants sailed east to build the railroads of the American West and to labor in western mines and fields (Reid 1968:42–45, 85–92; Daniels 1977:1–15; 1988:9–28, 100–154; 1990:239–264; 1996; García 1981:1–64; Brault 1986; McWilliams 1990:54–66; Sandmeyer 1991: 12–24; Zhu 1997:7–64).

Nativism

Between 1880 and 1914, nativism[4] varied considerably over time and across different groups of immigrants. Until the mid-1880s, xenophobia appears to have remained relatively low, the 1882 Chinese Exclusion Act notwithstanding.[5] Starting around 1885, however, nativism flared up and continued rising until around 1896. Beginning in 1885, for instance, whites in cities all over the West Coast rioted against the Chinese, and in the 1890s unemployed white farm workers in California violently expelled their Chinese "competitors" from the fields. Although anti-Italian violence seems to have been much less extensive than that directed against Asians and Mexicans, in 1891 a mob in New Orleans did lynch eleven Sicilians suspected of murdering the superintendent of police. Two years later, membership in the nativist American Protective Association also exploded (Saxton 1971:201–206, 229–232; Higham 1988:45–47, 68–69, 80–83, 91, 106–107; Takaki 1989:92; Daniels 1990:192; Becker 1991:31–45; Sandmeyer 1991:97–98; Bennett 1995:172–173; Zhu 1997:165–172; see also Handlin 1979:240).

From the turn of the century to about 1913, Americans seemed little concerned about the many immigrants arriving in the country.[6] During the first decade of the twentieth century, for example, editorials in the *New York Times* usually supported immigrants, even those from Japan and China. In 1914, however, national antiforeigner sentiments increased once again. And partly because of the Mexican Revolution, gratuitous, anti-Mexican violence became especially widespread in the Southwest starting in 1908 (Higham 1988:183; McWilliams 1990:108–109; Simon and Alexander 1993:242; Bennett 1995:179–181).

Though less frequently the victims of nativist violence, French Canadians, Irish Catholics, Jews, and other eastern Europeans suffered their share of ethnic prejudice and abuse during this period. With few exceptions, however, native-born Americans welcomed immigrants from Germany, Scandinavia, England, and Anglophone Canada (Baltzell 1964:109–142; Semmingsen 1978:133–134; McCaffrey 1984:105; Higham 1988:25–26, 66–67; Daniels 1990:160, 164–183, 258–264; 1997:39–40; Bretting et al. 1992; Sorin 1992:51–55; Simon and Alexander 1993:53, 84, 128–129, 198; Bennett 1995:169, 172–174; Smith 1997:364–365, 439, 442).

Economy

Overall, the U.S. economy grew enormously from 1880 to 1914, averaging about 4% growth per year. As industrial output soared, manufacturing continued to take over agriculture's former share of the economy. Real wages of industrial workers seem to have risen by about 25% in the 1880s, 6% in the 1890s, and 30% from 1900 to 1914. The major blot on this otherwise prosperous era was the Panic of 1893, a depression from 1893 to about 1897. This economic crisis saw unemployment rise to as high as 18.4% in 1894 (see Figure 2.1 and Table A1.1), and labor conflict become very widespread and bitter. The years 1883 to 1886 also witnessed a relatively mild "industrial depression." Another aberration from prosperity took place during the short-lived Panic of 1907, when unemployment reached 8.5%. The final downturn, also short-lived, occurred around 1914 as the beginning of World War I in Europe disrupted foreign trade and frightened financial markets (Smith 1955:399–407, 462–464, 491–492; Scheiber, Vatter, and Faulkner 1976:194, 221–223, 247, 255, 306–309, 317; Brownlee 1979:269–281, 320–321; Higham 1988:46).

1915–1924

Immigration

World War I brought immigration by Europeans to a virtual standstill. In their place, immigrants continued to arrive from Mexico, Canada, the West Indies, Japan, and the Philippines. With the end of hostilities, European immigration resumed, but it was never again to reach its prewar highs. Fleeing renewed pogroms in their homelands, many eastern European Jews immigrated to the United States in the early 1920s. From 1917 to 1924, however, increasingly restrictive American legislation on immigration began to alter the sources and number of newcomers dramatically. Although the 1917 literacy test eliminated few potential Americans, the quota-based Johnson Act of 1921 and, especially, the even stricter Johnson-Reed or "National Origins" Act of 1924 drastically reduced entries from southern and eastern Europe and prohibited any immigration from Asia[7] (Baltzell 1964:204; Reid 1968:41–44, 235–236; Daniels 1977:111; 1990:69, 278–284, 287–291, 310; Centro de Estudios Puertorriqueños 1979:111–112; Morrison and Zabusky 1980:40–43, 62–65, 105–109, 121–124; García 1981:41–60; Bade 1983b:22–23; Vega 1984; Bau 1985:41–42; Nieves Falcón 1987:20–25; Higham 1988:267, 273,

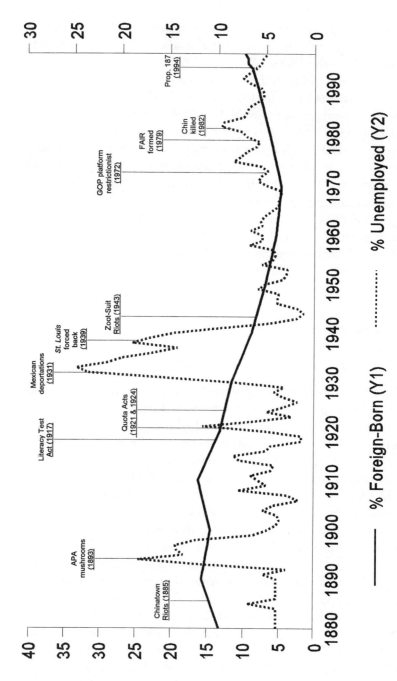

Figure 2.1. Nativism, foreign-born, and unemployment in the United States, 1880–1997. *Sources:* See Table A1.1.

— % Foreign-Born (Y1)   .... % Unemployed (Y2)

308–324; Takaki 1989:45–47, 315; Cohen 1990:182; McWilliams 1990:166–169; Barnett 1991; Rößler 1992; Simon and Alexander 1993:14; Bennett 1995:197, 217).

Nativism

From 1915 to 1924, nativism varied significantly over time as well as across groups of immigrants. All during the war, nativism remained moderately high. As Higham (1988:195) observes, "The struggle with Germany . . . called forth the most strenuous nationalism *and* the most pervasive nativism that the United States had ever known." The war years witnessed high anti-Semitism, anti-Mexican riots, widespread anti-German sentiment, and the enactment of legislation mandating a literacy test for immigrants. In 1918 miners lynched a German American in southern Illinois, and other ethnic Germans were publicly flogged or tarred and feathered during the war. During the Red Scare, the Department of Justice also beat up, arrested without stated cause, and/or deported hundreds of Russian immigrants (Baltzell 1964:186, 191–192; Handlin 1979:240, 259, 264; García 1981:189, 193–194; Calavita 1984:115–119; Bau 1985:41; Higham 1988:203, 209; Daniels 1990:160–161, 278; Luebke 1990: 31–50; Bretting et al. 1992:177–179; Sorin 1992:237–238; Simon and Alexander 1993:13–14; Bennett 1995:190–191).

Beginning in 1920, however, xenophobia exploded. In that year membership in the antiforeigner Ku Klux Klan skyrocketed. Amid a huge propaganda campaign to "Keep California White," in 1920 the state passed its anti-Japanese Alien Land Law.[8] This year also saw the beginning of Henry Ford's published, anti-Semitic diatribes, and three days of rioting against Italians in West Frankfurt, Illinois. In 1922, the year a Mexican was lynched in Texas, the *New York Times* observed that "the killing of Mexicans without provocation is so common as to pass almost unnoticed." Except for a short-lived dip in overall nativism for several months in late 1922 and early 1923, opposition to immigration continued at an almost hysterical level through the beginning of 1924. Articles in the *North American Review*, for example, "espoused the most extreme anti-immigrant sentiments." The U.S. Congress also passed the national-origins-based Quota Acts of 1921 and 1924 as well as the extension of the 1921 act in 1922. The 1921 act was "chiefly intended . . . to restrict the entrance of Jews from eastern Europe," and the

1924 sequel banned all immigration from Japan. Toward the end of 1924, however, xenophobia began to decline (Baltzell 1964:199, 201–204; Daniels 1977:82, 88–92, 95; 1990:280–283; 1997:122–143; Calavita 1984:144–146; Bau 1985:41–42; Higham 1988:264, 282, 289, 311–312, 315, 327; Takaki 1989:205; McWilliams 1990:109; Barnett 1991; Becker 1991:169–195; Simon and Alexander 1993:14, 60–63; Bennett 1995:208–210).

Of the various groups of immigrants from 1915 to 1924, Japanese and Mexican newcomers seem to have suffered the most severe native hostility. The only slightly more fortunate Filipinos encountered nativist agitation and violence in the western states, and Jews risked being lynched or having universities or potential employers reject them because of their background. With the exception of Germans during the war, on the other hand, immigrants from northwest Europe or English-speaking Canada found ready welcome in the United States from 1915 to 1924 (Baltzell 1964:210; Daniels 1977:1–2, 68, 87; 1990:238, 282–283, 357; Morrison and Zabusky 1980:99; Higham 1988:185–186, 278; McWilliams 1990:109; Simon and Alexander 1993:70; Bennett 1995:181, 206; Widdis 1998:346–351).

Economy

Both before and during direct American involvement in World War I, the U.S. economy boomed from the Allies' sudden demand for American food and munitions. Unemployment continued to decline until the end of 1919, bottoming out at a minuscule 1.4% (see Figure 2.1 and Table A1.1). The transition to a peacetime economy, however, contributed to the relatively severe depression of 1920–1922, when unemployment rose to almost 12%. Yet by 1923 the economy had recovered, beginning a period of prosperity that rivaled the wartime expansion (Smith 1955:492, 513–518, 532–535; Scheiber et al. 1976:317–327, 333–334; Brownlee 1979:365–389).

1925–1940

Immigration

With immigration from Asia illegal[9] and that from Europe heavily restricted, the share of "nonquota" newcomers from the Americas (mainly Mexico and Canada but also small numbers from Puerto Rico and other Caribbean islands)[10] increased significantly from 1925 to 1940. Just as the authors of the 1924 immigration act intended, those few Europeans who did manage to come to America during this period mainly originated from Ireland, Britain, Scandinavia, or Germany instead of from southern or eastern Europe. As the Great Depression intensified, migratory flows from most sources diminished until, from 1932 to 1935, net immigration became negative. Overall, the level of immigration from 1925 to 1940 hardly bears comparison with that from the first two decades of the twentieth century. Nazi persecution of European Jews, intellectuals, and dissidents nevertheless caused a small influx among these groups despite the very restrictive U.S. immigration policies (Reid 1968:34, 42–44; Centro de Estudios Puertorriqueños 1979:111–112; Bade 1983b:23; Vega 1984:135–198; Lookstein 1985:35–104; Breitman and Kraut 1987; Nieves Falcón 1987:24–27; Daniels 1990:124, 287–302, 310; McWilliams 1990:151–172; Röder 1992; Simon and Alexander 1993:14; Bennett 1995:238; Anderson 1998).

Nativism

Though beginning at a high level, nativism seems to have declined from 1925 to 1928. In 1925 the Ku Klux Klan continued its decline, and academic "race thinking" began losing its charm. New York City did witness an anti–Puerto Rican riot in 1926 and another serious anti–Puerto Rican disturbance in 1927. After the anti-Catholic campaign against Al Smith in 1928, however, WASP nativism seems to have gone into eclipse (McCaffrey 1984:159; Vega 1984:141–144, 151–152; Higham 1988:327–329; Bennett 1995:223–236).

Probably because of the restrictive Quota Acts and the negative or near-negative net immigration rate, opposition to most European and Asian immigrants seems to have remained low or moderate through the worst of the Great Depression. When the nativist author Madison Grant published *The Conquest of a Continent* in 1933, reviewers scoffed. Instead, the *New York Times* editorials in the 1930s generally sympathized with immigrants, and even the *North American Review* recommended increasing immigration in 1935. Yet perhaps because the Quota Acts did not exclude them, Mexican immigrants and their U.S.-born children suffered public hostility, government raids, and mass deportations around 1931 (Lipshultz 1971:10–16; Hoffman 1974; Guerin-Gonzáles 1985; Higham 1988:327, 413; Valdés 1988; McWilliams 1990:176; Simon and Alexander 1993:63–64, 215; Guerin-Gonzáles 1994:77–109; Barkan 1996:45–47).

From 1938 to 1940, anti-Semitism achieved "peak" levels, and generalized opposition to immigration also appears to have been high. Charles Coughlin began making anti-Semitic speeches in 1938, and the next year his followers attacked Jewish stores in Boston and New York. Apparently with substantial public backing, Roosevelt in 1939 forced hundreds of Jewish refugees on the ocean liner *St. Louis* to return to Nazi-dominated Europe. Close to half of the *St. Louis*'s former passengers eventually died in the Holocaust. A 1938 poll showed that 67.4% of the respondents opposed changing the country's restrictive immigration laws. One year later this proportion had risen to 83% (Morse 1968:270–288; Wyman 1968:14; Thomas and Morgan-Witts 1974; Lookstein 1985:81–104; Bennett 1995:xiv, 263–265; Barkan 1996:50–53; Korman 1998; Berger 1999).

Economy

From 1925 to 1929, the U.S. economy boomed. The real gross national product increased roughly 4% per year. Unemployment ranged from only 1.8% in 1926 to a modest 4.2% in 1928 (see Figure 2.1 and Table A1.1). Certain sectors of the economy (e.g., agriculture) and regions of the country failed to benefit much from this expansion, but on the whole the nation prospered (Smith 1955:532–537; Scheiber et al. 1976:334–347, 355; Brownlee 1979:384–399).

The stock market crash of October 1929 brutally ended the prosperous Roaring Twenties and ushered in the Great Depression of the 1930s, whose immediate effects lasted until at least 1940. From 1929 to 1933, when the depression reached its nadir, stocks lost close to 85% of their value. The economic devastation did not limit itself to stockholders, however. The rate of joblessness rose from 3.2% in 1929 to its all-time recorded high of 24.9% in 1933 (see Figure 2.1 and Table A1.1); even by 1940 unemployment had only declined to 14.6%. Conditions became so desperate that by 1934, 17 million Americans were receiving public relief. Beginning in 1933, the New Deal's public works and changes in monetary, fiscal, and regulatory policy may have improved the economy a little, yet the depression only really ended when the United States began massive production of munitions and armaments for World War II (Smith 1955:554–556, 565, 570–632; Scheiber et al. 1976:353–360, 389–391; Brownlee 1979:409–430).

1941–1945

Immigration

World War II brought a continued flow of Jews, intellectuals, and other refugees from Hitler's persecutions, though the numbers were small compared with how many victims could have been saved but were not. Trying to curry goodwill with its new wartime ally, the U.S. government lifted the ban on Chinese immigration in 1943 and gave China a nominal quota of 105 people per year. To alleviate its critical wartime labor shortage, the United States also instituted the *bracero* program, which allowed ostensibly temporary entry for over 100,000 Mexican agricultural and railroad workers. As in previous periods, a few Puerto Ricans continued to find work on the mainland (Baltzell 1964:316–317; Centro de Estudios Puertorriqueños 1979:124, 186; Mazón 1984:xi; Vega 1984:206; Bau 1985:42–43; Lookstein 1985; Breitman and Kraut 1987; Nieves Falcón 1987:30; Takaki 1989:370–378; Daniels 1990:296–306, 320; McWilliams 1990:237–240; Röder 1992; see also Morrison and Zabusky 1980:143–148).

Nativism

History does not seem to record many anti-immigrant actions for 1941. From 1942 to 1944, however, opposition to immigrants remained strong. Teenagers in New York City committed over thirty acts of anti-Semitic violence or vandalism during these three years. According to Wyman (1984:9), anti-Semitism rose in the early 1940s and peaked in 1944. In 1942 Roosevelt issued an executive order that forced Japanese immigrants into concentration camps, an action the Supreme Court supported in *Korematsu v. United States* (323 U.S. 214 [1944]). Also in 1942 a Michigan sheriff shot and killed a nineteen-year-old Mexican American cherry picker for playing an innocent prank on a female (Anglo) co-worker. During the 1943 "Zoot Suit

Riots," Anglo sailors and civilians chased, stripped, and beat up young Chicanos, all with the tacit approval or active collaboration of Los Angeles police. Abuses against Mexicans had become so frequent in Texas that in 1943 Mexico refused to send the state any more *braceros*. The fall of that year also saw widespread public opposition to refugees and immigrants. A 1944 poll rated Chinese immigrants moderately favorably, however, and by 1945 the public appears to have begun viewing immigrants in general more sympathetically. Anti-Semitism seems to have dropped as the end of the war neared. In April 1945 a Gallup poll showed that 70% of the respondents approved of providing temporary housing in the United States for refugees (Modell 1973; Houston and Houston 1974; Daniels 1981; 1990:303, 315–317; Mazón 1984; Wyman 1984:8, 264; Karst 1989:90–91; Takaki 1989: 389–393; McWilliams 1990:220–235, 241–242; Daniels, Taylor, and Kitano 1991; Simon and Alexander 1993:32; Bennett 1995:269–270).

Economy

By 1941 military production for World War II had finally ended the lingering economic effects of the Great Depression. In that year unemployment dropped to a relatively moderate 9.9%, and the jobless rate continued to fall until it reached 1.9% in 1945 (see Figure 2.1 and Table A1.1). Previously unemployed laborers became soldiers, sailors, and, especially, industrial workers helping to produce the $186 billion worth of wartime munitions. Although wage controls, rationing of consumer items, and shortages of raw materials imposed widespread hardships, the average American was still much better off economically during World War II than in the previous decade (Smith 1955:628–629, 638–645; Scheiber et al. 1976:404–413; Brownlee 1979:429, 451–454).

1946–1965

Immigration

From the end of World War II to the passage of the landmark Immigration Act of 1965, American immigration increased both in volume and national diversity. Starting from a little over 38,000 legal immigrants in 1945, the annual volume jumped to almost 109,000 in 1946 and continued to soar to just under 300,000 in 1965. Throughout this period the proportion of Europeans declined as the number of Asians and Latin Americans increased. Starting in 1946, a few Filipinos and Asian Indians could begin to immigrate to the United States, be naturalized, and bring in their families as nonquota immigrants. After the McCarran-Walter Act of 1952, citizens of the remaining Asian countries enjoyed privileges similar to those of the Chinese, Filipinos, and Asian Indians. Significant before 1945, Latin American immigration (e.g., from Mexico[11] and Puerto Rico) grew to roughly a fifth of all legal immigrants in the 1950s and two-fifths by 1965. Finally, hundreds of thousands of such refugees as the European displaced persons (DPs) of the 1940s and 1950s and the anti-Castro Cubans of the 1960s found safe haven in the United States (Glazer and Moynihan 1970:86–136; Centro de Estudios Puertorriqueños 1979:124–157, 186–187; Bau 1985:43; Nieves Falcón 1987:30–42; Takaki 1989:416–418; Daniels 1990:328–337; Simon and Alexander 1993:6, 15; Masud-Piloto 1996:19–56; see also Morrison and Zabusky 1980:161–171, 318–327).

Nativism

Mass nativism appears to have fallen steadily from 1946 to 1965. Signs reading "No Japs Allowed" or "No Japs Welcome" often greeted Japanese American internees returning home at the end of the war. While a Mexican could still be "killed with impunity" in Texas in 1946, the later historical record does not seem quite as filled with anti-Chicano violence. Strict segregation of Mexican students in the public schools also appears to have begun declining in the 1940s. In 1947 the New York City *World-Telegram* began a "smear" campaign against Puerto Rican immigrants, claiming they were "uncivilized," on welfare, and infected with tuberculosis and venereal disease. Although in the late 1940s *Reader's Digest* opposed admitting more DPs, the *New York Times* criticized the Displaced Persons Act's low ceilings and discrimination against Jews and Catholics. In 1946 Congress gave Asian Indians and Filipinos small quotas and made them eligible for naturalization. The 1952 McCarran-Walter Act entirely dropped the race-based ban on naturalization and immigration for Asians. By 1965 Congress had scrapped the national-origins system entirely (Lipshultz 1971:60–69; Vega 1984:226–230; Takaki 1989:405, 418–420; Daniels 1990:328–329, 338–344; McWilliams 1990:243–244, 252, 320–321; Simon and Alexander 1993:15–16, 169, 217).

Other available indicators of mass attitudes seem to confirm this decline in xenophobia. In 1947, 72% of the respondents said they would have voted against accepting 100,000 more European refugees. By 1953, 47% now approved of admitting 240,000 displaced persons, and a relatively low 39% held that the United States was letting in "too many" immigrants. Twelve years later, only 33% thought immigration should be "decreased." Californians voted to repeal the anti-Asian Alien Land Law in 1956. Anti–Irish Catholic sentiment had fallen so much that John F. Kennedy won the election for president in 1960.[12] In 1964, when vice-presidential candidate William Miller claimed Lyndon Johnson's generous program for immigration reform would open the "floodgates," Miller was attacked so severely that he withdrew his criticism. The political parties' campaign platforms, moreover, gradually changed from being silent or anti-immigration in the early 1940s to praising immigration in the early 1960s. In 1960 the Republican platform even urged "that the annual number of immigrants we accept be at least doubled" (McCaffrey 1984:163; Karst 1989:93; Takaki 1989:413; Daniels 1990:339–340; Simon and Alexander 1993:23–26, 34–37; Bennett 1995:320–321).

Economy

The U.S. economy grew steadily, though not spectacularly, from 1946 to 1965, with the 1960s outperforming the 1950s. More important, this period witnessed no extended depression and only mild, ephemeral recessions (1948–1949, 1953–1954, 1957–1958, and 1960–1961). Unemployment, moreover, never rose above 7%, usually remaining closer to 3% or 4% (see Figure 2.1 and Table A1.1). The most discordant element in this rosy economic picture was probably the chronic inflation that has become all too familiar to post–World War II generations (Scheiber et al. 1976:416–417, 424–429; Brownlee 1979:457–463; see also Smith 1955:657–659, 675–678).

1966–Present

Immigration

The passage of the Immigration Act of 1965 opened a dramatically new chapter in American immigration history. The act's abolition of the quota system as well as the increased prosperity of western Europe made for an ever-decreasing share of European immigrants. In their place came millions of Latin Americans and Asians, largely from developing countries. Not only did the 1965 act increase the share of non-European immigrants; it also boosted the number of immigrants overall. And although the nominal annual limits were themselves much greater than before 1965, they did not include the very large numbers of migrants exempt from numerical limitations. Often arriving in "chain migrations," family members of permanent residents compose the largest such group. The many waves of refugees form the next largest group, exemplified by the "Mariel boatlift" from Cuba in the early 1980s and the influx of Soviet Jews beginning in the 1970s. Finally, not everyone has entered with authorization. Undocumented migrants continue to cross over the Mexican-U.S. border, and many others arrive from Asia by air or sea. Some, such as many undocumented Irish, even initially came legally as tourists and simply overstayed their visas. In defiance of what they viewed as politically biased U.S. refugee policy, in the 1980s American members of the Sanctuary Movement also smuggled many Central American refugees into the country and sheltered them in churches and synagogues (Morrison and Zabusky 1980:346–349, 435–446; Bau 1985:9–37, 43–44; Muller and Espenshade 1985; Golden and McConnell 1986; Fetzer 1989:13–45; Morales 1989; Takaki 1989:419–423; Daniels 1990:307–327, 332–349, 350–370, 382–387, 400–402; Heer 1990; McWilliams 1990:320–321, 324–326; Reimers 1992:207–253; Simon and Alexander 1993:3–7, 11–12, 15–16; Branigin 1995; Barkan 1996:119–127; Masud-Piloto 1996:71–110; Simon 1997:59–79; O'Hanlon 1998:21; Rothenberg 1998:121–153).

Nativism

Available data leave some gaps, but nativism appears to have remained relatively low from 1966 through the end of that decade. The 1968

Republican platform, for example, "unreserved[ly]" supported the nondiscriminatory principles of the Hart-Celler Act of 1965 and pledged to make immigration law "still more equitable" (Simon and Alexander 1993:26).

By 1972, however, national opposition to immigrants had reappeared. In that year the GOP's platform called for a "halt [to] the illegal entry" of foreigners, or at least of those not "specially talented." After 1972 restrictionism seems to have declined and remained low through about 1978. Thus, a 1977 poll suggested that only 42% of Americans, a relatively small proportion, wanted less immigration. From 1979 to 1985, however, opposition to immigration reemerged, becoming a national political issue. The proportion of respondents supporting a reduction in immigration rose to 65% in 1981 and was still 66% one year later. The restrictionist Federation for American Immigration Reform (FAIR) was formed in 1979. U.S. English's campaign to make English the official language of the United States also took off during this period. Xenophobes beat Chinese-American Vincent Chin to death in Detroit in 1982, and blue-collar whites rioted against Latinos in Massachusetts in 1984. In the early 1980s Vietnamese fishermen along the Gulf of Mexico suffered violent opposition from white competitors. The normally pro-immigrant *New York Times* published a steady stream of editorials opposing Haitian refugees, undocumented Mexicans, and immigration in general in these years. *Reader's Digest* even spoke of "Our Immigration Nightmare" in 1983 (Daniels 1988:341–343; 1990:398; Takaki 1989:454, 481–483; McWilliams 1990:324; Simon and Alexander 1993:26, 41, 171, 222–225; Bennett 1995:363, 369–372).

Despite the fatal 1987 beating of an Asian Indian, in 1986 overall restrictionism declined significantly. Opposition to foreigners appears to have stayed relatively low through 1990. Although many recent Irish immigrants arrived "illegally," their presence did not seem to provoke any nativist backlash in the late 1980s. Only 49% of the respondents favored decreased immigration in 1986, and the figure was only slightly higher (53%) in 1988. In a dramatic shift, editorials in the *New York Times* resumed their normally pro-immigration tone from 1986 to 1990 (Takaki 1989:481; Daniels 1990:401–402; Simon and Alexander 1993:41, 225–229; O'Hanlon 1998:55–56).

Between 1991 and 1998, however, opposition to immigration seems to have risen and once again declined. By 1993, 64% of respondents said they wanted decreased immigration. In 1994, at around the peak of this nativist wave, California voters overwhelmingly passed the anti-undocumented-immigrant Proposition 187. The following year, however, the proportion of immigration opponents declined to 60%, and by 1997 the corresponding figure was only 48% (see Chapter 5 and Table A1.4; Espenshade and Hempstead 1995; Martin 1995; Hastings and Hastings 1997:191; Page 1997; Reimers 1998: 29–33).

Economy

Overall, the U.S. economy has grown slowly but very unevenly since 1965. Starting out very strong in 1966, economic growth gradually tapered off until 1969, when deficit spending induced by the Vietnam War caused the relatively mild recession of 1969–1970. Annual unemployment, for example, did not even exceed 5% for these two years (see Figure 2.1 and Table A1.1). The economy started recovering from 1971 to 1972, yet in 1973 the oil embargo by the Organization of Petroleum Exporting Countries precipitated the most severe recession since World War II. Lasting until 1975, this crisis caused widespread inflation and jobless rates approaching 9%. A recovery followed over the next four years, yet inflation and unemployment remained disturbingly high. Further increases in the price of oil in 1979 led to the recession of 1980 to 1982. Unemployment became increasingly worrisome, climbing to almost 10% for 1982. Tax reductions, larger defense budgets (with correspondingly larger budget deficits), and low savings rates fueled steady economic expansion from late 1982 to 1990.[13] In 1990 Gulf War–induced increases in oil prices once more caused a recession until 1991. Annual unemployment peaked at 7.5% in 1992, receded to 6.9% in 1993, and reached 4.9% in 1997 (Congressional Quarterly 1969:120–122; 1973:53–59; 1977: 49–56; 1981:205–209; 1985:27, 32; 1990:27–32; 1993:31–36; Slater 1996:xi–xiii; Bureau of Labor Statistics 1998:9).

Analysis of the Three Theories

Cultural Difference

The past 110 years of American immigration history do not support each of the three main explanations (i.e., cultural marginality or difference, economic self-interest or conditions, and contact or the proportion of foreign-born) equally. From 1880 to 1945 and 1966 to the present, native-born Americans' reception of a given group of immigrants does seem largely determined by how much the newcomers' culture diverged from the dominant WASP norm. Natives treated the highly distinct Chinese and Japanese abominably and the culturally similar British, Germans, and Scandinavians relatively well.[14] Relations between the United States and the country of origin appear to account for most outliers during these years (e.g., German Americans' sufferings during World War I and Chinese Americans' relatively decent treatment during World War II). The very mixed results for 1946–1965 (e.g., natives brutalized the moderately different Mexicans but behaved almost respectably toward the very culturally different Asians) could perhaps be attributed to the much greater number of Mexicans.

The American case might also suggest that nativism rises when a new wave of culturally distinct immigrants arrives. Pogrom-induced Jewish immigration from eastern Europe preceded the first Quota Act. The Zoot Suit Riots followed on the heels of the beginning of the *bracero* program. And the most recent era of nativism began about the time the post-1965 waves of Latin American and Asian immigration made themselves felt. Although Congress produced no landmark nativist legislation just after the 1906 wave of Russian Jewish immigration, the House narrowly rejected a literacy requirement that same year (Higham 1988:128–129; Daniels 1990:223–224).

Patterns of nativism across individuals, moreover, may also support the theory of cultural marginality. Cultural outsiders in American society often seemed more sympathetic to immigrants – perhaps the most marginalized "outsiders" of all – than the cultural "insiders" appeared to be. The Chicano labor leader J. M. Lizarras, for example, wanted to include Japanese as well as Mexican laborers in a planned American Federation of Labor (AFL) union in Oxnard, California. But the English American president of the AFL, Samuel Gompers,[15] agreed to grant Lizarras a charter only if the union "under no circumstances accept[ed] membership of any ... Japanese." Lizarras stood his ground, however, refusing "any other kind of charter, except one which will wipe out race prejudice and recognize our fellow [Japanese] workers as being as good as ourselves" (Takaki 1989:198–200).[16]

44

Comparing Caucasians' (or *haoles'*) views of Chinese in Hawaii to whites' attitudes toward Chinese in California tells a similar story. As Takaki (1989:39–40) suggests, white residents of Hawaii were themselves a greatly outnumbered ethnic minority on the islands: "Totaling only 6 percent of the population in 1878, [*haoles*] did not have a predominantly white society to preserve or defend." Not surprisingly, they urged their compatriots to "treat [Chinese immigrants to Hawaii] fairly." In the California of the 1880s, on the other hand, whites constituted almost 90% of the population. The violent hostility that Chinese workers encountered in California thus may have reflected native whites' felt "need to protect their white society" from the Chinese "threat to racial homogeneity."[17]

The major qualification to these findings for marginality theory seems to be that religious involvement may increase sympathy for immigrants regardless of one's religious identification (and, hence, regardless of one's own cultural marginality).[18] Across the variety of religions in America, greater commitment to religious ideals seems to promote pro-immigrant altruism. The (presumably white) Methodist clergy of San Francisco, for example, "as a body, denied the [nativists'] charges against the [largely non-Christian] Japanese." In fact, "Protestant churches . . . generally were the most vocal defenders of the Issei," the first-generation Japanese immigrants. Of course, some of this support for Asian immigrants might have also arisen from natives' desire to proselytize them (Daniels 1977:26). Yet even these ministers' belief that Japanese *could* be converted suggests much more respect for Asians than most nativists exhibited.[19]

American anti-immigrant rhetoric also points to the cultural causes of much restrictionism. One California judge of the 1920s claimed the Alien Land Act protected natives against immigrants who "substitute their philosophy of politeness and cunning for the enforcement of the 'golden rule'" and "bring to us their Oriental ideas and religion" (Daniels 1977:145). Even today, nativist Chilton Williamson Jr. (1996:115–116; see also Bork 1996:298–299) believes "the New Immigration of the 1980s and '90s" threatens the country's "culture and solidarity." "[T]he old WASP culture remains the only national culture worthy of the name," he contends. Such a "genuine American culture" is "incomparably superior to the . . . unsophisticated . . . proletarian and peasant cultures imported by the immigrant waves from the Civil War to the present."

Economic Conditions

American immigration history likewise reveals the effects of economic conditions. In prosperous times, natives usually tolerate immigrants. On the other hand, bursts of nativism have usually followed significant economic downturns (see Figure 2.1).[20] Membership in the American Protective Association skyrocketed during the Panic of 1893. Congress passed the first Quota Act during the depression of 1920–1922. The U.S. and state governments harassed and deported Mexicans and Mexican Americans during the worst of the Great Depression. And natives beat Vincent Chin to death during the severe recession of the early 1980s. One might of course view the second Quota Act and Proposition 187 as prominent exceptions to this general pattern. Both measures demanded at least a year of political "lead time" for passage, however, and both appear to have been sparked by earlier outbursts of recession-induced nativism. A critic might also wonder why the Zoot Suit Riots coincided with one of the lowest recorded unemployment rates in U.S. history. These anti-Chicano disturbances took place during the height of war-induced nationalism and paranoia (Mazón 1984:15–19), however, and therefore might not necessarily disconfirm economic theory.

Proportion of Foreign-Born

In contrast to cultural and economic factors, variations in the proportion of foreign-born in the population appear to explain over-time nativism poorly if at all. If the aggregate-level contact theory were correct, nativism should have peaked around 1910 and bottomed out around 1970 (see Figure 2.1). America of the 1990s, moreover, should only experience moderate nativism. Yet relatively few natives opposed immigration from 1900 to 1910, while the 1990s have arguably witnessed some of the most anti-immigrant political campaigns and legislation since 1924. Nativism was low around 1970, but the economy had been performing tolerably well (the mild recession of 1969–1970 notwithstanding), and the post 1965 wave of non-European immigration probably had not yet registered in the American psyche. Thus, economics and culture probably explain the low nativism of the early 1970s at least as well as the proportion of foreign-born does. Short-term, highly publicized bursts of culturally different immigration may boost xenophobia, but the simple number of immigrants in the population apparently does not.

Overall, this analysis of American immigration history has thus confirmed the cultural-marginality and economic theories. Yet the history of American nativism since 1880 does not provide much evidence for the over-time version of contact theory.

3

History of Attitudes toward Immigration in France

[T]he more we are invaded [by immigrants], the more our franc loses its value. . . . The experimentally demonstrated fact is that the Anglo-Saxon invasion has only one result, an increase in the cost of living. . . . We will end up vegetating in penury on soil which nature has blessed more than any other. . . . Beware of waking up one morning in a state of economic servitude! France will be nothing more than a colony.

> Journalist Gustave Téry, 1925 article
> in *l'Œuvre*, in Schor (1985:411)

A Christian church would have lost its soul and its reason for being if it did not put . . . divine law above all human eventualities. And divine law does not permit God-ordained families to be broken up, children to be separated from mothers, the right of asylum . . . to be ignored, respect for the individual to be infringed, and helpless people to be delivered to a tragic fate.

> National Council of the Reformed Church of
> France, in pastoral letter read in Protestant
> churches following the 1942 roundup of Jewish
> immigrants in Paris, in Bœgner (1989)

This analysis of French immigration history can only briefly outline the country's experience with immigrants since the end of the nineteenth century. For comprehensive histories of immigration into France during this period, see Dupâquier (1988a:214–227; 1988b), Noiriel (1988; 1996), Wihtol de Wenden (1988), Weil (1991), Lequin (1992; also previously published as Lequin 1988), and Schor (1996).

The works cited in the following paragraphs also provide good entrées into immigration during the specific periods.

1888–1914

Immigration

The aim of immigration into France from 1888, the beginning of significant governmental regulation of foreigners,[1] to the start of World War I in 1914 was to remedy the dramatic labor shortage caused by the country's continuing low birthrate. Until around the turn of the century, Belgians predominated, concentrating in the textile industry and mines of the north of France. Their numerical superiority was eventually surpassed by the many Italian laborers working in construction in the southeast and around Paris and in agriculture and maritime shipping near the Franco-Italian border. Besides these two nationalities, France also employed much smaller numbers of Spaniards, Swiss, and Germans (Perrot 1960; 1974:1:167; Tapinos 1975:4; Cross 1983:20–28; Dupâquier 1988a:214–216; Noiriel 1988:84–86; Wihtol de Wenden 1988:24; Lopez and Temime 1990:69–89; Lequin 1992:311, 326–332; Assouline and Lallaoui 1996a:12–53; Schor 1996:7–22).

Nativism

As Milza (1981:1:275) notes, "[t]he last three decades of the nineteenth century are marked in France by a strong upsurge in xenophobia toward foreign workers." Supporting Noiriel's claim (1988:258) that "at the end of the nineteenth century, xenophobic violence reache[d] an unheard-of intensity," Perrot (1960; see also 1974:1:170–173) documents eighty-two violent "incidents" (ranging from brawls to riots by as many as ten thousand people at a time) between natives and foreign workers from 1872 to 1893. At the southern town of Aigues-Mortes in 1893, for example, "the entire male population . . . masses in front of the town hall to demand the death of the 'Christos,' the principal derogatory term used for Italians during this period in the south of France. From there, armed with pitchforks and axehandles, the mob spills into the streets of the town and begins hunting Italians" (Milza 1979:25). A journalist covering the riots vividly describes the brutality with which the natives "hunted" the immigrants: "I have just been present at a scene of savagery without precedent and unworthy of a civilized people. At about 2:30 in the afternoon, in the middle of St. Louis square, in other words in the very center of Aigues-Mortes, a poor [Italian] wretch was attacked by a band of club-wielding brutes and literally had his brains beaten out. The maniacs didn't leave him until his skull was crushed to a pulp" (Vertone 1977:124). According to the government's figures, probably underestimated, these riots resulted in the deaths of eight Italians in addition to fifty or so injuries (Lopez and Temime 1990: 138; Schor 1996:25; see also Assouline and Lallaoui 1996a:80 –85).

From 1900 to the beginning of World War I, overall xenophobia seems to have declined compared with levels in the last decades of the nineteenth century. French farmers in Lorraine complained about the Poles' "excessive" Catholic zeal. Near the border with Belgium, French workers continued to threaten and harass Belgian immigrants, but such abuse does not seem to have reached the brutality of that meted out to Italians at Aigues-Mortes (Cross 1983:30; Lequin 1992:358, 380–381; Schor 1996:24–27).

Economy

As Figure 3.1 suggests, the French economy suffered a severe decline during the Grande Dépression of 1882–1896 but then gradually improved from 1897 to 1914. Although the depression of the late 1800s appears to have hurt the agricultural sector the most, the overall unemployment rate (measuring mainly industrial unemployment) reached a relatively high (for the time) 3.5% in the early 1890s. Starting in 1897, however, the economy began recovering, and after 1906 the growth rate accelerated rapidly (Caron 1979:29–30, 177–179; Asselain 1984a:161–163, 171–180; Bonin 1988:15–23).

1915–1918

Immigration

With the abrupt departure of many foreign workers for their homelands and of young Frenchmen for the front at the beginning of World

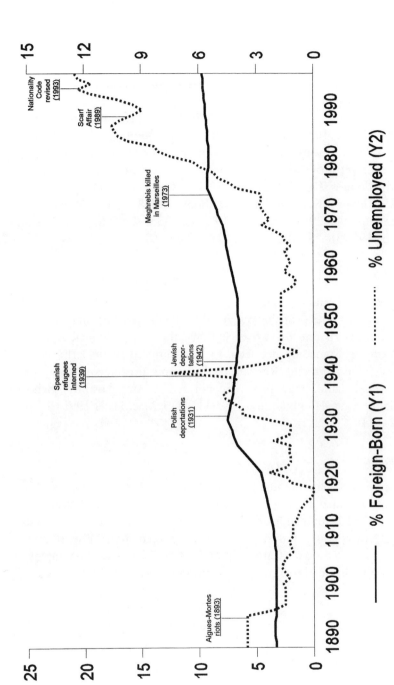

Figure 3.1. Nativism, foreign-born, and unemployment in France, 1888–1997. *Sources:* See Table A1.2.

Aigues-Mortes riots (1893)

Polish deportations (1931)

Spanish refugees interned (1939)

Jewish depor- tations (1942)

Maghrebis killed in Marseilles (1973)

Scarf Affair (1989)

Nationality Code revised (1993)

—— % Foreign-Born (Y1)   .... % Unemployed (Y2)

War I, France suddenly found itself without enough workers to support its agriculture, mining, and mushrooming munitions industry. In order to alleviate this shortfall, the French government recruited over 150,000 laborers from its colonies in North Africa and Indochina and contracted for over 200,000 workers from Spain, Portugal, Greece, Italy, and even China. Smaller numbers of ethnic Poles also aided the wartime French economy. At the end of hostilities, however, most of these various foreign workers were rapidly repatriated (Tapinos 1975:6; Mauco 1977:22; Cross 1983:33–41; Ageron 1985; Dupâquier 1988b:66–67; Ponty 1988:29–31; Wihtol de Wenden 1988:29–30; Lequin 1992:334–335; Le Moigne 1995:6; Schor 1996:38–44; MacMaster 1997:58–66, 68).

Nativism

Though relevant documentation appears rare, xenophobia toward most nationalities probably remained comparatively restrained during the war. With one or two exceptions, the many colonial subjects working in France do not seem to have suffered particularly severe abuses. German and Russian civilians and prisoners of war, on the other hand, may have encountered greater hostility (Schor 1985:69; 1996:41–44; Lequin 1992:335–336; MacMaster 1997:61–66, 122–124).

Economy

Despite or perhaps because of World War I, the French economy generally continued its prewar expansion from 1915 to 1918. Agriculture still lagged behind industry, but even the former sector appears to have grown slowly. Industry, meanwhile, posted annual growth rates of around 2% or 3% (Caron 1979:178–179). The overall unemployment rate declined to almost zero during the war (see Figure 3.1 and Table A1.2).

1919–1939

Immigration

Because of the catastrophic number of military casualties and the marked drop in births during World War I, France faced an even greater dearth of labor in 1919 than before the war. Several private organizations of employers, especially those forming the Société générale d'immigration, therefore recruited abroad for foreign replacements. Although Italians and Belgians continued to find work in France, the number of Polish and Spanish laborers increased dramatically in the interwar period. These two decades also witnessed the beginnings of a substantial peacetime work force from North Africa. Finally, the rise of National Socialism in 1930s Germany caused many Jews and dissidents to flee west to France, and Franco's victory in Spain in 1939 forced close to half a million Spanish refugees over the Pyrenees (Tapinos 1975:7–9; Mauco 1977:23–26; Cross 1983:52–63; Rovan 1983; Ageron 1985; Krieger-Krynicki 1985:45; Schor 1985:28, 37–39, 211–220, 613–626, 673–698; Dupâquier 1988b:96–98, 114–115; Lequin 1988:36–37; 1992:335–337, 409–412; Noiriel 1988:119, 152; Wihtol de Wenden 1988:36–38, 55; Bédarida 1991; Bennassar and Montbroussous 1991; Salgas 1991; Weil 1991:29, 49–50; Le Moigne 1995:7; Schor 1996:45–63, 103–109, 134–146).

Nativism

Anti-immigrant sentiment appears to have remained relatively restrained from 1919 to the end of the 1920s. In 1927 the legislature even allowed French women married to foreigners to retain French nationality for themselves and their children. The 1930s, however, witnessed a "wave of xenophobia" and even the murder of several immigrants. In the crisis year of 1931, striking French workers in northern France confronted Belgian "strikebreakers," hurling stones and bricks at them and even pitching several immigrants in the canals. France deported many Polish miners and their families between 1931 and 1936. Artisans, small-business owners, lawyers, and even doctors in the 1930s cried out against foreign-born competitors and sought "legal" protection for natives. No public outcry occurred, in contrast, when French authorities confined the Spanish refugees of 1939 in concentration camps[2] (Schor 1985:67–89, 391–546, 556, 561–562, 599–610, 675–698; Noiriel 1988:284–287; Borras 1991; Lagarde 1991; Decouflé 1992; Assouline and Lallaoui 1996b:72–81; see also Ponty 1988).

Treatment did vary according to the immigrant's nationality, however. In the 1930s, for example, French natives would habitu-ally use "tu," the informal or rude form of "you" in French, when addressing an African immigrant but would instead use "vous," the polite form, when speaking to a Belgian. Probably because of the recent conflict with France's neighbor "on the other side of the Rhine," "Germanophobia" also prevailed during the interwar years (Mauco 1977:32–33; Schor 1985:147–152; 1996:110–119; MacMaster 1997:125–133).

Economy

World War I had inflicted severe material and demographic damage on the country, yet France seemed to enjoy ever-increasing economic prosperity during most of the 1920s. One scholar even contends that during these years France "led the vanguard of European industrial progress" (Caron 1979:179; Asselain 1984b:13–29).

Although the worldwide depression beginning around 1929 or 1930 at first hurt France less than other countries, by 1931 the French were also beginning to suffer. From September 1931 to April 1932, French industrial production dropped 17%, and more than 250,000 workers (around 4%; see Figure 3.1) found themselves unemployed by the beginning of 1932. Economic conditions remained more or less grim through 1939 (Asselain 1984b:32–69).

1940–1945

Immigration

Though relatively little is known about foreigners in France during World War II, the two main trends seem to have been a reduction in their number and a radical deterioration in their conditions. Thou-sands of Algerians and Italians appear to have returned home at the beginning of the war, and the Nazis forcibly repatriated a few of the remaining Spanish refugees.[3] The Vichy regime, moreover, required almost fifty thousand foreigners to build fortifications for the German occupiers, and the Pétain administration rescinded the naturalizations of seven thousand Italians and six thousand Jews it deemed "undesir-able." Vichy also delivered over sixty thousand foreign Jews to the occupiers for deportation, the vast majority of whom perished in

54

Nazi death camps (Dupâquier 1988b:147, 159; Wihtol de Wenden 1988:79–80; Weil 1991:62, 72–73; Lequin 1992:414–415; Schor 1996:165–175).

Nativism

Because of the paucity of scholarship on the topic, estimating mass attitudes toward foreigners in France during World War II is difficult. The general public does not appear to have protested the gross violations of foreigners' rights or the Vichy government's various actions against Jews, however, and a reasonable guess is that xenophobia remained at least as high as during the 1930s. On the other hand, the French resistance did accept immigrants' help in struggling against Nazi occupation, and the French also appear to have viewed North African workers more or less positively (Ageron 1985; Wihtol de Wenden 1988:79–83; Lequin 1992:412–418; Assouline and Lallaoui 1996b:118–135; Schor 1996:167–179).

Economy

Despite a precipitous drop in French unemployment during German occupation (see Figure 3.1 and Table A1.2), World War II destroyed about 880 billion (1938 value) francs of the country's capital, or roughly one-quarter of the nation's wealth. The transportation system likewise suffered critical losses, and the war prevented the French from replacing aging equipment. The period thus hardly qualifies as prosperous (Caron 1979:195; Asselain 1984b:108).

1946–1974

Immigration

Once again facing a serious postwar labor shortage – due mainly to military and civilian casualties, the perennially low birthrate, and the rapidly expanding economy – France called on over two million foreign workers from 1946 to 1974 to fill its vacant positions in construction, public works, heavy industry, and domestic service. During this period, known as the Trente Glorieuses, the country drew its foreign laborers mainly from Spain, Italy, Portugal, and Morocco.

Beginning in the 1950s, smaller numbers of sub-Saharan Africans also found work in France (Tapinos 1975:13–15, 62, 98–99, 111–112, 126; Dupâquier 1988b:162–173, 463–465, 470–477; Wihtol de Wenden 1988:85; Weil 1991:558–559; Lequin 1992:421; Asselain 1995b: 69–76; Schor 1996:192–211).

Algeria's independence in 1962 forced the repatriation of close to one million French colonists, or pieds-noirs (literally "black feet"), back to metropolitan France. These immigrants tended to settle disproportionally in the cities of southern France, especially Marseilles. Roughly one hundred thousand harkis, or Algerian Muslims loyal to the French government, also accompanied the "Europeans" into exile (Tapinos 1975:55–58; Krieger-Krynicki 1985:27; Dupâquier 1988b:375, 459, 475; Jordi, Sayad, and Temime 1991:100–102, 106; Jordi 1995; Le Moigne 1995:9).

Nativism

From 1946 through the early 1970s, opposition to immigrants remained relatively restrained. Poll results even suggest that enthusiasm for immigration grew modestly from 1949 to 1965. In 1972 France criminalized racial discrimination in employment. A year later, however, opposition to immigrants exploded, leading to several deaths in Marseilles (Girard 1977; Gastault 1993; Schor 1996:223–229; see also Ageron 1985).

French xenophobes seem more likely to have targeted non-ethnic-European immigrants from 1946 to 1974. One French resident of Marseilles was quoted in 1973 as saying that "If this [North African immigration] continues, the children will end up speaking Arabic! Believe me, some of them [North Africans] should be killed. Here they're the kings" (Gastault 1993). European-origin, pied-noir refugees from Algeria were not always greeted with open arms, but they received a much warmer welcome than Berber- or Arabic-origin harki refugees (Jordi et al. 1991:101–106; Jordi 1995:36–57).

Economy

Although World War II left France's infrastructure devastated, reconstruction achieved such successes that from 1949 to the beginning of the 1970s the French economy experienced "unprecedented growth."

Compared with rates in later periods, unemployment remained modest, never rising above about 3% (see Figure 3.1 and Table A1.2). The crisis of 1973–1974, however, abruptly ended over two decades of robust expansion and set the stage for the increasingly severe decline of the years to come (Asselain 1984b:103–110; 1995b:362–366; Bonin 1988:245–249).

1975–Present

Immigration

Although in theory the French government "suspended" immigration in 1974, the reality since the mid-1970s belies official policy. First, hundreds of thousands of foreign workers have entered the country without authorization, and the government has sometimes seen fit to "regularize" them retroactively. Second, well over half a million spouses and children of foreign workers have immigrated to France since 1974. Finally, France has accepted the asylum claims of roughly 175,000 refugees. Foreigners arriving since 1974 have tended to come less from Europe and more from Africa (especially the sub-Saharan countries), Turkey, and Southeast Asia[4] (Tapinos 1975:119; Dupâquier 1988b:481–482, 488; Wihtol de Wenden 1988:194, 245; Weil 1991:124–128, 224–241, 354–358, 362–372, 376–377, 565–566; Lequin 1992:424–427; Le Moigne 1995:11, 16–17; Schor 1996: 230–247, 270–271).

Nativism

From 1975 to the present, French xenophobia has remained high (see Chapter 7), especially against North Africans. Refugees from Southeast Asia, however, seem relatively well received. During the 1989 "scarf affair," school authorities in Creil refused – with considerable public support – to admit three immigrant students who wanted to wear the traditional Muslim head covering (ḥijāb) for females. In 1993, furthermore, the parliament made acquisition of French nationality more difficult for second-generation immigrants[5] (Rovan 1983; Ben Jelloun 1984; Ageron 1985; Weil 1991:368; Wihtol de Wenden 1994; Gaspard and Khosrokhavar 1995:11–33; Schor 1996:248–284).

Economy

As Figure 3.1 illustrates, the years since 1974 have brought profound economic stagnation and ever-increasing unemployment. By 1997 the jobless rate had reached 12.5% (Statistics Directorate 1998:124) – roughly two and a half times that at the height of the Great Depression.

Analysis of the Three Theories

Cultural Difference

Support for a cultural form of marginality theory appears substantial. At any one time, French preferences for different nationalities of immigrants often do seem to follow a rough ranking of similarity to the dominant French culture. During the interwar period, such Europeans as Belgians, Swiss, and Italians enjoyed much more favor than such "exotics" as Levantines (originating in the countries east of the Mediterranean) and North Africans. Similarly, native-born Marseillans welcomed pieds-noirs more warmly than they did Berber- or Arab-origin Algerians in the 1960s. The intense "Germanophobia" of the interwar years (probably explained by previous German invasions of France) and the apparent preference for even Germanophone Swiss over the more "culturally similar" Italians in the pre–World War I era (perhaps a function of the Swiss immigrants' higher class) nevertheless remain exceptions to this trend (Schor 1985:138–174; Lopez and Temime 1990:117–126, 183–184; see also Tapinos 1975:40 and Lequin 1992:456).

Although "cross-sectional" versions of cultural marginality appear valid, "over-time" cultural explanations of xenophobia receive much less support in France than in the United States. If one views French immigration historically, those major immigrant groups which have been objectively closer to the French culturally have not necessarily been more easily tolerated than the culturally "strange" foreigners. Italians and Spaniards, both "Latin Catholics," would seem close to the French culturally, and North Africans and Southeast Asians, neither European nor predominantly Christian, much further removed. Yet, as incidents such as that in Aigues-Mortes demonstrate, the Italians were not necessarily better treated at the height of their immigration than the Maghrebis are today, at the height of theirs.[6] The cultural similarities with the Spanish refugees of 1939 did not cause a mass outcry when the French authorities confined them to concentration camps. "Culturally exotic" refugees from Southeast Asia, on the other hand, seem relatively well received. Of course, non-cultural factors (e.g., relations between France and the country of origin, political ideology, the state of the economy, cumulated experience with immigrants) may also help explain these differences in treatment. If one could evaluate the effects of these various factors all at the same time, an influx of culturally different immigrants may indeed have an independent influence on overall levels of nativism. Perhaps the Italians and Spaniards would have received better treatment if the French economy had not been ailing when they arrived, for example. This examination of the historical evidence should nonetheless warn against facile assertions that anti-immigrant sentiment is always and everywhere a function of objective cultural differences.[7]

In contrast, objective cultural differences (and, hence, often perceived threats to the dominant, "mainstream" culture) do seem to help explain why *individual* natives are more or less likely to support certain immigrants. French Jews of the 1930s appear to have supported foreign Jewish refugees slightly more faithfully than non-Jews did, and French Catholics seem to have appreciated more than other natives the devotion of the predominantly Catholic Poles. Having less stake in maintaining Catholic supremacy and recalling their own history of persecution as a religious minority, French Protestants seem to have far surpassed French Catholics in helping Jewish refugees escape deportation to Nazi death camps. French Protestants also appear less ambivalent than French Catholics about supporting today's predominantly Muslim immigrants (Hallie 1979; Schor 1985:144, 191; 1996:178; Fabre 1989; Bosc 1995; see also Gastault 1994 and Chapter 7).

Contrary to the cultural version of marginality theory, however, some French Catholic clergy and intellectuals have shown themselves to be pro-immigrant and pro-refugee, even when the foreigners are not Catholic or even Christian. Representatives of the Catholic Church spoke out in support of German Jewish refugees in the 1930s.

The archbishop of Lyon and such Catholic writers as François Mauriac and Jacques Maritain supported asylum for the anticlerical Spanish Communists. Several Catholic clerics in the 1970s fought for or even provided mosques for the many Muslim immigrants in their communities. Since the 1970s, Catholic clergy have proved themselves one of the most enduring sources of support for undocumented immigrants (Mauco 1932:534–536; 1977:143; Schor 1985:327–346, 618–619; 1996:177–179, 259–260; Wihtol de Wenden 1988:271; Weil 1991:296, 300; Lequin 1992:411; Gastault 1993; 1994; Siméant 1998:170–173).

Perhaps this dichotomy between rank-and-file Catholics (many of whom are presumably nonpracticing) and Catholic elites arises from a greater internalization among the clergy and intellectuals of the spirit of their religion and from a greater sense of cultural insecurity among the less-educated base (see Chapter 7). Among the elite, universal principles of compassion and solidarity with the oppressed would win out over any threat that the non-Catholic immigrants might pose to the supremacy of Catholicism in France. Having a more superficial understanding of Catholic Christianity, the laity might, on the other hand, be more likely to resist the immigrants' perceived efforts to replace them in their privileged cultural position.

Finally, although French antiforeigner rhetoric has historically been mainly economic, some members of the far right as well as several population experts – all members of the mainstream culture – have criticized immigration in explicitly cultural terms. Convinced of the superiority of the French culture, the extreme right of the interwar period feared a "bastardization" or "internationalization" of France by "elements whose culture and standard of living are inferior to ours." These right-wing critics also deplored the "imposition" on the French public of "the most mediocre [foreign] painters," in particular, Chirico, Miro, Chagall, and Picasso (Schor 1985:347–348, 356). The French immigration specialist Georges Mauco[8] (1932:555–558) likewise complains that foreigners "Europeanize" France and develop in the country "the taste for narrow discipline and the trend toward mechanization that are opposed to French humanism." "Don't the French race [sic] and culture," he asks, "risk suffering from this influx [of naturalized French citizens], this peaceful invasion?" And even the eminent French demographer Jacques Dupâquier (1988b:551) fears a future in which France will be "cut in two, its national identity threatened, with an aging majority, withdrawn into its values and acquired rights, and a young Islamic minority, poorly integrated and more or less aggressive."

Economic Conditions

Evidence for the second, or economic, theory is even more overwhelming than in the United States. Every major economic crisis (see Figure 3.1) since 1888 has provoked an upsurge in antiforeigner sentiment. The Grande Dépression of 1882–1896 unleashed what was probably the most extreme outbreak of anti-Italian sentiment and violence in French history. The Great Depression of 1929–1938 produced another major wave of xenophobia and deportations, even though violence seems to have been less frequent. The crisis of 1973–1974 coincided with the "racist blaze of 1973." The continuing economic crisis of the 1980s and 1990s, moreover, seems to have provoked an increasingly alarming public rejection of immigrants. The intervening periods of absolute or relative prosperity, in contrast, generally seem to lack such marked hostility to foreigners (Rovan 1983; Schor 1985:547–709; 1996:26; Noiriel 1988:261–262; Wihtol de Wenden 1988:220–379; Jordi et al. 1991:109–111, 174–183; Weil 1991:112–115, 158–318; Decouflé 1992; Lequin 1992:399–412; Gastault 1993; Commission nationale consultative des droits de l'homme 1994; see also Chapters 5 and 7).

Proportion of Foreign-Born

Again confirming the American results, contact theory performs poorly in France. At least at the "macro," or national, level, the percent foreign-born does not seem to explain over-time variations in French opinion toward foreigners. As Figure 3.1 illustrates, the proportion of foreign-born was highest in the 1930s (over 7%) and since the 1960s (officially from 7.4% to 9.4%), and lowest from around 1888 to 1906 (about 3.3%).

The late nineteenth century, however, was notorious for its xenophobia and the number and brutality of its anti-immigrant riots. During the two periods with the highest proportion of foreigners, on the other hand, the natives do not clearly seem more hostile (if greater hostility is possible!). The 1930s and the post-1960 period certainly witnessed high nativism as well, but even the "racist blaze" of 1973 (Gastault 1993) does not quite equal the brutality of an Aigues-Mortes. Of course, rising average levels of education in the past hundred years may have also reduced the likelihood of xenophobic violence. Yet contact theory would have still predicted more violence in the 1930s than actually occurred.

The public may nevertheless need a concrete object (i.e., real immigrants) about which to form a meaningful opinion. Where there are virtually no immigrants, it is not surprising that natives either have no stable views on immigration or at least usually have no markedly anti-immigrant sentiments. It is no wonder, for example, that most of the anti-Italian "incidents" of the late 1800s occurred near the border with Italy, where the Italians were concentrated, rather than in Brittany, where the foreign population was all but nil. Although the presence of *some* immigrants (e.g., at the *départemental* level) may thus be a prerequisite for significantly anti-immigrant attitudes, *over-time* variations in the size of this foreign presence (again, if we assume that the region contains enough immigrants to justify speaking of a "foreign presence" at all) do not seem to explain changes in attitudes toward immigrants very well (Perrot 1974:1:171; Dupâquier 1988a: 217–219; 1988b:135–137; Lopez and Temime 1990:185; Lequin 1992:329–332, 457–458).

Overall, then, the French case strongly supports the economic and cultural-marginality explanations of anti-immigrant sentiment but provides little evidence for theories stressing the proportion of immigrants in the population. With the minor exception of over-time cultural differences, these results parallel the American findings.

4

History of Attitudes toward Immigration in Germany

It may sound chauvinistic: "Germany for the Germans." But it is not meant to be. These words harbor a basic truth, and the failure to recognize that truth will be bitterly avenged should migration continue at the same pace. If we grant permits to foreign workers to the extent desired by the employers, we are heading for serious trouble. Interbreeding with all these alien elements can only spell disaster for the purity of the Germanic tribes. May Providence protect Germany from witnessing the spectacle of her own native sons stunted and wasting away – in favor of foreign nationals!

> Leipzig professor Stieda, 1910 address to Sixth
> Labor Exchange Congress, in Herbert (1990:28)

As a minority in the Reich, we have not forgotten how we were treated and for this reason alone, not to speak of higher considerations and deeper motives, we shall never lend a hand to forge weapons used today against the [eastern European] Jews, tomorrow against Poles, and the day after tomorrow against the Catholics. . . . Don't expect our support in making it possible for you to exult: "We got rid of the Jews. Now bon voyage to the Catholics!"

> Catholic Center Party politician Ernst
> Lieber, parliamentary speech from 1894–1895
> session, in Wertheimer (1987:38)

This chapter provides a sketch of the history of immigration in Germany over the past one hundred plus years.[1] For more comprehensive, single-volume introductions to this history, see Bade (1983b, 1992a) and Herbert (1990). For more detailed treatment of specific periods, see the references cited in the summaries.

1880–1913

Immigration

The first major wave of foreign workers into the newly founded Germany[2] was that of ethnic Poles from Russia and Austro-Hungary. As a result of mass migration either to German urban centers in the West or to other countries abroad (mainly the United States), East Prussian agriculture suffered from an acute labor shortage, or *Leutenot*. Despite the addition of German workers from the eastern agricultural regions, the expanding industries in western Germany (especially the Ruhr region) also faced a critical lack of laborers, or *Arbeiternot*. The Poles helped alleviate both of these labor shortages, working during the growing season on the farms of eastern Germany and year-round in the mines and factories of the Ruhr as *Ruhrpolen*. Although other nationalities also found work in Germany from 1880 to the outbreak of World War I, ethnic Poles from Russia, Austro-Hungary, and even what was then eastern Germany were the dominant "non-German" work force (Kleßmann 1978:12–22; 1992; Bade 1983b:23–24, 29–33; 1992b; Dohse 1985:29–43; Herbert 1990:11; Kulczycki 1994).

Millions of eastern European Jews also migrated west through and to Germany after 1881. Fleeing poverty and pogroms, most Jewish immigrants simply transited the German Reich on their way to countries such as the United States. Other eastern European Jews, however, sought sanctuary and a wide variety of jobs in Germany (Wertheimer 1987:11–12, 21, 91–102; Daniels 1990:223–225; Blank 1992).

Nativism

Polish workers in the pre–World War I years suffered from pitifully poor housing, considerable public hostility, and often severe physical abuse. Social conservatives and religious Germans lashed out at Prussian employers for housing Polish workers in "haylofts, horse stables, or cattle sheds, or in some structure or other in the farmyard." Such poor lodging often caused the workers to "suffer horribly from the cold." Especially among ethnic German workers, the "culturally despised . . . Polacks" became an object of widespread "prejudice and discrimination." Beginning in 1885, Prussian authorities deported at least twenty thousand Polish immigrants and their families. In 1913 the prince-bishop of Breslau submitted to the Prussian Ministry of Culture a long and detailed list of physical abuses against foreign workers. In one reported incident, for example, the "supervisor struck the [Polish] worker with his riding whip because he had lost hold of his plow." The worker's boss also "attempted to ride him down with his horse" and later, with the aid of the foreman, "beat [the Pole] so heavily with a whip over his head and back that the man . . . was unable to work for six days" (Neubach 1967:125–131; Kleßmann 1978:51; Herbert 1990:9–85; Bade 1992b; Blank 1992; Brubaker 1992:131, 223).

Eastern European Jewish immigrants faced comparable hostility. The German government summarily expelled roughly ten thousand foreign Jews around 1885 and targeted Russian Jews for deportations again from 1905 to 1906. A petition calling for the end of most Jewish immigration and of many civil rights for Jews received close to 250,000 signatures in 1881, while anti-Semitic "patriotic" and business associations flourished. In 1913 the German Reichstag passed a law making German nationality almost completely a function of having German "blood" (*jus sanguinis*),[3] thus excluding all ethnically Jewish or Polish immigrants (Neubach 1967:125–131; Wertheimer 1987:60–62; Blank 1992; Brubaker 1992:114–137).

Economy

From 1880 to about 1895, the German economy suffered from the severe Great Depression (see Figure 4.1 and Table A1.3), with unemployment rates perhaps as high as 15%. Beginning in 1896 the economy stabilized, however, and relative prosperity prevailed until the recession of late 1913 (Kitchen 1978:161–172, 266; Braun 1990:22).

1914–1918

Immigration

At the start of World War I, the Prussian government prevented all foreign workers from enemy countries from returning home. The

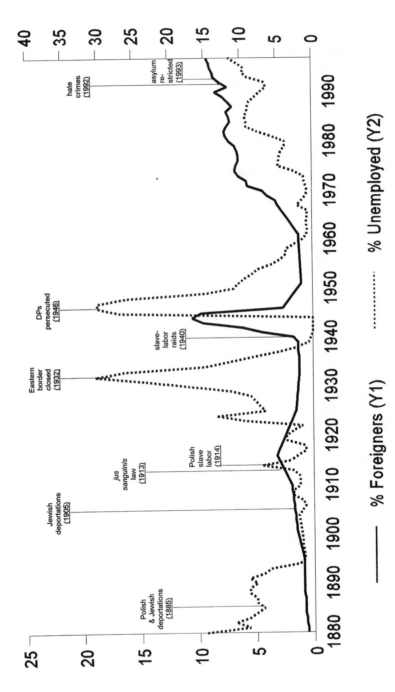

Figure 4.1. Nativism, foreigners, and unemployment in Germany, 1880–1997. *Sources*: See Table A1.3.

—— % Foreigners (Y1)   ·········· % Unemployed (Y2)

mainly Russian Poles then remained in Germany as forced agricultural laborers for the duration of the war, helping to replace the
Germans serving in the military or killed in battle. These forced
laborers were later joined by the over two million prisoners of war
(POWs), mainly from Russia, France, and England, captured between
1914 and 1918. Although the German authorities also tried to force
civilians from occupied Belgium to come to work in German industry, this attempt at coercion proved a failure (Herbert 1985:24–35;
1990:87–119).

Nativism

These forced laborers received their share of hostility and abuse, not
the least of which was being prevented from returning home. Poles,
however, appeared to suffer harsher treatment than some other
nationalities. In 1915, for example, the armed forces command center
in Münster noted that the "number of complaints [of poor treatment]
among Belgian workers is not anywhere near what it is among the
Russian Poles." Germans in general appeared unconcerned about the
fate of foreign workers during World War I. Few natives complained
in 1914 about the Poles being forced to remain in Germany, although
the German public does seem to have noticed the forced conscription
of Belgian civilians (Dohse 1985:77–81; Herbert 1985:24–35, 113,
117; 1990:87–119).

Economy

Although the start of World War I in 1914 saw a relatively high unemployment rate of 7.2% (see Figure 4.1), later periods of the war witnessed severe labor shortages. Beginning in 1916, shortages of food
and long working hours led to serious labor unrest (Henning 1978:11;
Braun 1990:25–31).

1919–1932

Immigration

Despite the often high overall levels of German unemployment
during the Weimar Republic, farms in eastern Germany continued to

rely on Polish migrant workers. Many ethnic Poles remained in the Ruhr region as well. Germany also employed a few foreign workers from Czechoslovakia, Holland, and Austria, and in the 1920s Berlin sheltered as many as three hundred thousand refugees from the Russian Revolution (Kleßmann 1978:172–177; Bade 1980; Herbert 1990:121–126; Schlögel 1998:78–110).

Nativism

While public opposition to Poles appeared weaker than before World War I, the German right continued to protest the Poles' efforts to maintain their culture. Particularly offensive to ethnic Germans in the Ruhr were Polish-language secondary schools, especially once the economic crisis began. In 1932 Germany closed its eastern border to migrant farm workers. Hostility to the Russian refugees in Berlin, meanwhile, does not seem to have been especially strong (Kleßmann 1978:172–174; Herbert 1990:127; Schlögel 1998:78–110).

Economy

With few exceptions, Germany's economy enjoyed relative stability from 1919 to 1923 and almost achieved real prosperity during the Golden Twenties from 1924 to 1929. From 1929 to 1932, however, the country experienced perhaps the most severe depression in its history (see Figure 4.1; Henning 1978:11–12, 51–140; Braun 1990: 33–77).

1933–1945

Immigration

The Nazi period of 1933 to 1945 brought one of the largest and probably the most exploited number of foreigners, or *Fremdarbeiter*, in German history. As the expanding armaments industry and later World War II caused ever greater demands for labor, the Nazis forced millions of POWs and civilians from occupied Europe to work in German industry. In 1940 Nazi authorities began raiding Polish schools, cinemas, towns, and whole cities in search of slave laborers. Especially under Allied bombardment toward the end of the war, the forced laborers faced a horrific working environment, and many thousands either died from the brutal conditions or were simply murdered. At the end of the war, many of the surviving *Fremdarbeiter* became the stateless "displaced persons," who gradually found new homes around the world (Homze 1967; Dohse 1985:119–134; Herbert 1985; 1990: 127–192; Jacobmeyer 1992).

Nativism

The largely eastern European forced laborers in World War II encountered deliberate, mass starvation, nightmarish working conditions, draconian punishments, and a populace that was often more hostile than the workers' own employers. Forced laborers from western Europe, however, often fared slightly better (Herbert 1985; 1990:127–192).

Economy

From Hitler's rise to power in 1933 until the beginning of World War II in 1939, the overall German economy improved dramatically (see Figure 4.1 and Table A1.3). Although unemployment exceeded 26% in 1933, by 1939 militarization and the beginning of the war had practically abolished male joblessness (Nazi ideologues frowned on women working outside the home). During the war itself, severe labor shortages became the rule, but the many war-induced economic dislocations hardly qualify this period as one of economic prosperity. As the Germans' defeat neared in 1944, the country's economy finally collapsed (Henning 1978:141–184; Braun 1990:78–143).

1946–1973

Immigration

As part of Germany's defeat, roughly twelve million ethnic Germans, or *Vertriebene*, were driven out of eastern Europe – including those parts of Poland and Russia that had belonged to Germany before the war – into the area of today's Federal Republic. The ten million who survived the trek were forced to begin their lives from scratch in the war-devastated Germany, causing even more hardships for the "native

Germans" who were compelled to receive them. Especially before the building of the Berlin Wall in 1961, roughly four million East German *Übersiedler* also fled to West Germany, adding to the West Germans' problems of integrating so many "nonnatives" (Kulischer 1948: 266–268, 282–287; Lemberg and Edding 1959; Bade 1992c; Benz 1992; de Zayas 1994; Thorwald 1995; Bade, Meier, and Parisius 1997).

As Germany's postwar economic recovery, or *Wirtschaftswunder*, heated up, the country once again faced a severe shortage of labor. Beginning in the 1950s and continuing into the 1970s, the government therefore recruited thousands of "guest workers," or *Gastarbeiter*, from southern Europe, especially Turkey, to work in the Federal Republic.[4] Although their stay was originally supposed to be temporary, millions of these "guests" eventually brought their families as well and so today constitute what is probably the largest group of immigrants in Germany (Mehrländer 1974; Heckmann 1981; Bade 1983b:82–95; 1992e; Dohse 1985:181–200; Herbert 1990:201–235; Şen 1993).

Nativism

Public reception of the two early groups of newcomers appears to have differed greatly. Despite the Allies' widespread fears of a severe native German backlash against the expellees, such an explosion failed to materialize, and their relatively successful integration ranks with the *Wirtschaftswunder* as a postwar German "miracle." In contrast, the German public seems to have transferred their suppressed rage at the Allied occupiers and the postwar devastation onto the displaced persons. Even the German police delighted in persecuting them (Herbert 1985:341–345; Kleinert 1990; Benz 1992; Jacobmeyer 1992; Bade et al. 1997:159–168).

The two later groups of immigrants also encountered widely different welcomes. Coming from the former East Germany, the *Übersiedler* were rapidly and easily assimilated into West German society. Indeed, West German citizenship law did not even consider them immigrants. The Turks were not so lucky, however. Scores of opinion polls, hundreds of anti-Turkish hate crimes, and the ubiquity of vicious "Turkish jokes" all testify to the extreme public opposition that most *Gastarbeiter* have faced in the Federal Republic (Wallraff

1985:108–114; Bade 1992c; Brubaker 1992:169; Leggewie 1992; Morris 1993; Kürsat-Ahlers 1996; *Los Angeles Times* Wire Service 1997; see also Chapter 8).

Economy

Although the immediate postwar German economy can only be described as catastrophic, by the mid-1950s the *Wirtschaftswunder* was bringing renewed prosperity (see Figure 4.1). The economy continued to enjoy relatively good health until the time of the oil crisis in 1973 (Henning 1978:185–244; Braun 1990:144–173).

1974–Present

Immigration

With the fall of the Iron Curtain in the late 1980s, millions of persecuted ethnic Germans in eastern Europe now had the option of returning to their ethnic homeland in the Federal Republic. Originating mainly from Poland, Romania, and the ex–Soviet Union, thousands of such *Aussiedler* have emigrated west to begin new lives as "Germans among Germans." The end of the Cold War has also allowed tens of thousands of ex-Soviet Jews to settle permanently in Germany (Bade 1990; 1992c; Runge 1995; Chapin 1997:23–24).

Germany's relatively generous pre-1993 asylum policy also brought thousands of asylum seekers, or *Asylbewerber*, in the 1980s and 1990s. Largely from Romania, Turkey, the former Yugoslavia, and various developing countries in Africa, Asia, and the Middle East, these asylum seekers receive food and housing at least until their cases are decided. Even after having had their applications rejected, many remain in the country illegally, or the government nevertheless allows them to stay until the situation in their homeland improves (Bade 1992d; Axt 1997; Chapin 1997:18–23).

Nativism

Public reception of these foreigners continues to vary widely by the ethnic origin of the immigrant group.[5] On the whole the *Aussiedler* have provoked relatively little serious reaction and receive full

German citizenship upon arrival. Ex-Soviet Jews, on the other hand, face popular anti-Semitism and Neo-Nazi vandalism of their synagogues and cemeteries. Asylum seekers probably fare much worse, however, often exchanging political persecution in their homeland for another form of terror in Germany. During the 1992 wave of hate crimes, skinheads[6] and other hoodlums beat up or burned out hundreds of such *Asylbewerber* and Turkish immigrants, causing several deaths. Partly in response to this violence, in 1993 the German parliament tightened the constitutional requirements (Article 16) for obtaining asylum (Bade 1992c; 1992d; 1997; Brubaker 1992:165; Bundesministerium des Innern 1993:72–78, 91–94; Svoray and Taylor 1994; Human Rights Watch 1995; Runge 1995:32–33, 98–100; Willems 1995; Kurthen, Bergmann, and Erb 1997; Watts 1997:61–69, 260–261; Laster and Ramet 1998).

Economy

From the 1974–1975 recession to the present, Germany has generally suffered from an increasingly ailing economy. Unemployment rates, for example, have risen to levels similar to those during the Great Depression of the late nineteenth century (see Figure 4.1; Braun 1990:169–222).

Analysis of the Three Theories

Cultural Difference

Immigrants' cultural marginality or difference, often perceived by natives as a threat to the German culture, seems to have a large effect on acceptance of foreigners. At a given time, public reception of the major groups of foreigners appears largely determined by how similar the group's culture is to that of the Germans. In employing eastern European seasonal workers before World War I, the Prussians seem to have accorded the less culturally different ethnic Masuren more respect than the more culturally "threatening" ethnic Poles and the ethnic Jews. Similarly, the German population of the Nazi era appears to have accepted the western and northern European forced laborers more readily than the Slavic ones. In the immediate post–World War

II period, the largely eastern European DPs faced much more severe hostility than the ethnic German expellees. Today Turkish *Gastarbeiter* and non-European and Romanian-"Gypsy" *Asylbewerber* suffer much more abuse than the ethnic German *Aussiedler* (Töppen 1969: 482–508; Kleßmann 1978:20, 73; Weber 1983:230–250; Herbert 1990:200).

German immigration history does not demonstrate that waves of culturally divergent immigrants are the principal cause of nativism, however. The arrival of the first waves of Turkish *Gastarbeiter* in the 1950s and 1960s did not coincide with widespread xenophobia. The influx of non-European asylum seekers in the 1990s did occur at the same time as the dramatic rise in hate crimes and the restriction of asylum (see Figure 4.1). Rational-choice theorists would counter, however, that the severe recession of the early 1990s and the economically traumatic unification with the former East Germany were more likely to blame. The massive "immigration" of Slavic slave laborers in World War II certainly coincided with unspeakably brutal treatment of most foreigners. Yet critics might contend the war effort itself was at least partly responsible.

Nevertheless, cultural factors do appear to affect which *individual* natives are more or less opposed to foreigners. Among the German clergy of the late nineteenth and early twentieth centuries, Catholics seemed much more concerned for the welfare of foreign workers than the Lutherans were. As Just (1990) notes, a "principal reason" for this difference was "certainly that the great majority of the foreigners, the Poles, Ruthenians, and Italians, were Catholic." German Catholics were better able to "see in the foreigner a fellow human being, especially when it was a matter of 'co-religionists.'" Lutheran churches, on the other hand, were more likely "energetically to support" the Prussian government's efforts "either to exclude or to Germanize strangers and national minorities."

Even under National Socialism such a dynamic seems to have been at work, much to the consternation of the authorities. An SS intelligence report from 1939 complains about German Catholic priests who would habitually shake hands with Polish Catholic POWs or forced laborers in front of the church after mass. Some priests would even ask their parishioners for donations for the Poles, and in general the "excessively friendly attitude of the Catholic clergy and that part of the population under their influence toward the Polish POWs has on several occasions produced infuriation among the National Socialist population" (Herbert 1985:70–71).

Yet, at least since 1945, even the very mainstream, *evangelische* clergy and active laity have sometimes supported immigrants. Despite belonging to the most established and arguably most powerful religious tradition, some Protestant leaders harshly criticized the deplorable conditions of guest workers in the 1960s. More recently, *evangelische* ministers in Mannheim joined with Muslim leaders and city officials to help alleviate the public's anti-Islamic prejudices. Without such efforts, city residents' misconceptions about Muslims might have made building Mannheim's large mosque impossible.[7] And many Protestant pastors direct the "church asylum" movement's civil-disobedience campaigns on behalf of non-European refugees (Herbert 1990:215–216; Just 1993; Mucan 1999).

This minor qualification aside, the rhetoric of German nativists further supports the cultural interpretation. One 1885 newspaper article opposing Polish workers, for example, claimed:

> A Polonization is taking place in certain regions that had previously been won over to Germanic customs, culture, and language. A wave of Polish immigration is inundating our eastern provinces [in Prussia]. . . . All this forces upon us the question as to whether it is not in fact necessary – in the interest of self-preservation – to close the door tightly on any further expansion of Polish culture and their national-political conception. (Bade 1983a; Herbert 1990:11)

Of course, the author was probably just as much concerned about the resurrection of a Polish state carved out of Prussian territory (hardly an idle fear, given later events) as about a decline of German national traditions. Much of such anti-Polish rhetoric nevertheless proceeded on the assumption that Germans were on a "higher cultural level" than the "Slavic" foreign workers (Bade 1992b).

In a similar spirit, the anti-immigrant Heidelberg Manifesto of 1981 warns of a "foreign infiltration [*Überfremdung*] of our language, our culture, and our national traditions [*Volkstum*]" by the "influx of many million foreigners and their families." It then calls for the "return of the foreigners to their ancestral homeland" and "the founding of a nonpartisan and ideologically independent league" whose mission is to "preserv[e] . . . the German people [*Volk*] and their spiritual identity on the basis of our Christian-Western heritage" (Bade 1983b:112).

Economic Conditions

Turning to the second main theory of public acceptance of immigrants, we find substantial evidence for the effect of economic conditions (see Figure 4.1). The *Wirtschaftswunder* provided good economic conditions during the relatively uneventful integration of the *Vertriebene* and most of the *Übersiedler*. The economic devastation of the immediate postwar period and the recession of the 1990s, on the other hand, coincided with the persecution of the displaced persons, the burst of hate crimes against *Gastarbeiter* and *Asylbewerber*, and the restriction of asylum. During the Great Depression of the 1880s, the Prussian government deported foreign Poles and Jews. And in response to the worst of the depression of the 1930s, Germany closed its eastern border. Perhaps the major outlier is the deportation of Jews during the relative prosperity of 1905, but twentieth-century German history suggests many obvious reasons for this exception (Braun 1990:144–152, 165–174).

Proportion of Foreign-Born

Finally, an examination of the percentage of the population that is foreign lends very lukewarm support to theories of contact. As Figure 4.1 and the underlying data in Table A1.3 suggest, the proportion of foreigners in general was highest during the latter stages of World War II (*Fremdarbeiter*) and in the 1980s and 1990s (mainly the *Gastarbeiter*). Although the *Vertriebene* were technically German citizens, one might also view them as a large immigrant group in the decade or two following the end of World War II. According to the Statistisches Bundesamt (1956:45), *Vertriebene* accounted for 16.7% of the West German population in 1951. The lowest levels of foreigners, on the other hand, come mainly from the late nineteenth-century *Kaiserreich*. The long period in which the *Übersiedler* arrived in West Germany is on average one with a moderate number of foreigners.

The high percentage of foreigners in the population might help explain the poor treatment of DPs, *Asylbewerber*, *Gastarbeiter*, and *Fremdarbeiter*. This contact variable seems much less useful, however, in accounting for the relatively good treatment of the *Vertriebene* and *Aussiedler*, groups that arrived during periods with high levels of foreigners. This theory would also have trouble explaining the Polish and Jewish deportations before World War I and the relatively sudden increase in anti-immigrant activity after 1990.

In general, then, the German case strongly supports the cultural and economic explanations of nativism. What evidence German history appears to provide for contact theory is probably a spurious reflection of cultural difference and economic conditions, however.[8] With little variation across the three countries in this study, then, immigration history since the 1880s suggests that immigrants are at particular risk of attack if they come from a culture that is especially different from the host country's. Individual natives who belong to the dominant cultural (i.e., linguistic, ethnic, religious) group, moreover, appear less likely to come to the aid of the foreign-born than are more culturally "marginal" natives. In all three countries, however, increased religious activity seems to foster sympathy for immigrants even among members of the dominant or majority religion. Again across the United States, France, and Germany, economic downturns usually spark renewed opposition to immigrants and immigration, whereas prosperity generally attenuates such hostility. In none of the three countries, in contrast, does an increase in the overall proportion of immigrants consistently appear to cause xenophobia.

Where the three countries diverge most markedly is probably in their response to a fresh wave of culturally different immigrants. Whereas a rapid influx of such newcomers seems to have provoked nativist outbursts in the United States, analysis of French and German immigration history fails to duplicate these results. Were migrant flows in the three countries not correlated with such confounding factors as the state of the economy, one might be able to determine the true effect of a new wave of culturally divergent immigration. Qualitative analysis of immigration history as it is, however, probably does not allow us to conclude one way or the other.

PART II

Quantitative Analysis

The single most startling implication of our analyses is for those who justify apprehension about immigration in economic terms. Although debate continues about the economic consequences of immigration, there is increasing acceptance of the view that rather than taking jobs from nationals, immigrants add needed elements to the work force. . . . Added to this is the evidence from our study which demonstrates that except in the United States, opinion toward immigrants is weakly related or unrelated to economic variables of any kind: employment status, income or economic concern. Such patterns suggest that portraying immigrants as economic predators is at best ill-informed and at worst a conscious effort to substitute inflammatory rhetoric for substantive responses to real economic issues.

Political scientist Marilyn Hoskin (1991:146)

In contrast to the qualitative, historical investigation in Part I, the next four chapters use quantitative time-series and cross-sectional models to isolate the causes of post-1980s public opinion on immigrants, immigration policy, and anti-immigrant political movements. Exchanging a rich historical narrative for a larger universe of cases, these chapters permit more rigorous analysis and thus more certainty about our findings.

To reflect this change in methods, Part II uses slightly different interpretations of the three major theories. Chapter 5's relatively short time-series models of attitudes toward immigration policy and anti-immigrant parties are not well suited to testing marginality, at least in its cultural form. Over-time fluctuations in real income and the unemployment rate stand in for economic self-interest, however.

Over-time variations in the immigration rate and the percentage of the population that is foreign or foreign-born represent contact theory.

The cross-sectional analyses in Chapters 6 to 8 also use slightly different versions of the three main explanations. Variables representing cultural forms of marginality include being born outside the country of residence and belonging to a racial, ethnic, or religious minority. Where data permit, these models also include perceived cultural threat as an intervening variable. In other words, such models hypothesize that being culturally marginalized oneself will make one less likely to perceive immigrants as a threat to the dominant culture and so will reduce one's opposition to immigration.

Models in Chapters 6 to 8 likewise test economic self-interest. Analysis of this second major theory looks at factors such as income, personal financial well-being, employment status, occupational prestige, and, where possible, perceptions of the national economy and of the economic threat immigrants supposedly pose to natives.

Finally, these chapters assess the validity of contact theory. Here relevant variables include, as data allow, increases in the number of immigrants in an area, personal contact with immigrants, and the number of foreign-born in one's region or neighborhood or at one's workplace. Besides examining those variables used to evaluate the three main explanations of immigration-related attitudes, the cross-sectional models usually estimate the effects of demographics, such as education and gender.

Each of the three cross-sectional chapters first briefly describes the three main forms of nativism to be studied: "negative affect," or hostile feelings toward immigrants; opposition to immigration or immigrant rights;[1] and support for anti-immigrant political movements or parties (i.e., California's Proposition 187 for the United States, the National Front for France, and the Republikaner for Germany). Most of the balance of each chapter then discusses the results for each major theory in turn (i.e., marginality, especially in its cultural form; economic self-interest; and contact). Each country's chapter concludes with a tabular and narrative summary of the major findings for that particular nation.

5

Over-Time Opposition to Immigration and Support for Nativist Political Movements

[In 1920], as part of a general adjustment to peacetime conditions, two factors which time and again in American history had encouraged anti-foreign outbreaks vividly reappeared. One was economic depression, the other a fresh wave of immigration.

Historian John Higham (1988:266–267)

The unavoidable conflicts caused by mass migration became acute only when unemployment in the host countries became chronic. In the era of full employment, which probably will never return, millions of immigrant workers were recruited. Almost ten million immigrants from Mexico came to the United States, three million from the Maghreb to France, and five million to the Federal Republic [of Germany], including almost two million Turks. This migration was not merely tolerated; it was emphatically welcomed. Opinion changed only when structural unemployment rose despite increasing prosperity.

Essayist Hans Magnus Enzensberger (1992:56)

Whereas single-time-point, or "cross-sectional" models of attitudes toward immigrants are common (Hoskin 1991), over-time or "time-series" work is virtually nonexistent. Yet such analysis seems at least as relevant for immigration policy as cross-sectional modeling is. Politicians are probably just as likely to pay attention to the mean level of mass opposition to immigration as to which particular sectors of the public are more or less opposed to accepting further immigrants. And popular notions of the causes of attitudes toward immigration seem just as likely to contain implicit time-series arguments (e.g., "Proposition 187 passed because the California economy was in a recession") as cross-sectional ones (e.g., "all of the unemployed voted for Le Pen").

Methodological considerations also call for over-time analysis. In particular, several possible causes of attitudes toward immigration do not vary over individual respondents but do fluctuate over time at the national or aggregate level. Single-time-point models cannot really measure the effects of the monthly or annual immigration rate. The national unemployment *rate* (as opposed to an individual's employment status) also fluctuates over time but not across respondents.

Methods

Unfortunately, this theoretically and methodologically important time-series analysis is hampered by lack of data on the variable to be explained. In the United States, no true time series on immigration or related issues seems to exist. Examination of the American data is therefore limited to examining correlation coefficients. Where relatively long time series exist, however (as for support for anti-immigrant political parties in France and Germany), the analysis proceeds to traditional time series and even ARIMA (autoregressive integrated moving average) modeling.

As in the historical sections, the selection of potentially causal variables depends on which statistics are available and on which particular measures fluctuate significantly over time instead of across respondents. The German time-series models, for example, examine the influence of variations over time in the proportion of the population that is non-German. Yet later cross-sectional models (see Chapters 6–8) will instead estimate the effects of having many foreigners living in one's neighborhood.

In particular, this chapter tests economic-self-interest theory by examining the effects over time of the national unemployment rate, the percent change in real disposable income per capita, and the percent change in real hourly wages. The analysis operationalizes contact with immigrants (e.g., whether personal or more indirectly via the media) as the national immigration rate (or some minor variant) and the proportion of the population that is foreign or foreign-born. Although one might have also liked to study the influence of more cultural factors, monthly breakdowns of the foreign population by country or region of origin were not usually available. Cultural determinants of immigration attitudes, moreover, rarely show much variation during the relatively short periods for which we have time-series data.

These over-time versions of economic-self-interest and contact theories do not necessarily assume the same causal process postulated for cross-sectional models. We may find that increasing unemployment rates or declining real income coincides with surges in overall nativism. Yet such over-time effects might not necessarily result simply from more unemployed or poor individuals in the population. Equally plausible explanations for such time-series results include "sociotropic" (based on perceptions of the economy) phenomena or changes in elite discourse (see Zaller 1992). Comparison with later cross-sectional analyses can, of course, help narrow down the possibilities, but definitive answers to this "macro-micro" question will probably have to wait for further research.

A similar caveat applies for contact theory. If time-series models suggest that high immigration rates cause greater overall xenophobia, one must not necessarily conclude that more frequent personal contact between immigrants and natives is the culprit. While such an interpretation might seem plausible, at least absent American-style segregation, so would a theory holding that the greater symbolic presence of immigrants (e.g., in the media, elite political discourse, and everyday conversation) is to blame. Again, later cross-sectional modeling should help untangle some of these theoretical possibilities.

The United States

To situate analysis of American attitudes toward immigration, Figure 5.1 plots the few over-time data available for the United States (see Table A1.4). Overall, the proportion of Americans favoring less immigration seems to have hovered at about 45% from 1953 through 1977. From 1977 to the early 1980s, this proportion rose to 71%. It then declined through 1986, bottoming out at 54%. After 1986 anti-immigration sentiment gradually rose to 64% in 1993 before falling to 48% by 1997. Despite its reputation as a "land of immigrants," then, the United States has not been especially pro-immigration.

Because these U.S. data do not constitute a true time series, statistical analysis must remain relatively rudimentary. We can, however,

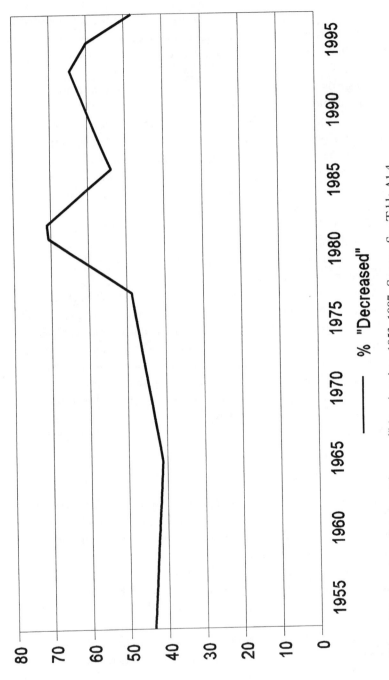

Figure 5.1. Americans favoring "decreased" immigration, 1953–1997. *Sources*: See Table A1.4.

Table 5.1. *Correlation Coefficients of Americans Favoring*
"Decreased" Immigration

Variable	Bivariate r	Partial r
Change in real disposable income per capita (%)	−.855**	−.733**
Unemployment rate (%), differenced once	.570*	.531
Immigrants admitted per 1,000 U.S. residents, differenced once	−.603*	−.154
Foreign-born (%), differenced once	.362	.539
t	10	10

Note: Correlation coefficients statistically significant at the .05 level are in bold. Partial correlation coefficients reflect controls for two of the other potential causes of attitudes. (The series contained too few time points to control for all three of the other potential causes at once.) For the raw data on which these correlations are based, see Table A1.4; for further details on the models, see Appendix 2; and for a description of the dependent variable, see Appendix 4.
*p < .10, two-tailed test; **p < .05, two-tailed test.
Sources: Gallup, CBS News/*New York Times*/Tokyo Broadcasting System, and Princeton Survey Research Associates Polls, 1953–1997.

calculate partial correlation coefficients between opposition to immigration and detrended[1] versions of each of the four independent variables.

As Table 5.1 suggests, percent change in real disposable income per capita is the only variable that appears to affect opposition to immigration. The negative, statistically significant partial correlation (r = −.733) between a given year's mean change in real disposable income and that same year's mean opposition to immigration thus suggests that increases in disposable income produce corresponding declines in the percentage of Americans opposing immigration.

The other causal hypotheses receive little or no confirmation. Variations in the proportion of foreign-born in the United States fail to yield any statistically significant correlations. Although the detrended unemployment and immigration rates achieve statistical significance at the relatively lax .10 level, neither survives controls for any two of the remaining variables. According to the data available in

1998, only changes in real income influence overall levels of American nativism.

This relatively simple analysis of the American data obviously cannot match the sophisticated time-series models in the French and German sections. Yet correlational methods probably represent the most complex technique the available data will stand. Should more complicated methodology yield similar results for France and Germany, moreover, this correlational analysis for the United States might increase our confidence in our findings.

France

Except for the dramatic jump in French support for Jean-Marie Le Pen and his Front national during the 1995 presidential elections (see Figure 5.2 and Table A1.5), the French view of Le Pen and his anti-immigrant party has remained more or less constant since 1984.[2] Previously almost completely insignificant, the Front national rose to relative prominence in the early 1980s arguably because of an economic crisis and the established French political elites' legitimation of the party as a more or less acceptable political player (Schain 1987; see also Charlot 1986; Loch 1990:11–23; Camus 1996; Perrineau 1996). As Figure 5.2 illustrates, the proportion of French respondents who have a "good opinion" of the party has closely paralleled the percentage who would like to see Le Pen "play an important role" in the future.

To attempt to explain fluctuations in these two forms of French nativism, this section estimates the effects of changes in the real hourly wage (the closest available French equivalent of real disposable income per capita), the unemployment rate, and gross immigration using ARIMA, or sophisticated time-series, models. Interested specialists will find further technical details in Appendix 2.[3]

In a result reminiscent of the American analysis, Table 5.2 reports that increases in real hourly wages[4] substantially reduce support for the Front national (percent change[5] = −35.8). Surprisingly given the findings in Chapter 7, soaring unemployment rates also appear powerfully to drive up support for the Front (percent change = 30.3). The number of immigrants admitted, in contrast, seems to have no statistically significant[6] effect.

Even though support for the Front and approval of Le Pen follow

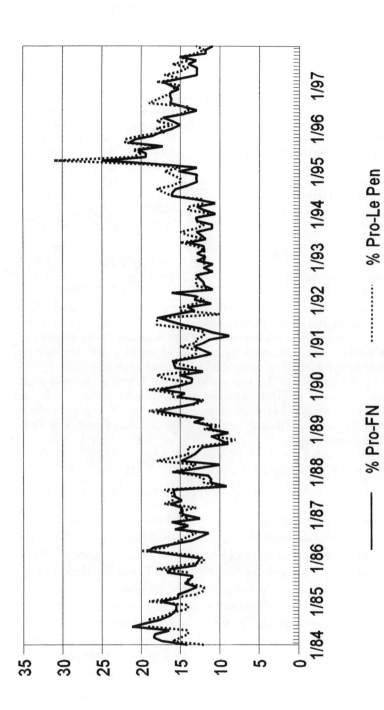

Figure 5.2. French support for the Front national and approval of Le Pen, 1984–1997. *Sources*: See Table A1.5.

Table 5.2. *ARIMA Models of French Support for the Front national and Approval of Le Pen*

Variable	Support for Front national	Approval of Le Pen
Change in real hourly wage (%)	**−3.228****	−1.075
Unemployment rate[a] (%)	**42.729****	−5.361
Gross immigration[a]	−3.360	−1.949
Autoregression term (lag 1)		.415**
Autoregression term (lag 6)	.280**	
Constant	.133	14.314**
t	72	84
R^2	.196	.178
Durbin-Watson statistic	2.418	1.900

Note: Substantive coefficients statistically significant at the .05 level are in bold. Support for Front national differenced once. Change in wage has nominal two-month lead. Unemployment rate has nominal one-month lead for FN model and one-month lag for Le Pen model. Gross immigration smoothed (with 1-period moving average) and lagged seven months for FN model and smoothed for Le Pen model. For the raw data on which these models are based, see Table A1.5; for further details on the models, see Appendix 2; and for a description of the dependent variable, see Appendix 4.
[a]Natural logged and ordinarily and seasonally differenced once, then ordinarily differenced again.
*p < .10, two-tailed test; **p < .05, two-tailed test.
Sources: SOFRES/*Le Figaro* Polls, 1985–1992.

parallel tracks (see Figure 5.2), no potential cause achieves significance in the Le Pen model in Table 5.2. This finding may suggest that public views of Le Pen respond more to the momentary "gaffes" of this incendiary French politician (see Mayer and Perrineau 1993) than to such structural changes as the state of the economy.

These French data therefore indicate that increases in the real hourly wage (more or less equivalent to real income per capita) and decreases in the unemployment rate may reduce voting for anti-immigrant parties. These effects might not extend to support for anti-immigrant politicians, however. The amount of immigration, in contrast, seems to have no significant effects on either form of nativism. These findings thus confirm popular French notions that voting for the Front national is partly a reaction to high unemployment rates.

Germany

The percentage of Germans intending to vote for the anti-immigrant party "Die Republikaner" (see Figure 5.3 and Table A1.6) has remained relatively low since the group's founding in 1983 (see Lepszy 1989; Leggewie 1990; Veen, Lepszy, and Mnich 1993), never exceeding 10% of the population.[7] General opposition to foreigners, on the other hand, is more prevalent. At its peak in the summer of 1991, the proportion of German respondents finding the presence of foreigners "not OK" even represented a bare majority.

According to some observers, many of the deepest troughs and highest peaks in support for the Republikaner (and perhaps in opposition to foreigners as well) arise from political events. The first spike of nationwide Republikaner support in early 1989, for instance, may have occurred because of the party's surprisingly good showing in the Berlin *Land* elections of January 1989 (Lepszy 1989; Roth 1990). When around the beginning of 1990 the German political debate turned from the "asylum-foreigner problem" to the question of German unification, support for the Republikaner and their antiforeigner proposals seems to have dropped (Falter 1994:160; see also Roth 1990). The resurrection of the "asylum-foreigner" theme in late 1991 and early 1992 seems to have, in turn, boosted support for this radical-right party. The gradual decline of this theme in public debates and its replacement with the "unemployment problem" may have also contributed to the downward trend of support for the Republikaner since the middle of 1992 (Falter 1994:160).[8] The revisions to the German Basic Law's asylum provisions in July 1993 (Harenberg 1993:81) may have also hurt the Republikaner by creating the impression that the "asylum problem has been solved."

While recognizing the validity of these political explanations, this chapter nonetheless tests whether more structural variables influence German attitudes as well. In particular, the models in this section include as potential causes the percentage of the western German population that was foreign, the monthly unemployment rate in western Germany (i.e., the "old Federal states"), and the percent change in real disposable income per capita for this same region

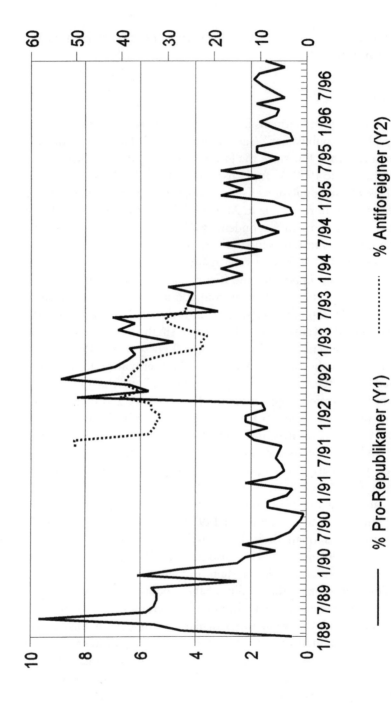

Figure 5.3. German support for the Republikaner and opposition to foreigners, 1989–1996. *Sources*: See Table A1.6.

—— % Pro-Republikaner (Y1)   ·········· % Antiforeigner (Y2)

Table 5.3. *Traditional Time-Series Model of German Opposition to Foreigners*

Variable	Opposition to Foreigners
Change in real disposable income per capita (%)	−.591**
Unemployment rate (%), differenced once	−.646
Foreigners (%), differenced once	13.758
Firebombing, lagged one month	**−6.369****
Constant	−.644
t	23
R^2	.567
Durbin-Watson statistic	2.592

Note: Substantive coefficients statistically significant at the .05 level are in bold. Opposition to foreigners differenced once. For the raw data on which these models are based, see Table A1.6; for further details on the models, see Appendix 2; and for a description of the dependent variable, see Appendix 4.
*p < .10, two-tailed test; **p < .05, two-tailed test.
Source: Politbarometer West, 1991–1993.

(for the raw data, data sources, and related calculations, see the appendixes).

Both ARIMA and traditional time-series analysis produced no statistically significant effects of any of the potential causes on support for the Republikaner.[9] In a confirmation of the American and French results, however, Table 5.3 suggests that increased real income does strongly reduce Germans' likelihood of opposing foreigners (percent change = −21.5).

Because the two years of the opposition-to-foreigners series witnessed several fatal and internationally publicized Neo-Nazi attacks on foreigners, the model in Table 5.3 controlled for such hate crimes as well. If such an attack occurred in the previous month,[10] opposition to foreigners appears to fall (percent change = −27.8) even more markedly than for disposable income. Fire-bombing of foreigners by a few Neo-Nazis thus seems to increase the mass public's sympathy for immigrants. This finding hardly represents a recommended way to reduce public xenophobia, however.[11]

For the third time, the most reliable determinant of over-time changes in immigration-related attitudes seems to be fluctuations in real income. Despite the much-heralded expectations for high unemployment rates and large influxes of foreigners, neither of these hypotheses received confirmation in the German data.

Discussion

The overall message of this chapter is simple: the only substantive over-time variable that ever produces unambiguous, statistically significant results is the percent change in real disposable income per capita or real hourly wages. Neither of the contact variables (percent foreign and the immigration rate) had any effect on opposition to immigration or immigrants or on support for anti-immigration political parties. And only in France did increases in the unemployment rate boost support for a nativist political party.

Popular notions of anti-immigration sentiment may thus be correct in assuming that "poor economic conditions produce xenophobia." Yet the most critical economic variable seems to be real disposable income instead of unemployment. Not armies of the unemployed but rather something (e.g., a perceived decline in the national economy or increased elite scapegoating of immigrants) associated with a thinner collective pocketbook seems more likely to boost overall levels of opposition to immigration.

The findings from this chapter may further suggest that opposition to immigration and voting for radical-right, anti-immigrant parties are driven less by the particularly disadvantaged few than by the public as a whole. Although relatively few people are unemployed at a given time, everyone in the society can respond to changes in the amount of money he or she has to spend. Such a view would also mesh with some theories of xenophobia and support for extremist parties, theories that see right-wing voters more as "protesting" against current hardships than as upholding the radical ideology of the extremist party (see Roth 1989; Falter 1994:136–156).

At least at the national level, explanations of anti-immigration sentiment that stress the number of immigrants in the population seem to fall flat. In neither the American nor the German time-series analyses does the estimate for the proportion of nonnatives achieve statistical significance. And neither the American nor the French data confirm that high immigration rates lead to anti-immigrant backlash. At least in the short run, then, simply how many immigrants live in a country does not seem to matter for the native population's attitudes toward them.

6

Recent Attitudes toward Immigration in the United States

A country that loses control of its borders isn't really a country anymore. The Constitution of the United States obligates the federal government to protect the states from foreign invasion, and our government is derelict in that constitutional duty. If we can send an army halfway around the world to defend the borders of Kuwait and Saudi Arabia, why can't we defend the borders of the United States? I will build a security fence and we will seal the border of the country cold and we will stop illegal immigration in its tracks if I am elected.

> Presidential candidate Patrick Buchanan,
> National Conference of United We Stand America,
> August 12, 1995, in Federal News Service (1995)

In short, the negative consequences of any level of immigration which is politically imaginable at present are at most speculative, rather than documented. Therefore, a policy which is both prudent and also consistent with these observations would be to increase immigration quotas in a series of increments of significant size – perhaps half a percent, or one percent, of total population at each step – to check on any unexpected negative consequences, and to determine whether demand for admission ever exceeds the supply of places.

> Economist Julian Simon (1989:348)

To complement the previous chapter's analysis of shifting support for immigration over time ("time-series analysis"), this and the following two chapters examine variations in support across different respondents ("cross-sectional analysis"). The present chapter concentrates on why Americans disagree about immigration, and Chapters 7 and 8 investigate recent French and German attitudes, respectively. This chapter's analysis examines how well the three theories explain these U.S. data. Within a given section, the analysis tests a single theory against models of three main forms of nativism: negative affect, or a general disliking of immigrants; opposition to pro-immigration or pro-immigrant policy; and support for California's Proposition 187.

To increase readability, only the most important discussion of the data analysis appears in the body of this chapter. Interested specialists, however, will find such further technical details as sampling procedures, precise statistical modeling, and specification of the variables in the appendixes.

First, a few descriptive statistics might help situate the analysis. U.S. data suggest that Americans view immigrants in general with very lukewarm affection. In the panel portion of the 1992 American National Election Study,[1] valid respondents rated "immigrants" on average at 56.73 on a 100-point "feeling thermometer" (see Table 6.1). Particular groups of relative newcomers to the United States received slightly higher ratings. The mean for Asian Americans was 59.18, and that for Hispanic Americans an even higher 60.65. Ratings for legal immigrants, Latinos, and Asian Americans exceeded those for such relatively disliked groups as conservatives (55.73), Christian fundamentalists (55.19), big business (54.99), labor unions (54.79), and feminists (53.66) but were narrowly surpassed by those for the more favored southerners (65.40), blacks (65.11), Catholics (64.66), Jews (64.21), and members of the women's movement (61.74). "Illegal immigrants," in contrast, ended up dead last (35.88).

The American mass public's views on immigration policy appear equally ambivalent, if not outright anti-immigration. In the 1986 CBS News/New York Times National Survey, only 8.0% of the respondents claimed to support an increase in immigration, as opposed to 53.8% for a decrease and 38.2% for no change. Similarly, only 7.6% of the respondents supported the admission of more political refugees. Yet 44.2% said the government should not admit more, and 48.1% claimed that the U.S. admission policy should depend on the circumstances. As with affect, undocumented immigration seems to provoke especially strong responses from many native-born U.S. citizens. When asked about "illegal aliens," 33.1% of the interviewees

Table 6.1. *"Feeling Thermometer" Ratings of Various Groups*

Group	Average Rating
Whites	71.10
Poor people	70.46
Police	69.77
Military	69.60
Environmentalists	67.30
Southerners	65.40
Blacks	65.11
Catholics	64.66
Jews	64.21
Women's movement	61.74
Hispanic Americans	**60.65**
Asian Americans	**59.18**
Immigrants	**56.73**
Conservatives	55.73
Christian Fundamentalists	55.19
Big business	54.99
Labor unions	54.79
Feminists	53.66
Congress (U.S. Senate and House of Representatives)	51.67
People on welfare	51.51
Liberals	51.23
Lawyers	49.83
Federal government in Washington	48.71
Gay men and lesbians (homosexuals)	36.46
Illegal immigrants	**35.88**

Question Text [Variables 5316–5340]: "Please turn to page three of this booklet. I'd like to get your feelings toward some of our political leaders and other people who are in the news these days. I'll read the name of a person and I'd like you to rate that person using something we call the feeling thermometer. Ratings between 50 degrees and 100 degrees mean that you feel favorable and warm toward that person. Ratings between 0 degrees and 50 degrees mean that you don't feel favorable toward the person and that you don't care too much for that person. You would rate the person at the 50 degree mark if you don't feel particularly warm or cold toward that person. If we come to a person whose name you don't recognize, you don't need to rate that person. Just tell me and we'll move on to the next one."

Source: American National Election Study, Full Panel Survey, 1990–1992.

appeared to support deporting otherwise law-abiding undocumented immigrants, in contrast to 60.6% who apparently held that such foreigners deserve to remain in the United States. More than a third (35.3%) of the respondents even agreed with the suggestion that the army replace the U.S. Border Patrol if this agency proves incapable of stopping "illegal" migration from Mexico.

Nativism usually wins the day, moreover, on support for political movements opposed to immigration or immigrants. On election day 1994, 59% of California voters approved Proposition 187, which would have made undocumented immigrants ineligible for various public services (Martin 1995). Fortunately for the state's *indocumentados*, in 1997 a federal district judge declared almost all of Proposition 187's provisions unconstitutional (McDonnell 1997), and two years later Governor Gray Davis decided to withdraw the state's appeal of the 1997 ruling (Nieves 1999).

Marginality Theory

As suggested in Chapter 1, marginality theory predicts that belonging to a religious, ethnic, or racial minority (e.g., being Catholic, Jewish, Latino, African American, or Asian American), being poor or unemployed, coming from an immigrant family, suffering from declining finances, or being a woman reduces nativism.[2] Such variables should have an especially strong effect on those nativist attitudes which most closely approximate persecution of a clearly defined group of victims. Among the three forms of American nativism examined in this chapter, support for Proposition 187 should probably show the greatest marginality effects. Negative affect should show the least, and policy preferences should reveal a moderate level of marginality influences. Arguably, depriving poor undocumented immigrants of publicly funded medical care and education is closer to persecution than merely disliking them. Believing that immigration should be reduced probably falls somewhere in between. At least as an intervening factor, perceiving that immigrants threaten the dominant U.S. culture should also increase nativism.

Measures

To test marginality and the other theories, this chapter analyzes an "anti-immigrant affect" index based on general feelings about immigrants and "Hispanic Americans." This section also looks at an "opposition to immigration" scale based on questions about admitting more immigrants and refugees and enforcing immigration laws.[3] The "support for Proposition 187" variable comes from whether California voters reported choosing yes on this 1994 ballot initiative. As throughout this book, higher values of such variables indicate greater nativism. (For further details on the specification of variables, see Appendix 4.)

Overall, Table 6.2 suggests that cultural forms of marginality do significantly reduce nativism. As predicted, however, policy preferences and support for Propsition 187 show these marginality effects more markedly than does anti-immigrant affect.

Religion

In the predominantly Protestant Christian United States, such religious minorities as Jews and Catholics should feel marginalized and, hence, disproportionately support immigrants. Indeed, being Jewish strongly reduces opposition to immigration and support for Proposition 187 among the respondents in these samples. The coefficient for Jewish identification fails to reach statistical significance in the survey of affect, on the other hand, suggesting that religious marginality plays less of a role in forming people's basic liking or disliking of immigrants. The estimate for being Catholic tells a similar story. Belonging to this religious minority significantly decreases opposition to immigration and support for Proposition 187. Probably because Jews represent a smaller proportion of the U.S. population than Catholics, the effect of being Catholic only achieves about half the strength of that for being Jewish. And just as for being Jewish, being Catholic has no statistically significant effect on anti-immigrant affect. The results for nonreligious respondents replicate the findings for Catholics: not belonging to any religion in the disproportionately religious United States moderately reduces opposition to immigration and support for Proposition 187 but has no statistically significant effect on anti-immigrant affect. Belonging to an "other religion" strongly decreases support for the proposition but fails to reach statistical significance in the models for affect and opposition to immigration. Although the lack of an effect on affect matches the pattern for the other major religious variables, the failure of the "other

Table 6.2. Determinants of Anti-Immigrant Affect, Opposition to Immigration, and Support for Proposition 187 in the United States

Independent Variables	Anti-Immigrant Affect[a]		Opposition to Immigration[b]		Support for Proposition 187[c]	
	Estimate[d]	Std. Err.	Estimate[d]	Std. Err.	Estimate[e]	Std. Err.
Catholic	-.658	2.684	-.620***	.148	-.561***	.091
Other Christian			.191*	.104		
Jewish	-7.301	9.274	-1.476***	.384	-1.086***	.148
Other religion	-2.000	5.647	-.230	.361	-1.018***	.143
No religion	.044	3.206	-.612**	.302	-.858***	.099
Foreign origin	-5.359*	3.186	-.717**	.294	.104	.085
Latino	-23.705***	4.210	-.720***	.235	-1.620***	.149
African American	-14.774***	3.449	-.340	.238	-.711***	.139
Asian American	1.373	9.170			-.483***	.183
Native American	.563	9.620				
Other race	-1.148	3.194	-.168	.371	.044	.193
Poor	1.402	2.712	-.032	.207	-.174	.107
Rich	-1.061	2.514	.277	.188	.102	.078
Finances declined	2.911	2.606			.122	.076
Finances improved	-.939	4.638			.066	.084
Unemployed			-.144	.354		
Professional/manager	-5.855*	3.147				
Manual laborer	2.590	4.205				

Table 6.2. (cont.)

Independent Variables	Anti-Immigrant Affect[a]		Opposition to Immigration[b]		Support for Proposition 187[c]	
	Estimate[d]	Std. Err.	Estimate[d]	Std. Err.	Estimate[e]	Std. Err.
Nonpaid worker	−1.639	3.044	−.124	.193	−.343*	.200
Sec. school graduate	−9.261***	2.967	−.766***	.221	−.896***	.202
University graduate	−18.394***	3.814	−.326**	.127	−.260***	.065
Female	−.454	2.149	−.014	.142	−.182*	.100
Age ≤ 30	.698	2.694	.602***	.182	.240***	.092
Age ≥ 60	−3.620	3.084	−.094	.158		
South	3.136	2.771				
Constant	97.612***	4.058	9.000***	.222	1.329***	.215
R^2	.085		.104			
% correctly predicted					63.6%	
n	1,036		985		4,310	

[a] Model analyzes American National Election Study Full Panel Survey, 1990–1992.
[b] Model analyzes 1986 CBS News/*New York Times* National Survey.
[c] Model analyzes November 1994 *Los Angeles Times* Exit Poll.
[d] Coefficients are unstandardized ordinary least-squares regression estimates. Higher values of the dependent variable indicate greater nativism.
[e] Coefficients are logistic regression estimates. Value 1 for dependent variable = yes vote on Proposition 187.
* p ≤ .10; ** p ≤ .05; *** p ≤ .01.

religion" variable to influence policy preferences may stem from the relatively few (n = 29) "other religious" respondents in this sample. The anti-immigration effect of "other Christian" in the policy model might appear to disconfirm marginality theory, but experience suggests such respondents are most likely Protestants (e.g., "nondenominational," "just Christian," "born-again") and hence part of the religious majority.

Ethnicity

As marginality predicts, belonging to a minority ethnicity or "race" or originating in an immigrant family (i.e., having at least one foreign-born parent) likewise lessens nativism. Being Latino forcefully reduces all three forms of anti-immigration sentiment, hardly surprising to anyone at all familiar with U.S. immigration politics. More surprising to many observers is that being African American substantially diminishes dislike of immigrants and support for Proposition 187. Tracing one's ancestry to Africa does not appear to have had any effect on opposition to immigration per se, possibly because American blacks might have been less likely to see immigrants as victims in 1986, the year of the CBS News/*New York Times* poll, than in the 1990s, when the other two surveys were conducted. Being Asian American modestly reduced support for Proposition 187 but had no statistically significant effect on anti-immigrant affect. These results for Asian Americans thus confirm the general rule that marginality has a stronger effect on support for anti-immigrant political movements than on anti-immigrant affect. Neither "Native American" nor "other race" achieved statistical significance, but the affect and policy surveys probably contain too few relevant respondents (n = 12 for each poll and category) for a fair test of these potential causes. The *Los Angeles Times* Exit Poll does include 124 valid "other race" respondents, but this category may be too ethnically heterogeneous for any firm conclusions. "Foreign origin" produces a pattern opposite to most cultural variables, reducing anti-immigrant affect and opposition to immigration but having no effect on support for Proposition 187. Perhaps the Proposition 187 debate in California so targeted non-Anglos of whatever nativity that third- or fourth-generation Latinos, for example, felt just as threatened as first-generation Mexican Americans (the survey only includes U.S. citizens).

Perceived Cultural Threat

As least as an intervening factor between these cultural-marginality causes and Americans' dislike of immigrants,[4] the perception that immigrants somehow "threaten" the dominant U.S. culture[5] may further exacerbate xenophobia. According to the path analysis in Figure 6.1, such a cultural threat substantially increases respondents' dislike of immigrants (percent change = 14.2). Cultural threat, in turn, largely appears to be a symptom of belonging to the dominant ethnic and religious group (i.e., white Protestant Christians), being an "old-stock" American, and lacking an advanced education. Because they themselves do not belong to the dominant culture, ethnic and religious minorities seem less troubled by the additional cultural diversity that immigrants might bring. Higher education, moreover, may teach students the value of minority culture and thus reduce their fear of immigration-induced cultural pluralism. (Alternatively, education might simply teach people to disguise their prejudices.) The negative coefficient for the effect of being a "nonpaid worker" (percent change = −4.9) seems puzzling but might suggest that remaining outside the traditional workplace insulates one from the culturally based anti-immigrant rhetoric prevalent there.

Economics

In contrast to cultural forms of marginality, economic manifestations performed poorly. Being unemployed or poor, suffering declining personal finances, and working as a manual laborer all failed to yield any statistically significant results in Table 6.2. At least, pending the findings for France and Germany, we should question the validity of an economic form of marginality theory.

Education and Gender

Both relevant demographic variables support the marginality explanation. Having earned a college degree powerfully reduces all three forms of reported nativism. Because economic self-interest makes the same empirical prediction, however, this finding does not help us adjudicate between marginality and the economic interpretation. Relatively marginalized in a male-dominated society, American

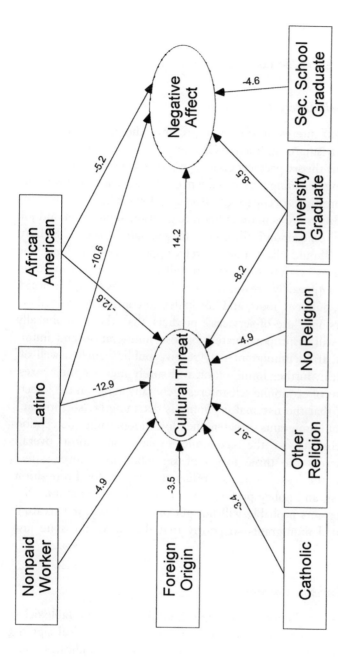

Figure 6.1. Path analysis of cultural threat and negative affect in the United States. *Note:* Path coefficients represent percent change. Only statistically significant coefficients (at .10 level) shown in diagram, although all variables included in actual regressions.

women are somewhat more likely to support immigration and oppose Proposition 187. As with most of the cultural-marginality variables, these gender effects do not carry over to anti-immigrant affect.

Economic Self-Interest

Economic self-interest probably represents the major alternative theory of nativism. As outlined in Chapter 1, the usual "labor-market" version of this theory predicts greater overall xenophobia from being poor, suffering declining personal finances, lacking a job, and working in a low-prestige occupation. Because low-skilled immigrants allegedly inflict more economic harm (e.g., wage depression and job displacement) on economically disadvantaged natives, such U.S.-born respondents should disproportionately oppose immigration. The "use-of-services" variety of economic self-interest focuses more on immigrants' supposedly greater use of public services (e.g., Medicaid, food stamps, public schools, and hospitals). In contrast to the "labor-market" version, "use-of-services" predicts that the economically advantaged will disproportionately oppose immigration and immigrant rights. If an immigrant may receive public benefits, well-off Americans fear, further immigration will surely increase their taxes. Both versions of economic self-interest generally agree on the effects of believing that the national economy is declining (a "sociotropic" effect) or that immigrants threaten one's livelihood. Either perception should, according to the economic explanation, boost overall nativism. Across the three forms of xenophobia, however, affect should show the least economic influence, support for Proposition 187 the most, and policy preferences an intermediate amount. Disliking immigrants probably will not get one's job back, but treating undocumented immigrants so poorly that they leave the state just might.[6]

Objective Economic Condition

Despite these predictions, only one economic variable in Table 6.2 – working as a professional or manager – achieves statistical significance. The negative sign for this occupational category indicates, contrary to the "use-of-services" version, that enjoying high occupational prestige moderately *decreases* dislike of immigrants. Unfortunately, the surveys for policy and for Proposition 187 do not allow us to compare the effect of being a professional or manager on the other two forms of nativism. The available evidence suggests, however, that being unemployed, being rich or poor, or suffering from declining or improving personal finances has no direct influence on Americans' immigration-related attitudes.

Sociotropic Effects

The data only allow us to test the sociotropic variation of economic theory on anti-immigrant affect. Yet here again, economic theory does not match reality. Neither perceiving an improved national economy nor sensing a national economic downturn has any statistically significant effect on hostility to immigrants (p = .65 and .26, respectively). Unfortunately, the American surveys do not appear to contain a viable measure of relative deprivation.

Perceived Economic Threat

Despite these dismal results, models of subjective economic threat may provide the strongest evidence for economic self-interest. Even if one controls for the usual economic, cultural, and demographic variables, believing that recent immigrants are likely to take away Americans' jobs may[7] modestly boost anti-immigrant affect (percent change = 8.1, p ≤ .001). The data reported in Figure 6.2 tell a similar tale, indicating that perceived economic threat may powerfully increase opposition to immigration as well (percent change = 27.4). This belief that immigrants economically threaten natives appears to stem from being poor or African American, belonging to a religion, and lacking even a high school diploma. Particularly interesting is the effect of being African American, which simultaneously increases perceived economic threat and *decreases* opposition to immigration. Perhaps African Americans' relatively disadvantaged economic status makes them more fearful of competition from low-skilled immigrants. The cultural and political marginality of many American blacks, on the other hand, might make them less sympathetic to racially tinged political campaigns against immigration.

The role of education in Figure 6.2 also demands attention. According to these data, having a high school or, especially, a college

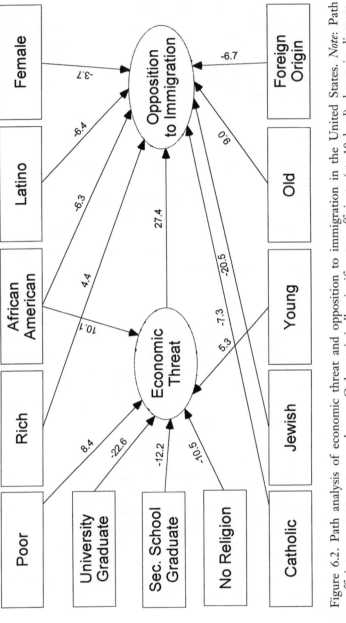

Figure 6.2. Path analysis of economic threat and opposition to immigration in the United States. *Note:* Path coefficients represent percent change. Only statistically significant coefficients (at .10 level) shown in diagram, although all variables included in actual regressions.

education dramatically reduces the sense of economic threat from immigration. At least according to this model,[8] education nonetheless has no direct effect on Americans' opposition to immigration. These findings may suggest that education gives students the occupational skills they need to avoid the low-prestige vocations filled by many immigrants. Alternatively, advanced schooling may teach Americans enough economics or critical-thinking skills to recognize the fallacy in the simplistic formula "one employed immigrant equals one unemployed native." Why lacking a religious affiliation appears to decrease perceived economic threat seems hard to explain. Perhaps this effect would prove spurious if one were able to correct for any bidirectional causation between opposition to immigration and perceived threat.

Although the apparent effect of perceived economic threat appears large in Figure 6.2, the best evidence available indicates that perceived *cultural* threat may have an even greater impact on overall nativism. Unfortunately, the CBS News/*New York Times* survey lacks any measures of cultural threat. If one includes both types of threat (as well as the usual controls) in a single analysis of anti-immigrant affect, however, the direct effect of cultural threat (percent change = 12.9, $p \leq .001$) seems roughly twice as influential as that for economic threat (percent change = 6.9, $p \leq .001$). And while cultural threat achieves moderate strength in Figure 6.1 (percent change = 14.2), in a parallel analysis economic threat appears significantly weaker (percent change = 8.1, $p \leq .001$).

Contact Theory

According to the final theory, close, cooperative, equal-status contact with individual immigrants should decrease hostility toward them. If natives instead interact with the foreign-born more superficially, increased contact should increase nativism. Among the three forms of nativism, anti-immigrant affect should prove most susceptible to contact effects. Working together with María or Yong might foster warmer feelings toward Mexican or Korean immigrants but not necessarily change one's views on immigration policy dramatically.

Regional-Level Contact

Analysis of the 1992 American National Election Study suggests that contact indeed influences Americans' feelings about immigrants. The effect of living in a county with many foreign-born residents (b = −.756, SE = .344, percent change = −17.0) does not necessarily confirm contact theory, however. According to this model, living in Dade County, Florida (45.1% foreign-born in 1990, the maximum in the data set), instead of Monroe County, Arkansas (0.1% foreign-born, the minimum), would cause one to like immigrants 34.0 points (on a 200-point scale) or 17.0% *more*. Normally, one would expect the percentage of immigrants in the county to measure superficial instead of close contact. Instead, this variable behaves as if it were tapping into "good" contact with newcomers. Perhaps U.S. counties are not as rigidly segregated by nativity as one might fear (White and Omer 1997). Maybe people living in the same county participate as functional equals in the same parent-teacher associations or sports clubs, for example. Because counties should be economically and socially more homogeneous than larger areas (e.g., states), interaction at the county level might also be more likely to occur among people of relatively equal social status. Native, middle-class suburbanites might find it easier to like the middle-class immigrants with whom they interact in their neighborhood than to appreciate the working-class foreign-born who cannot afford to leave the center city.

A parallel analysis of the Proposition 187 vote yields similar results. According to this second model, living in a region (one of eight major areas in California; see Appendix 4) with a high percentage of foreign-born residents in 1990 substantially *reduced* a Californian's likelihood of voting yes on the initiative four years later (b = −.052, SE = .010, percent change = −16.4). Contrary to contact theory, then, regional-level contact seems to decrease both dislike of immigrants and support for Proposition 187. Such contact appears to have an equally strong influence, moreover, on both forms of nativism.

Alternative Explanations Not Adequate

One cannot explain away these pro-immigrant effects as arising merely from immigrant-friendly natives moving into counties with many foreigners. "Two-stage least-squares" and "simultaneous Logit," the statistical techniques used to estimate these models (see Appendix 2), already correct for such a possibility. Nor do these findings evaporate if one contends that the surveys' interviewers might have been more likely to interview ethnic minorities (or "new Americans" themselves) if the interviews occurred in counties with high levels of immigrants; the models also control for foreign origin and ethnic background. Whereas a Cuban American living in New Hampshire may well feel more warmly toward immigrants than her old-stock Yankee neighbors do, the model for affect suggests that Cuban Americans in Miami would, all else being equal, like foreigners even more than she.

In contrast to the results for affect and Proposition 187, analysis of policy preferences does not yield similar contact effects. At least without corrections for bidirectional causality (i.e., for the possibility that natives who support immigration will disproportionately choose to live in "ethnic" neighborhoods; see Appendix 2), the number of immigrants in one's "community" has no statistically significant influence (b = .224, SE = .144, p > .10) on support for immigration. Knowing recent immigrants personally may boost support for immigration in general (b = −.236, SE = .076, percent change = −5.9), but this result may also spuriously reflect pro-immigrant respondents' seeking out immigrants to befriend.[9]

Discussion

As Table 6.3's summary of this chapter's findings suggests, cultural-marginality explanations of xenophobia and nativism usually perform better than ones based on economic marginality, economic self-interest, or contact. Even more than being a battle over whose job will be saved or whose pocketbook will benefit, U.S. immigration politics seems to bring into question the ascendancy of the tradition-ally dominant majority's cultural values. In the face of perceived threats to their cultural hegemony, Anglophone, white, old-stock Protestants (America's "insiders") appear to react with outbursts of hostility to immigrants (a prominent group of marginalized outsiders), opposition to immigration, and support for such anti-immigrant political movements as Proposition 187. As Chapter 2's history of American immigration politics makes plain, this pattern is nothing new.

Across the different forms of nativism, cultural marginality appears less likely to influence affect than to determine policy preferences and

Table 6.3. *Summary of Chapter's Findings*

Variables	Marginality	Economic Labor Market	Economic Use of Services	Contact
Cultural				
Perceived cultural threat	√*		ø*	
Catholic minority	√		ø	
Jewish	√		ø	
Other religion	ø		√	
No religion	√		ø	
Foreign origin	√		ø	
Latino	√		ø	
African American	√		ø	
Asian American	√		ø	
Native American	ø		√	
Other race	ø		√	
Economic				
Perceived economic threat		√*		
Poor	ø	ø	ø	
Rich	ø	ø	ø	
Finances declined	ø	ø	ø	
Finances improved	ø	ø	ø	
Unemployed	ø	ø	ø	
Professional/manager	ø	√	ø	
Manual laborer	ø	ø	ø	
Nonpaid worker	ø	ø	ø	
Perceived decline in national economy			ø	
Perceived improvement in national economy			ø	
Contact				
Proximity/region				ø
Proximity/neighborhood				ø*
Personal contact				√*
Demographic				
Sec. school graduate	√		√	
University graduate	√		√	
Female	√		ø	

Note: √ = on average, data confirm theory's prediction. ø = on average, data do not confirm theory's prediction. * = result provisional because not corrected for bidirectional causality.

support for anti-immigrant political movements. Although the evidence remains more ambiguous for economic variables, a similar pattern seems to hold for at least perceived economic threat. The influence of contact, however, does not appear to change systematically across the three forms of nativism.

7

Recent Attitudes toward Immigration in France

[We must not] accept that certain communities . . . reject our culture and try to impose theirs on us. . . . We must not tolerate . . . the evolution toward a multiethnic, multiracial, and multicultural society. . . . Multiethnic and multiracial, yes, multicultural, no!

> Former Interior Minister Charles Pasqua,
> in *Le Monde* (1993)

We have had enough of watching the growing contempt for, distrust of, and hostility toward immigrants. We have had enough of the ideologies that justify these attitudes. It is not possible to entertain the slightest doubt about the attitude of Christ toward foreigners, toward immigrants, toward society's disenfranchised.

> Cardinal Albert Decourtray, in Tincq (1992)

As with the preceding chapter on the United States, the analysis of the French data is divided into three main sections, each of which examines how well the three theories presented in Chapter 1 explain the data. Within a given section, the analysis tests a single theory against models of the main forms of French nativism: anti-immigrant affect; opposition to pro-immigrant policies; and support for Jean-Marie Le Pen's Front national party.[1]

As for the previous chapter, a few descriptive statistics should help situate the regression analysis to come. Just as the foreign-born do in the United States, immigrants to France encounter widespread hostility. Table 7.1 demonstrates that immigrants fall at the very bottom of French people's "sympathy" ratings.[2] Although immigrants from Asia (primarily Southeast Asians such as the Vietnamese) hardly enjoy

Table 7.1. *Sympathy toward Various Groups*

Group	Valid Percent Saying "somewhat sympathetic"
Catholics	50.0
Blacks of South Africa	34.7
Antilleans	33.0
Protestants	32.3
Jews	32.0
Asians	**28.7**
Muslims	**22.3**
Arabs	**21.0**

Question Text: For each of the following categories of people, tell me whether you are somewhat sympathetic, somewhat unsympathetic, or neither one nor the other.

Source: 1985 "Racism" Survey by Institut Français d'Opinion Publique.

a warm reception in France (only 28.7% of respondents viewed them as "sympathetic"), Muslim and "Arab" (primarily North African) newcomers encounter the most contempt (22.3% and 21.0% "sympathetic," respectively). The 1988 Eurobarometer 30[3] also reveals the French public's lack of enthusiasm for immigrants. Among valid French respondents in this survey, 13.0% found people "of another nationality . . . disturbing." On average, valid interviewees in this same poll also rated North Africans at 44.5 on a feeling thermometer with a range of 0 to 100.

Nor does the French mass public wholeheartedly support immigrant rights. In the 1988 Eurobarometer, 25.2% of the valid respondents did not believe the "right to asylum" should always be respected. When asked about non–European Community (EC) nationals living in France, 26.1% of the French sample thought such immigrants' rights should be further "restricted," and 46.2% opted for the status quo. Only 27.7% supported extending immigrant rights.

But perhaps most alarming is the proportion of French citizens willing to support Le Pen's vehemently anti-immigrant party, the

Front national. Le Pen garnered 15% of the votes cast in the first round of the 1995 presidential election (Simmons 1996:111). And at his highest level of recorded public support in April 1995, 31% of *Le Figaro's* usable respondents hoped Jean-Marie Le Pen would play an "important role" (presumably in French politics) in the future (see Table A1.5).

Marginality Theory

In the French context, marginality theory predicts that belonging to a religious minority (e.g., not being Catholic), coming from an immigrant family, being poor or unemployed, suffering from declining finances, working as a manual laborer, or being a woman will attenuate nativism. As in the United States, these variables should especially influence support for the National Front and, less strongly, opposition to immigration. Voting for a vindictive, anti-immigrant politician such as Le Pen arguably comes much closer to persecution than does despising *sales Arabes* (though the latter psychologically paves the way for the former). At least as an intervening variable, believing that immigrants threaten traditional French culture should boost nativism as well.

Measures

To test the three main theories, this analysis uses an "anti-immigrant affect" scale based on respondents' feelings about "North Africans" and "people of another nationality." This section also examines an "opposition to immigration" index based on questions about respecting the right to asylum, extending the rights of non-EC immigrants, and facilitating naturalization. The "support for the Front national" variable comes from a feeling thermometer for Le Pen and a series of questions on whether the Front's leader would be the best person to solve France's various problems. Higher values of these variables represent increased nativism. (For further details on the specification of variables, see Appendix 4.)

As Table 7.2 documents, cultural manifestations of marginality appear to influence French views on immigration significantly. Across the three forms of nativism, cultural marginality seems particularly

Table 7.2. *Determinants of Anti-Immigrant Affect, Opposition to Immigration, and Support for the Front national in France*

Independent Variables	Anti-Immigrant Affect[a]		Opposition to Immigration[a]		Support for Front national[b]	
	Estimate[c]	Std. Err.	Estimate[c]	Std. Err.	Estimate[d]	Std. Err.
Non-Catholic	-.987***	.264	-.548***	.106	-2.596***	.374
Foreign origin	-.363	.239	-.172*	.096	.376	.486
Poor	-.148	.301	-.024	.122	-.284	.514
Rich	.223	.360	.172	.145	.345	.321
Finances declined	.120	.254	.158	.103	-.297	.578
Finances improved	-.208	.341	-.136	.138	.243	.634
Unemployed	.358	.500	.096	.194		
Professional/manager	-1.732***	.456	-.693***	.180	-2.347***	.782
Manual laborer	.010	.418	-.004	.167	-.475	.713
Nonpaid worker	-.441	.345	-.228	.140	-.011	.424
Sec. school graduate	-.765**	.334	-.139	.134	-2.566***	.471
University graduate	-.571	.404	-.218	.165	-3.798***	.444
Female	.051	.252	-.144	.101	-1.496***	.309
Age ≤ 30	-.210	.279	.161	.110	1.344***	.398
Age ≥ 60	.560	.358	-.083	.149	-1.213***	.469
Constant	8.139***	.383	2.186***	.151	4.011***	.356
R^2	.093		.107			
n	794		673		2,645	

[a] Model analyzes 1988 Eurobarometer 30.
[b] Model analyzes 1995 SOFRES French National Election Study.
[c] Coefficients are unstandardized ordinary least-squares regression estimates. Higher values of the dependent variable indicate greater nativism.
[d] Coefficients are Tobit regression estimates. Higher values of the dependent variable indicate greater support for the Front national.
* p ≤ .10; ** p ≤ .05; *** p ≤ .01.

likely to affect opposition to immigration and support for the Front national.

Religion

Not belonging to the Catholic majority distinguishes itself as the most powerful cultural variable across all three versions of nativism (see Table 7.2), a result reminiscent of the results for being a religious minority in the United States. Whether Jewish, Protestant, or agnostic, one seems much less prone to oppose France's predominantly Muslim immigrants if one is not symbolically allied with the country's dominant religion. Though the effect of being non-Catholic on anti-immigrant affect is not trivial either (percent change = −7.6), the corresponding influence on opposition to immigration (percent change = −13.7) proves even greater. For technical reasons,[4] the estimated percent change for support for the Front national (7.0%) is not directly comparable with those for affect and policy. The effect of being non-Catholic on support for the Front might nonetheless be stronger than that for affect, especially because religious affiliation affects this form of nativism more powerfully than any other factor except for having a university education.[5]

Foreign Origin

The remaining cultural variable in Table 7.2, foreign origin, has no statistically significant effect on anti-immigrant affect. This form of cultural marginality does, however, modestly reduce opposition to immigration (percent change = −4.3). This disparate influence across different types of nativism thus confirms our original hypothesis about the varying effect of marginality across the three main manifestations of xenophobia.

Perceived Cultural Threat

A more psychological variable, perceived cultural threat, may[6] powerfully boost opposition to immigration (percent change = 43.3; see Figure 7.1) and moderately increase anti-immigrant affect (percent change = 32.8).[7] Figure 7.1 suggests that being Catholic, being a male, and interacting in the traditional workplace all produce such perceived

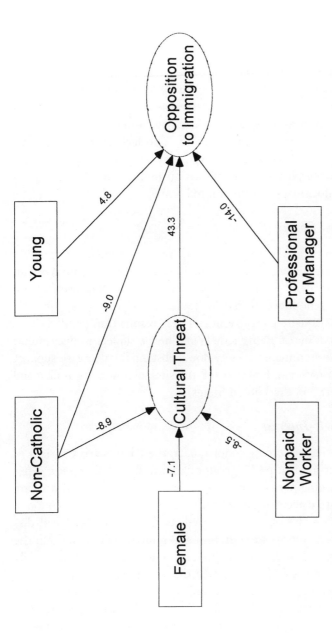

Figure 7.1. Path analysis of cultural threat and opposition to immigration in France. *Note*: Path coefficients represent percent change. Only statistically significant coefficients (at .10 level) shown in diagram, although all variables included in actual regressions.

threat. The effects of being a religious minority and a nonpaid worker thus parallel the determinants of Americans' cultural threat (see Chapter 6). On the other hand, the French model for cultural threat does not replicate the effects of originating in an immigrant family or having earned a university degree. Because the French poll contains no separate measure of ethnicity, cross-national comparison of "foreign origin" becomes problematic. The lack of an educational effect in the French sample, however, may suggest that higher education in France places less emphasis on multiculturalism and anti-racism than do colleges in the United States.

Economics and Gender

In contrast to cultural forms, economic manifestations of marginality produce few significant changes in nativism. Poverty, unemployment, and poor finances all fail to produce statistically significant effects on any form of xenophobia listed in Table 7.2. Working as a manual laborer yields equally paltry results. These results thus parallel those for the United States. Being female and hence subject to discrimination in a male-dominated society does substantially decrease support for the Front national, however (cf. the similar results for policy and Proposition 187 in the United States).

Economic Self-Interest

As for the American cross-sectional data, the labor-market variant of economic self-interest posits greater nativism from being poor, experiencing declining personal finances, being unemployed, and working in a low-prestige occupation. The use-of-services variety of economic self-interest, on the other hand, predicts that the well-off will disproportionately oppose immigration and immigrant rights. As in the previous chapter, both versions of economic self-interest generally agree on the effects of believing that the national economy is declining or that immigrants threaten one's livelihood. The two variants of economic self-interest likewise concur on the nativistic effects of perceived relative economic deprivation. Across the three forms of xenophobia, however, anti-immigrant affect should show the least economic influence, support for the Front national the most, and policy preferences an amount in between.

Objective Economic Condition

Yet, in a confirmation of the American results, the only economic variable in Table 7.2 to achieve statistical significance was working as a professional or manager. The estimates for this occupational category indicate, again contrary to the use-of-services version of economic theory, that working in a high-prestige occupation substantially reduces hatred of immigrants (percent change = −13.3), opposition to immigration (percent change = −17.3), and support for the French National Front (−6.3). Although comparison with the Tobit model (Tobin 1958) for the Front national is hazardous, occupying a high-status job does seem to have a slightly greater effect on French respondents' policy preferences than on their liking or disliking of immigrants. In contrast to working as a professional or manager, being poor, suffering from declining finances, being unemployed, or working as a manual laborer had no effect in any of the models in Table 7.2. These results strongly contradict the popular French perception that the unemployed, for example, disproportionately support the neofascist Front national and its "France for the French" rhetoric.

Sociotropic Effects and Perceived Relative Deprivation

Individuals' objective economic conditions thus appear to play little role in determining attitudes toward immigration. The average French person's economic *perceptions*, on the other hand, do seem strongly tied to one's immigration-related views. The Kinder-Kiewiet sociotropic model (1981) finds uniform support in the data. The statistically significant percent change for the effect of believing that the French economy has declined equals 6.3 for affect, 6.2 for policy, and 4.4 (not strictly comparable) for support for the Front national. Across all three forms of French nativism, then, perceiving a national economic downturn may[8] modestly increase xenophobia. At least for affect and policy,[9] perceiving that immigrants are doing better economically than people such as oneself may also stimulate strong nativist reactions (percent change for relative deprivation = 23.7 for affect and 27.3 for policy).

Perceived Economic Threat

Figure 7.2 illustrates the possible[10] relationships among perceived economic threat, opposition to immigration, and their various causes. As in the United States, believing that immigrants threaten natives' or one's own job dramatically increases opposition to immigration (percent change = 26.0) as well as dislike of immigrants (percent change = 28.9; similar path analysis not shown). Believing that immigrants do *not* threaten natives' jobs in turn appears to arise from having a secondary school (percent change = −15.5) or university degree (percent change = −15.1),[11] not belonging to the Catholic majority (percent change = −12.0), and working as a professional or manager (percent change = −10.7). Suffering personal financial decline, however, modestly increases one's sense of economic threat (percent change = 6.9). The effects of personal finances and occupation on economic threat seem consistent with economic theory. Education may reduce threat by teaching about the economic advantages of a large consumer base and an adequate supply of labor – both of which immigration can provide. The effect of religious affiliation, in contrast, seems harder to explain. Perhaps nonreligious French people (the majority of the "non-Catholic" category) receive generalized pro-immigration cues (including those rooted in economics) from the anticlerical milieu to which many of them belong. Finally, at least in the French case, economic threat seems to play as large a role as cultural threat in producing opposition to immigration. If one simultaneously looks at the apparent effects of cultural versus economic threat, the two forms of threat achieve almost exactly the same percent change (30.2 for economic and 29.8 for cultural; $p \leq .001$).

Contact Theory

The third theory predicts that close, cooperative, equal-status contact with individual newcomers (e.g., at the workplace) should reduce negative feelings toward them. If, on the other hand, native-born French people interact with immigrants more casually or symbolically (e.g., in most neighborhoods or at the regional level), such contact should boost nativism. And despite the American results, anti-immigrant

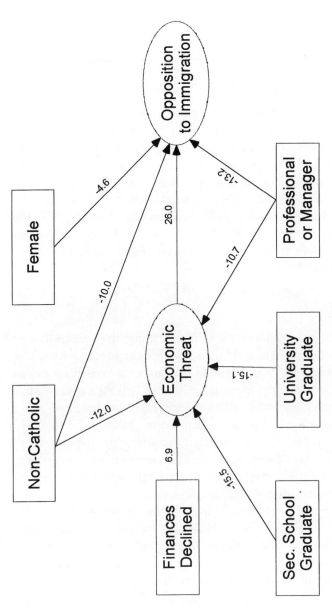

Figure 7.2. Path analysis of economic threat and opposition to immigration in France. *Note:* Path coefficients represent percent change. Only substantive, statistically significant coefficients (at .10 level) shown in diagram, although all variables included in actual regressions.

affect should in theory show more contact effects than the other two forms of nativism do.

Contact at the Workplace or in the Neighborhood

Overall, the French data partly support these predictions. Contact theory appears least useful in explaining contact with immigrants at the workplace or in the neighborhood (*quartier*). Interacting at either of these locales failed to produce any statistically significant effects on French respondents' anti-immigrant affect (b = .254, SE = .269 for workplace; b = −.288, SE = .240 for neighborhood) or opposition to immigration (b = −.109, SE = .108 for workplace; b = −.025, SE = .098 for neighborhood).[12] These French results thus confirm the American findings for the effect of interaction at the neighborhood or "community" level.

Regional-Level Contact

Contact theory seems more useful in explaining the French data on proximity at the regional level. Despite opposite results for the U.S. model of affect and Proposition 187, living in a French *région* (see Appendix 4) with a high proportion of foreign nationals appears modestly to *increase* both anti-immigrant affect (percent change = 7.5, p ≤ .05) and opposition to immigration (percent change = 7.7, p ≤ .10), even after correction for bidirectional causation (see Appendix 2). At the more restricted, *département* level, furthermore, high proportions of foreign citizens likewise boost support for the Front national moderately (percent change = 10.2, p ≤ .05).

These regional-level French findings thus generally confirm the original formulation of contact theory; the increased "casual" contact presumably measured by the regional variables breeds dislike of immigrants, opposition to immigration, and support for the National Front. As seen in the previous chapter, however, the strength of any contact effects does not seem to change systematically across the three types of nativism.

Although the French results for regional-level proximity mostly support contact theory, they still conflict with the U.S. findings for affect and Proposition 187. It is not completely clear why high percentages of immigrants in an American county seem to produce

Table 7.3. *Summary of Chapter's Findings*

Variables	Marginality	Economic Labor Market	Economic Use of Services	Contact
Cultural				
Perceived cultural threat	√*		ø*	
Non-Catholic minority	√		ø	
Foreign origin	√		ø	
Economic				
Perceived economic threat			√*	
Poor	ø	ø	ø	
Rich	ø	ø	ø	
Finances declined	ø	ø	ø	
Finances improved	ø	ø	ø	
Unemployed	ø	ø	ø	
Professional/manager	ø	√	ø	
Manual laborer	ø	ø	ø	
Nonpaid worker	ø	ø	ø	
Perceived decline in national economy		√		
Perceived improvement in national economy		√		
Perceived relative economic deprivation		√*		
Contact				
Proximity/region				√
Proximity/neighborhood				ø*
Proximity/work				ø*
Demographic				
Sec. school graduate	√		√	
University graduate	ø		ø	
Female	ø		√	

Note: √ = on average, data confirm theory's prediction. ø = on average, data do not confirm theory's prediction. * = result provisional because not corrected for bidirectional causality.

pro-immigrant or anti–Proposition 187 feelings when high proportions of foreigners in a French *région* or *département* appear to increase nativism. Perhaps immigrants (as opposed to native-born African Americans) in the United States are less strictly segregated than the foreign-born are in France. Interaction in U.S. counties might then represent "good" or close contact, whereas most contact in the more segregated French regions would remain "casual" and hence produce hostility toward immigrants.

Discussion

As Table 7.3 indicates, cultural-marginality explanations of French xenophobia and nativism generally fare better than theories based on economic marginality or economic self-interest. Not belonging to the Catholic religious majority, not perceiving recent immigrants as a threat to France's culture, and not originating in a *français de souche* (old-stock French) family all attenuate various forms of nativism. Immigration politics in France appears to turn just as much on whether the country's culture will remain primarily Catholic and European as on whether most native-born French workers will be able to find jobs. In other words, in the French mind Maghrebi immigrants represent at least as much of a threat to France's dominant culture as Muslims as they do to the French labor market as low-wage, relatively unskilled employees.

As in the United States, cultural marginality appears less likely to influence affect than to determine policy preferences and support for anti-immigrant political movements. Patterns across the three main forms of xenophobia seem harder to discern for economic self-interest and especially contact theory. Perhaps any such patterns were less obvious because the forms of contact and economic self-interest often varied significantly across the three varieties of nativism.

8

Recent Attitudes toward
Immigration in Germany

> Our land is not a country of immigration. We say NO to a
> "multicultural" society, and thus to a multiethnic state. We say NO
> to voting rights for foreigners, including for EC citizens.
>
> Republikaner party platform of January 1990, in
> Republikaner (1990:18)

> Through the cross-border migratory events of recent decades the
> Federal Republic of Germany has long since become a country
> of immigration, even if not in the same sense as the "classical"
> overseas countries of immigration.
>
> Historian Klaus J. Bade (1994b:52)

Overall, the previous two chapters have generally supported cultural
marginality but as often as not disconfirmed economic marginality,
economic self-interest, and contact theory. In this final cross-sectional
chapter, we repeat the analysis on German data. The chapter also
investigates how well the three main theories presented in Chapter 1
explain reality. Within each section, the analysis tests one theory
against models of the three main forms of German xenophobia: anti-
immigrant affect; opposition to pro-immigrant policies; and support
for the Republikaner party.

As in the two earlier chapters, some descriptive statistics set the
stage for the later regression analysis. In general, foreigners in
Germany are not particularly well liked (see Table 8.1). In the
American Jewish Committee–commissioned EMNID poll "Einstellungen gegenüber Juden und anderen Minderheiten,"[1] for example,
the percent of valid respondents who said they would prefer not to

Table 8.1. *Desirability of Various Groups as Neighbors*

Group	Valid Percent Saying "rather not"
East/West Germans (Ost-/Westdeutsche)	9.1
Jews (Juden)	18.9
Vietnamese (Vietnamesen)	**28.5**
Turks (Türken)	**33.9**
Africans (Afrikaner)	**34.2**
Poles (Polen)	**37.1**
Arabs (Araber)	**45.5**
Gypsies (Zigeuner)	63.9

Question Text [Question 110]: What are your feelings about having the groups that I am about to read off in your neighborhood? Would you like to have the given group as neighbors, doesn't it matter to you, or would you rather not have them as neighbors? (Was empfinden Sie, wenn Sie die Gruppen, die ich Ihnen gleich vorlese, in Ihrer Nachbarschaft haben? Möchten Sie die jeweilige Gruppe als Nachbarn haben, ist Ihnen das egal oder wollen Sie sie lieber nicht als Nachbarn haben?)
Source: 1994 Einstellungen gegenüber Juden und anderen Minderheiten Survey.

have foreigners of various nationalities in their neighborhood (*Nachbarschaft*) was 28.5% if the foreigners were Vietnamese, 33.9% if Turks, 34.2% if Africans, 37.1% if Poles, and 45.5% if Arabs. In contrast, the valid respondents appeared relatively friendly toward Jews (18.9% of the respondents said they would prefer not to have Jews as neighbors) and Germans from the opposite half of the reunited country (i.e., former West Germans toward former East Germans; only 9.0% of all valid respondents claimed not to want their ethnic brethren as neighbors). The respondents exhibited even more hostility, on the other hand, toward Roma/Sinti, or "Gypsies," many of whom hold German nationality (63.9% of the interviewees preferred not to have such "strangers" as neighbors).

Mass political attitudes exhibit similar levels of opposition to pro-foreigner policies. Of the valid respondents in the 1992 Institut für praxisorientierte Sozialforschung (IPOS) poll "Einstellungen zu aktuellen Fragen der Innenpolitik," a bare majority (52.93%) agreed that it was "not OK" that many foreigners were living in Germany;

72.0% also claimed to believe that the German provisional constitution needed to be amended to prevent abuse of the right of political asylum, and 63.9% held that only a limited number of politically persecuted asylum seekers should be granted asylum in the country; yet, on the other hand, 77.5% seemed to approve of the right of asylum in the abstract.

Finally, open support for the anti-immigrant political party the Republikaner appears quite low. Only 5.2% of the valid 1992 IPOS respondents said they would vote for this party if the legislative elections were to take place the following Sunday.

Marginality Theory

For western Germany,[2] marginality theory predicts that coming from an immigrant family, being poor or unemployed, suffering from declining finances, working as a manual laborer, or being a woman will reduce nativism. Since Catholics and *Evangelische* are about evenly divided in western Germany (Harenberg 1993:306–307), however, religious affiliation should not matter for these two denominations. As in the United States and France, marginality variables should especially influence support for anti-immigrant political movements (here, the Republikaner) and, less strongly, opposition to immigration. Voting for a Neo-Nazi political party such as the Republikaner arguably approximates persecution more closely than does disliking Turks. And, at least as an intervening predisposition, believing that immigrants threaten traditional German culture should also increase nativism.

Measures

To test the three major theories, this chapter uses an "anti-immigrant affect" scale based on German respondents' feelings about "Turks" and "people of another nationality." This section also looks at an "opposition to immigration" index based on questions about respecting the right to asylum, extending the rights of non-EC immigrants, and facilitating naturalization. The "support for the Republikaner" variable comes from feeling thermometers for Franz Schönhuber and the Republikaner as well as a series of questions on one's ranking of the various German parties. Higher values of these variables represent increased nativism. (For further details on the specification of variables, see Appendix 4.)

Foreign Origin

As Table 8.2 documents, the German data generally confirm a cultural version of marginality theory. Coming from an immigrant family substantially reduces anti-immigrant affect (percent change = −14.4) and opposition to immigration (percent change = −11.2),[3] a result that confirms the American models of affect and policy and the French model of policy. That the effect of "foreign origin" appears to have a greater effect on Germans' policy preferences than on French respondents' opposition to immigration[4] (percent change = −4.3) may suggest that nonethnic Germans feel more marginalized than do nonethnic French people. Perhaps Germany's pre-2000 *jus sanguinis* citizenship laws made any nonethnic Germans feel that full acceptance is impossible. France's more *jus soli* nationality policy, in contrast, might allow immigrants to feel more incorporated into the French nation (see Brubaker 1992). These German results do not seem to support marginality theory's original hypothesis about the different effects across the three forms of nativism, however. Contrary to the American and French results (see Tables 6.2 and 7.2), originating in an immigrant family has a greater impact on affect than on policy preferences in the German sample. Perhaps German society, then, rejects nonethnic Germans even more decisively than – until January 2000 – Germany's *jus sanguinis* policy prevented them from obtaining German passports.[5]

Religion

Across the three forms of German nativism, being Catholic has no effect on anti-immigrant affect or opposition to immigration but does appear to increase voting for the Republikaner. Whereas the first two findings fit marginality theory, the third seems to disconfirm it. As Roth (1989) suggests, however, this result is almost certainly spurious. Having originated as a splinter group of the Bavarian-based Christian Social Union (Kitschelt 1995:216–217), the Republikaner should enjoy a disproportionately Catholic following simply because Bavaria is predominantly Catholic. Indeed, after controlling for living

Table 8.2. *Determinants of Anti-Immigrant Affect, Opposition to Immigration, and Support for the Republikaner in Germany*

Independent Variables	Anti-Immigrant Affect[a]		Opposition to Immigration[a]		Support for Republikaner[b]	
	Estimate[c]	Std. Err.	Estimate[c]	Std. Err.	Estimate[d]	Std. Err.
Catholic	-.368	.249	-.040	.104	1.238***	.416
Other religion					2.663	2.060
No religion					.081	.814
Foreign origin	-1.871***	.499	-.449**	.205		
Poor	-.616*	.360	-.492***	.152		
Rich	-.347	.373	-.068	.156		
Finances declined	.351	.436	.046	.172	1.846**	.754
Finances improved	.277	.306	.007	.125	-.484	.431
Unemployed	.879	.701	.000	.289	1.411	1.536
Professional/manager	-.240	.435	.009	.180	-1.824***	.652
Manual laborer	.623	.459	-.053	.200	1.915**	.913
Nonpaid worker	-.140	.398	.057	.171	-.443	.582
Sec. school graduate	-1.815***	.442	-.523***	.186	-3.780***	.908
University graduate	-1.441***	.395	-.494***	.162	-2.916***	.768
Female	-.096	.265	-.148	.111	-1.118***	.423
Age ≤ 30	-.277	.302	-.061	.125	.279	.533
Age ≥ 60	1.269***	.373	.339**	.159	.939	.573
Constant	7.635***	.415	2.572***	.177	5.638***	.569
R²	.118		.079			
n	669		539		1,935	

[a] Model analyzes 1988 Eurobarometer 30.

[b] Model analyzes 1990 German Election Panel Study.

[c] Coefficients are unstandardized ordinary least-squares regression estimates. Higher values of the dependent variables indicate greater nativism.

[d] Coefficients are Tobit regression estimates. Higher values of the dependent variable indicate greater support for the Republikaner.

* p ≤ .10; ** p ≤ .05; *** p ≤ .01.

in Bavaria, the coefficient for "Catholic" ceased to be statistically significant (b = .649, SE = .418).

Neither "other religion" nor "no religion" reached statistical significance in the Republikaner model, but the number of respondents (17) in the first category may be too small for any firm conclusions. The size of the nonreligious category, on the other hand, does appear large enough (142 respondents) for analysis. Perhaps because western Germany lacks the kind of conflictual church-state relations common in the United States and, especially, France (see Soper and Fetzer, in press), nonreligious Germans might feel less marginalized than their American or French equivalents (not being religious in those two countries does reduce opposition to immigration and support for anti-immigrant political movements). But further testing on other data is probably required before reaching any definite conclusions.

Perceived Cultural Threat

Despite contradictory cross-national results for economic marginality, perceived cultural threat does not produce conflicting effects in different countries. As in the United States and France, the apparent[6] nativistic influence of believing that immigrants threaten the dominant culture remains robust and very powerful (percent change = 48.2 for policy and 34.2 for affect; p ≤ .001 for both estimates). Figure 8.1 further demonstrates that this sense of threat originates in belonging to the dominant ethnic German majority (percent change = –15.1 for "foreign origin"), being over fifty-nine years old (percent change = 9.9), enjoying a comfortable income (percent change for poor = –6.3), being *evangelische* (percent change for Catholic = –5.2), and lacking a secondary school education (percent change for "secondary school graduate" = –9.5). Because the underlying data come from the same Eurobarometer survey, comparison of Figure 8.1 and the equivalent diagram for France (Figure 7.1) may prove instructive. One major difference is that the two educational variables strongly influence Germans' sense of cultural threat but have no influence on French respondents' perceived threat. Such findings may suggest that the French educational system less effectively instills an appreciation for cultural diversity than does the German (or the American; cf. Figure 6.1). Whereas originating in an immigrant family powerfully reduces

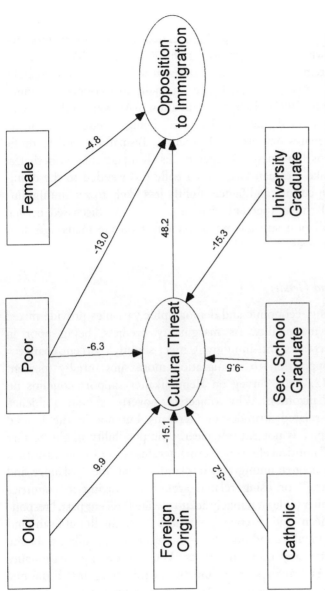

Figure 8.1. Path analysis of cultural threat and opposition to immigration in Germany. *Note:* Path coefficients represent percent change. Only statistically significant coefficients (at .10 level) shown in diagram, although all variables included in actual regressions.

Germans' sense of threat (percent change = −15.1), ethnic origin has no effect in the French sample. As argued already, Germany's lack of an acknowledged immigration tradition or (until 2000) a *jus soli* citizenship regime may make "foreignness" much more socially suspect in Germany than in France, a traditional country of immigration (Lequin 1992).[7] Religious affiliation matters in all three countries. In the United States and France, being a religious minority usually attenuates nativism. Of course, Bismarck's anti-Catholic *Kulturkampf* is long past. Vestiges of disadvantage may nonetheless suffice to make German Catholics a trifle less wedded to the dominant German culture and hence slightly less likely to see immigrants as a cultural threat (percent change = −5.2). As discussed earlier, religious affiliation still has no direct effect on Germans' affect or policy preferences.

Economics and Gender

The remaining, economic and demographic variables provide mixed support for marginality. As marginality predicts, being poor in Germany decreases anti-immigrant affect slightly (percent change = −4.7) and opposition to immigration more substantially (percent change = −12.3; the survey on Republikaner support contains no measure of income). Why objective poverty should influence immigration-related attitudes in Germany but not in the United States or France is not entirely clear. One possibility might be that "responsible" political elites[8] in Germany refuse (for obvious historical reasons) to scapegoat immigrants by claiming that "die Ausländer sind unser Unglück"[9] or using related arguments. Living in countries without a similar (at least publicly acknowledged) recent past, "responsible" American and French politicians – both Republican and Democratic, Gaullist and Socialist – might be more willing to blame immigrants for any economic woes. While economic marginality might lead the German poor to sympathize with immigrants, economic scapegoating of immigrants by American and French leaders might overpower the pro-immigration effects of poor respondents' economic disenfranchisement. Being poor, then, would reduce nativism in Germany but have no net effect in the United States and France.

Two other economic variables, experiencing poor personal finances[10] (b = 1.846, SE = .754) and working as a manual laborer (b = 1.915, SE = .913), also achieved statistical significance in the Republikaner model but in a direction contrary to marginality's predictions (i.e., they increased such support). As in the United States and France, working as a professional or manager decreased at least one form of nativism (in Germany, support for the Republikaner), but this finding also disconfirms the economic form of marginality. Finally, being a woman supports marginality theory by moderately reducing support for the Republikaner (b = −1.118, SE = .423; see Leggewie 1990:16–17).

Economic Self-Interest

As for the American and French cross-sectional models, the labor-market version of economic self-interest predicts increased xenophobia from being poor, experiencing poor personal finances, being out of work, and working in a low-prestige occupation. The use-of-services variety, in contrast, hypothesizes that being better-off will boost opposition to immigration and immigrant rights. As in Chapters 6 and 7, both versions of economic self-interest usually concur on the effects of believing that the national economy is poor or that immigrants threaten natives' livelihood. The two variants of economic self-interest likewise agree on the anti-immigrant effects of perceived relative economic deprivation. Among the three forms of xenophobia, however, affect should show the least economic influence, support for the Republikaner the most, and policy preferences an intermediate amount.

Objective Economic Condition

In a significant departure from the American and French results (and from earlier cross-national analysis by Hoskin 1991:141), Table 8.2 displays several statistically significant economic effects. The substantial anti-Republikaner influence of working as a professional or manager (b = −1.824, SE = .652) does match similar findings in the United States and France. But only in Germany does working as a manual laborer increase nativism, very noticeably boosting support for the Republikaner (b = 1.915, SE = .913). Critics might nonetheless point out that "manual laborer" has no effect on affect or policy preferences. Skeptics might similarly write off the large pro-Republikaner effect of poor finances (b = 1.846, SE = .754) as a spurious manifestation of the slightly different question wording (finances "bad" versus "declined"; see Appendix 4). The pro-immigrant impact of being poor, on the other hand, cannot be so easily explained away. Unemployment represents the major continuity across the three countries, failing to achieve statistical significance. But in confirmation of economic self-interest, support for the Republikaner does reveal greater economic effects than do affect or policy preferences.

The divergence between the effect of income in Germany and its influence in the United States and France could conceivably have more than one cause. As discussed earlier, leading German politicians' greater hesitancy to scapegoat immigrants might help explain some of the results for being poor in the three countries. *How* politicians and other activists rhetorically attack the foreign-born might also account for the different effects of income. While much political discourse in the United States and France focuses on the labor-market effects of immigration (e.g., "immigrants are taking our jobs"), the immigration debate in Germany tends to concentrate more on the use of services (e.g., "asylum seekers are raising our taxes by living off the state"). As both economic marginality and the use-of-services variant of self-interest predict, being well-off in Germany would thus make one less likely to support immigration than it would in the other two countries.

Perceived Relative Deprivation

If several of individual Germans' objective economic conditions appear to help determine immigration-related attitudes, so too do some of the Germans' economic *perceptions*. Believing that immigrants are doing better economically than people such as oneself may, for example, powerfully stimulate the Germans' dislike of immigrants and opposition to immigration (percent change for relative deprivation = 28.5 for affect and 21.1 for policy). Because correction for two-way causation between nativism and relative deprivation proved impossible, however, one should view such results with caution.

Sociotropic Effects

In contrast to the French results but parallel to the American findings, perceptions of the national economy have no impact on German nativism. Greater overall prosperity in the United States and western Germany (Harenberg 1993:69) may well explain this new cross-national difference. Perhaps sociotropic phenomena manifest themselves most prominently when the national economy is performing poorly.

Perceived Economic Threat

Finally, Figure 8.2 diagrams the potential[11] interrelations among perceived economic threat, opposition to immigration, and their various determinants. Just as in the United States and France, believing that immigrants threaten natives' or one's own job strongly increases opposition to immigration (percent change = 34.2) as well as dislike of immigrants (percent change = 36.7; path analysis not shown).[12] As in the other two countries, a secondary school education (percent change = -19.2) appears to reduce this sense of economic threat substantially. Only in the United States, however, does a university education appear markedly more powerful than just a secondary one in reducing economic threat (compare Figures 6.2, 7.2, and 8.2). Perhaps what really reduces economic threat is the kind of socioeconomic analysis taught at the undergraduate level in the United States but at the earlier *lycée* or *Gymnasium* level in France or Germany.

Education aside, economic threat appears to have few common causes in all three nations. Particularly puzzling is the pro-threat effect of poverty in the United States (percent change = 8.4) but its antithreat impact in Germany (percent change = -7.5). Also noteworthy is how unemployment appears to increase Germans' economic threat noticeably (percent change = 16.2). But without correcting for bidirectional causation, firm conclusions about the true causes of perceived economic threat must remain tentative.

Simultaneously including only perceived economic threat and perceived cultural threat in the German model of policy produces a percent change for economic threat (26.4) that is slightly smaller than for perceived cultural menace (36.2). In France, by contrast, economic threat (percent change = 30.2) appeared about as influential as cultural threat (percent change = 29.8; see Chapter 7). Perhaps just as for perceptions of the national economy, relative economic prosperity weakens the effects of economic threat relative to other causes.

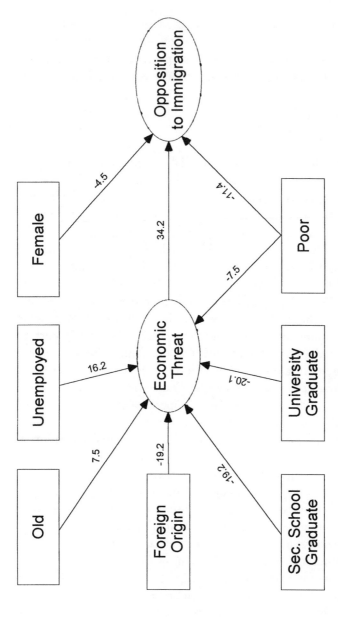

Figure 8.2. Path analysis of economic threat and opposition to immigration in Germany. *Note*: Path coefficients represent percent change. Only statistically significant coefficients (at .10 level) shown in diagram, although all variables included in actual regressions.

Contact Theory

The Allport-Pettigrew version of contact theory holds that close, cooperative, equal-status contact with individual immigrants reduces hostility toward them (see Pettigrew 1986). More casual interaction with the foreign-born, on the other hand, should intensify xenophobia. And – at least in theory – affect should reveal more contact effects than do the other two types of nativism.

Contact at the Workplace or in the Neighborhood

In general, German data tend to support these predictions about the type of contact. Interacting with immigrants at the workplace appears to reduce opposition to immigration substantially (percent change = –19.4, p ≤ .01) but has no statistically significant effect on anti-immigrant affect. Proximity at the German workplace thus supports contact theory by reducing opposition to immigration but disconfirms this explanation's prediction of an even greater pro-immigrant effect for affect. Though the American surveys contained no measure of workplace proximity, these German results do conflict with the French findings of no effect at all for this contact variable. Perhaps contact at the German workplace is more likely to be equal-status and/or cooperative (e.g., if immigrants are better integrated on the job) than in France and thus more likely to reduce nativism.

The French (and American) data also differ from the German surveys on the effect of "neighborhood" proximity. Whereas living in a neighborhood with many immigrants affects neither affect nor policy preferences in France (see Chapter 7), in Germany increased proximity at the neighborhood level appears[13] to *increase* anti-immigrant feelings moderately (percent change for affect model = 10.5, p ≤ .05; no corresponding effect for policy model).

The Puzzle of French versus German Results

This difference between the French and German results seems all the more puzzling because the data come from the same Eurobarometer survey and because residential segregation appears much less prevalent in Germany than in France (Thränhardt 1994). In Germany, in other words, the relatively integrated housing should be *less* likely than in France to foster "casual" contact and *more* likely to encourage "good" or close, equal-status interactions. Instead, however, the data suggest that proximity in (relatively unsegregated) German neighborhoods boosts dislike of immigrants but has no effect in (relatively segregated) French communities.

If the French and German samples of Eurobarometer 30 were truly comparable, one might be tempted to discard contact theory as completely worthless. Linguistic analysis of the precise question wording for the "neighborhood"-proximity variable, however, may help explain these surprising cross-national results. The English "master" questionnaire for Eurobarometer 30's item on residential proximity (Variable 0241) reads, "From this list [show list] I would like you to tell me if there are many such people, a few, or none who live in your neighborhood . . . people of another nationality?" (Reif and Melich 1991:88). Yet while the French version translated "neighborhood" as *quartier* (Reif and Melich 1991:461), the German questionnaire instead used *Nachbarschaft* (EMNID 1988).

Although both the French and the German words are reasonable translations of the English "neighborhood" (Robert and Collins 1978: 2:397; Messinger 1988:2:429), the German word probably implies a much smaller area than does the French. According to the authoritative French dictionary *Le Petit Robert* (Robert 1986:1576), a *quartier* is an "administrative division of a city" or the "part of a city that has its own appearance and a certain unity." The dictionary gives as an example the *Quartier Latin* in Paris, the large university and literary district in the French capital. Such a district might approximate a city ward in the United States. The area of a *Nachbarschaft*, on the other hand, seems much more restricted. The standard German dictionary *Duden-Universalwörterbuch* (Drosdowski 1989:1049–1050; see also Messinger 1988:1:382) defines a *Nachbarschaft* as "the totality of the neighbors [*Nachbarn*]." The German approximation of the English "neighbor," moreover, means "someone who lives in one's [immediate] proximity and whose house or property lies [immediately] next to one's house or property." Essentially, a *quartier* approximates one's housing development, village, or city ward, while a *Nachbarschaft* includes only one's very close (e.g., next-door) neighbors.

If French and German respondents perceived this difference in size, the different translations may help explain the divergent results for France and Germany. If one assumes that most residential contact between natives and immigrants remains superficial, one might expect greater anti-immigrant effects from more frequent encounters. Because living next door to an immigrant family would make for more frequent contact than simply residing in the same city ward, the German *Nachbarschaft* variable should therefore produce stronger anti-immigrant reactions than the French *quartier* indicator.

Perhaps the most serious critique of this analysis is that living "right next door" to an immigrant family should change not only the frequency of contact but also the quality of interaction. Wouldn't next-door neighbors tend to invite each other over for dinner, go to the park together, and baby-sit each other's children? Not necessarily, if my experience living in the Parisian suburbs is any indication. Although one ethnic French family I knew lived literally "on the other side of the wall" (the house was attached to a large apartment complex) from a family of Portuguese immigrants, contact generally remained limited to greeting each other on the street and occasionally asking to borrow some flour. To the best of my knowledge, neither family ever invited the other over for dinner or engaged in any close, cooperative activities together. Although my relevant experience in Germany is more limited, interaction with one's *Nachbarn* appeared equally "casual" in Allport's terms.[14] Especially when natives harbor latent resentment toward immigrants to begin with, having foreigners move in "right next door" as in Germany might thus provoke a stronger xenophobic reaction than having them relocate into one's village or housing development as in France. Such reactions might prove all the more vehement if the natives lack the means to move elsewhere (cf. American "white flight").

Regional-Level Contact

French and German results for contact also differ somewhat at the regional level. In Germany, living in a *Land* (roughly equivalent in size to a French *région*) with a high percentage of immigrants seems to increase dislike of them modestly (percent change = 10.4, $p \leq .05$) but has no effect on policy preferences or support for the Republikaner.[15] Living in West Berlin, where 11.36% of the population was foreign in 1987, for example, should on average make one 1.35 points (on a 13-point scale) more hostile to immigrants than if one lived in Schleswig-Holstein, where only 3.01% of the population was foreign

Table 8.3. *Summary of Chapter's Findings*

		Economic		
Variables	Marginality	Labor Market	Use of Services	Contact
Cultural				
Perceived cultural threat	√*		ø*	
Catholic	√		√	
Other religion	ø		√	
No religion	ø		√	
Foreign origin	√		ø	
Economic				
Perceived economic threat			√*	
Poor	√	ø	√	
Rich	ø	ø	ø	
Finances declined	ø	ø	ø	
Finances improved	ø	ø	ø	
Unemployed	ø	ø	ø	
Professional/manager	ø	ø	ø	
Manual laborer	ø	ø	ø	
Nonpaid worker	ø	ø	ø	
Perceived decline in national economy			ø	
Perceived improvement in national economy			ø	
Perceived relative economic deprivation			√*	
Contact				
Proximity/region				ø
Proximity/neighborhood				√*
Proximity/work				√*
Demographic				
Sec. school graduate	√		√	
University graduate	√		√	
Female	ø		√	

Note: √ = on average, data confirm theory's prediction. ø = on average, data do not confirm theory's prediction. * = result provisional because not corrected for bidirectional causality.

in 1987. Both the German and, especially, the French models for the effect of regional contact on nativism thus differ from the corresponding American analysis (see Chapter 6). As suggested in the previous chapter, our best guess is that this difference stems from the possibly greater segregation of immigrants in Germany and, above all, France.

Discussion

As Table 8.3 suggests, cultural-marginality explanations of German xenophobia usually perform at least as well as theories based on economic marginality, economic self-interest, or contact. Believing that immigrants threaten the dominant German culture correlates strongly with increased hostility to foreigners and their political cause. Coming from a non-German ethnic group, on the other hand, appears to increase positive feelings for immigrants and support for the rights of the foreign-born. Because Protestants and Catholics are more balanced in western Germany, being Catholic does not seem to produce the kinds of pronounced pro-foreigner effects one often observes among religious minorities in France and the United States (see Chapters 6 and 7; the apparent pro-Republikaner effect of being Catholic seems to be a spurious reflection of region).

The German data reveal no strong difference in the effect of cultural marginality on the three forms of nativism, a result in some tension with the American and French results. The relative paucity of cultural variables in the German samples may nonetheless make cross-national comparisons of cultural effects provisional. As in the U.S. and French analyses, however, contact's influence usually did not seem to vary systematically across the three main forms of xenophobia. And as in the United States, economic variables generally seem more influential in shaping policy views and support for anti-immigrant political movements than in determining affect.

9

Culture, Nationality, and the Future of Nativism

> If a man be gracious and courteous to strangers, it shews he is a citizen of the world, and that his heart is no island cut off from other lands, but a continent that joins to them.
>
> Francis Bacon ([1625] 1994)

> After the history of the 20th century – which is one of the most brutal, violent centuries on human record – to resurrect the ghost of xenophobia, racism, hatred of the other, is exposing oneself once more to the worst crimes of our age. One would have thought these lessons had been learned.
>
> Mexican novelist Carlos Fuentes, in O'Connor (1997)

Analysis has usually supported cultural forms of marginality theory and, slightly less frequently, confirmed some forms of economic self-interest. Perhaps because the available indicators were far from ideal, however, the data did not validate contact theory very often.

Overall Results

Historical Analysis

Table 9.1 summarizes the relatively clean results of the historical analysis from Chapters 2, 3, and 4. As cultural-marginality theory predicted, natives warmly welcomed immigrant groups whose culture approximated the traditions of the dominant group of natives in each country. In spite of economic theory's contrary prediction, immigrants

Table 9.1. *Summary of Results for Historical Analysis*

Variables	Marginality	Economic	Contact
Cultural difference between immigrants and natives of dominant ethnicity	√	ø	
Wave of culturally different immigrants	ø	√	
Depression/recession	ø	√	
Percent Foreign-Born			ø

Note: √ = on average, data confirm theory's prediction. ø = on average, data do not confirm theory's prediction.

whose backgrounds diverged most widely from inlanders' cultural "norm" almost always suffered the most severe hostility from the native-born during any given period. Except in the United States,[1] waves of culturally different immigrants do not appear to have boosted xenophobia. Over time, the historical record also confirms economic theory. Periods of economic prosperity – at least in the United States and France – brought with them greater overall tolerance of foreigners, whereas depressions or recessions most often provoked widespread nativism. The proportion of foreign-born in a country's population, on the other hand, does not appear to have caused fluctuations in the overall level of restrictionism.

Times-Series Analysis

Chapter 5's time-series models yield similar results (see Table 9.2). Suitable cultural indicators were not available, but increases in the percent change in real disposable income or wages per capita do seem to reduce opposition to immigration and support for anti-immigrant political movements. Yet the data do not show that the second economic indicator, the unemployment rate, has any consistent effect on these immigration-related attitudes. The analysis likewise fails to confirm that either of the contact variables (percent foreign-born and the immigration rate) influences these over-time forms of nativism.

Table 9.2. *Summary of Results for Time-Series Models*

Variables	Marginality	Economic	Contact
Economic			
Real disposable income per capita		√	
Unemployment rate		ø	
Contact			
Percent foreign-born			ø
Immigration rate			ø

Note: √ = on average, data confirm theory's prediction. ø = on average, data do not confirm theory's prediction.

Cross-Sectional Analysis

As befits the number of datasets analyzed and potential causal variables examined, results for the cross-sectional analysis in Chapters 6, 7, and 8 make concise summaries difficult. Not only do findings occasionally differ across countries, but results may also vary according to the type of dependent variable (i.e., affect toward immigrants, preferences on immigration policy, or support for anti-immigrant political movements). At the risk of some distortion or oversimplification, Table 9.3 nevertheless "averages" the cross-sectional findings across countries and over all three types of dependent variables.[2] This table is thus based on the corresponding summaries (Tables 6.3, 7.3, and 8.3) in each of the respective cross-sectional chapters.

Contact

If Table 9.3 contains no completely obvious theoretical winner, it does have a prominent loser. Only individual contact (personal contact or proximity/work) confirmed contact theory, and even there, this effect may well disappear if one were to control for bidirectional causation. Unfortunately, statistically correcting for pro-immigrant people simply choosing to associate closely with immigrants proved intractable. One may, of course, read the overall effects for regional-level contact as either disconfirming contact theory or suggesting that such interaction depends on the amount of residential segregation:

Table 9.3. *Summary of Results for Cross-Sectional Models*

Variables	Marginality	Economic		Contact
		Labor Market	Use of Services	
Cultural				
Perceived cultural threat	√*		ø*	
Non-Catholic minority	√		ø	
Catholic minority	√		ø	
Jewish	√		ø	
Other religion	ø		√	
No religion	√		ø	
Foreign origin	√		ø	
Latino	√		ø	
African American	√		ø	
Asian	√		ø	
Native American	ø		√	
Other race	ø		√	
Economic				
Perceived economic threat		√*		
Poor	ø	ø		ø
Finances declined	ø	ø		ø
Unemployed	ø	ø		ø
Professional/manager	ø	√		ø
Manual laborer	ø	ø		ø
Nonpaid worker	ø	ø		ø
Perceived decline in national economy		ø		
Perceived relative economic deprivation		√*		
Contact				
Proximity/region				ø
Proximity/neighborhood				ø*
Proximity/work				√*
Personal contact				√*
Demographic				
University graduate	√		√	
Female	ø		√	

Note: √ = on average, data confirm theory's prediction. ø = on average, data do not confirm theory's prediction. * = result provisional because not corrected for bidirectional causality.

the more a region is segregated by nativity, the more contact will increase nativism.

This poor showing does not necessarily mean that the Allport-Pettigrew theory of contact is false, however. As Pettigrew points out (1986), many so-called disconfirmations of contact theory have "either measured only in part or ignored altogether . . . the relevant conditions" for tolerance-producing intergroup contact. Such a criticism seems especially apropos in secondary analysis of public-opinion surveys. One could probably find one or more violations of the Allport-Pettigrew guidelines in every cross-sectional contact variable in Table 9.3. Certainly at the regional and neighborhood levels, the relevant "authorities, custom or law" (Pettigrew 1971:30) fail to support close interaction between natives and immigrants. If anything, these "norm makers" support de facto segregation by nativity. For the workplace, moreover, our surveys do not tell us whether immigrants and natives possessed "equal status in the situation," sought "common goals," or depended "cooperatively upon each other" (Pettigrew 1971:29–30). Violation of any one of the four requirements can invalidate a strict test of contact theory. Perhaps one should only attempt to evaluate this explanation using a formal experimental design. On the other hand, examining the indicators in Table 9.3 may still have some value since some of the more popular explanations of nativism rely upon such contact variables (e.g., "native French people started voting for Le Pen when all the Algerians moved into their neighborhood").[3]

Marginality

When the remaining two theories make contradictory predictions, marginality posts a slight lead over economic self-interest (whether the labor-market or use-of-services variant). The two major theories' predictions conflict for nineteen of the potential causes in Table 9.3. Yet, although the data disconfirm fourteen of the predictions of economic theory, the results fail to support only ten of the expectations of marginality theory.

Marginality appears most powerful when formulated in cultural terms (e.g., perceived cultural threat, religious identification, nativity, ethnicity, or race). In general, outsiders by economic situation or gender do not seem to behave much differently from corresponding insiders. At least before one corrects for bidirectional causation, believing that immigrants threaten the dominant culture appears to increase an individual's sympathy for anti-immigrant campaigns. Belonging to a religious minority or "outsider group," conversely, tends to increase tolerance for immigrants, outsiders by nativity. Religious outsiders in all three predominantly Christian countries, Jews strongly support pro-immigrant policies in the United States. If the French and German samples had contained enough Jewish respondents for separate analysis, the corresponding dummy variable would probably have been pro-immigrant as well. In general, the Catholic variable also confirmed cultural-marginality theory. A religious minority in the United States, American Catholics showed themselves to be relatively pro-immigration. In France, however, the overwhelmingly Catholic majority proved decidedly anti-immigrant. When the Protestant and Catholic forces are more or less equally matched, as in western Germany, however, this denominational divide makes little difference. The overall results for "other religion" proved disappointing for cultural theory, yet the usually small number of respondents in this category might have made definitive confirmation or disconfirmation problematic.

Those respondents who themselves were naturalized citizens or who had recent roots in the country also exhibited markedly pro-immigration views. Less tied to the dominant cultures in each country, they apparently felt less threat from the diverse cultural practices that today's immigrants might bring. In France, where racial or ethnic survey questions as such are rare, the "foreignness" variable also serves as a proxy for non-French ethnicity. Not themselves *français de souche*, these French citizens "by choice" also seem less likely to fear any immigration-induced alterations in traditional French culture.

In the United States, the three largest ethnic or racial minorities likewise appear ceteris paribus less anxious about further immigrant "reinforcements" of ethnic minorities. U.S.-born Latinos should obviously welcome their ethnic cousins from Mexico, Central America, Cuba, and Puerto Rico more warmly than Anglos would. Asian Americans should likewise be more willing to oppose campaigns against recent Chinese immigrants. What is more surprising, however, is that (again, multivariately) even African Americans oppose attacks on immigrants more strongly than whites do. A racial minority subject to widespread discrimination and prejudice, American blacks apparently find it prudent to oppose whites' campaigns against immigrant minorities as well.

The two smaller ethnic categories (i.e., "Native American" and "other race") produced more anomalous results. No "averaged" estimate for one of these groups deviated from zero. Since relatively few respondents belonged to these smaller ethnic categories, the sample size may not have been large enough to register any statistically significant effects. Alternatively, the "other race" category might have contained too much ethnic diversity for meaningful results. True Native Americans (e.g., Lakota, Ojibwe) might have been confused in the surveys with non-American-Indian "superpatriots" who also feel compelled to label themselves "Native Americans" (see discussion of the *Los Angeles Times* Poll in Appendix 2).

These results for ethnicity and race at first seem to run counter to earlier studies of American attitudes toward immigration. Simon and Alexander (1993:40), for example, find that "[p]ersons of . . . a minority racial category are more likely to be anti-immigration." This hostility arises, the authors believe, because "[i]mmigrants . . . [are perceived as] competing with [native-born racial minorities] for jobs, housing, benefits, and their children's place in institutions of higher learning." Such analysis, however, restricts itself to bivariate relationships between race and immigration-related attitudes. On average, native-born racial minorities may well dislike immigrants more than American whites do. Yet one must not conclude from this datum that being a racial minority *causes* anti-immigrant sentiments. Rather, racial minorities in the United States are most likely more hostile to immigrants because these native-born minorities are less likely to be well educated, of high occupational prestige, or Catholic. In fact, the analysis in this book suggests that between, say, two equally prosperous Protestant physicians – one white and the other black – the African American doctor would be more tolerant toward immigrants. Belonging to a racial minority, by itself, tends to decrease xenophobia. The chief reason why the multivariate results in my study seem to conflict with the bivariate ones in the research by Simon and Alexander is that being a racial minority in today's United States unfortunately correlates very positively with suffering socioeconomic disadvantages.

Economic Self-Interest

The data also partly support economic self-interest, but not the way popular explanations would have it. Overall, individual unemployment has no effect, just as aggregate unemployment usually has no influence in Chapter 5's time-series models. Nor does having a higher income relative to other respondents seem to reduce nativism (for similar cross-national results, see Hoskin 1991:77–94).

This last variable reveals yet another area of political behavior to suffer from a "macro-micro problem" (Norpoth, Lewis-Beck, and Lafay 1991). Time-series analysis from all three countries suggests that an increase in the percent change in real disposable income or wages per capita reduces aggregate opposition to immigration and support for anti-immigrant political movements. Yet cross-sectional differences in personal income are probably not driving these aggregate results; as we have seen, individual income usually has no effect. The sociotropic hypothesis fails to reconcile these conflicting results since perceptions of the economy usually have no effect on individuals' nativism (see Table 9.3). Perhaps the most plausible remaining hypothesis is that political elites and their media allies rhetorically scapegoat immigrants whenever the economy declines (Cornelius 1982; Citrin et al. 1997; for another solution to the macro-micro problem, see Kramer 1983). Unfortunately, rigorous testing of such an explanation is outside the scope of this book.

Education

Finally, the demographic variables produced few surprises. As many previous studies have demonstrated (see, e.g., Hoskin 1991:147), increased education powerfully decreases reported opposition to immigration. The path diagrams in Chapters 6 and 8 indicate that some of education's effect may act through reducing people's fear of cultural threat from immigrants. The path diagrams for economic threat may also support Hernes and Knudsen (1992; see also Hernes and Knudsen 1989), however. According to these scholars, higher education also instills greater confidence in one's ability to "compet[e] successfully in the labor market" and hence to be able to absorb any competition from immigrants. At least on average, however, gender did not produce any significant effects.

The strong and robust pro-immigration effect of higher education may help explain the seemingly large disjunction between official immigration policy and mass public opinion. Although politicians certainly take notice of popular nativism, usually their actions are not nearly so restrictionist as the populace seems to want. As Simon and Alexander (1993:246; see also Lee 1998) note in the American context, "If public opinion polls dictated immigration policies, the restrictionist legislation of the 1920s and 1950s would have remained in place." Yet perhaps the highly educated and hence disproportionately pro-immigration elites dismiss much popular nativism as simply the isolationist and ethnic prejudices of ill-informed hoi polloi (but see Holsti 1996:192–195). Leading economists (see Moore and Simon 1989) and politicians might support immigration because it is "good for the country and its economy" even if the average citizen "doesn't recognize this fact."

Variations across Forms of Nativism

Across the three forms of nativism, cultural marginality and economic self-interest usually tended to have a greater effect on policy or support for anti-immigrant movements than on anti-immigrant affect. The results were reversed for contact, however, which generally had a greater impact on affect than on the other two types of nativism. These secondary predictions of the three major theories thus found some confirmation in the data.

Few Conflicting Results across Countries

Another striking result of this study is that the three nationalities behaved very similarly despite large differences in culture, history, and experience with immigration. Overall findings from the historical and time-series analyses usually remain the same regardless of country. The number of unexplained cross-national differences in results from the cross-sectional models also seems surprisingly low.

Further Testing of Marginality Theory

This book's relatively strong support for at least the cultural variant of the marginality explanation may suggest further testing of this little-examined theory. Economic self-interest (see Green and Shapiro 1994) and contact interpretations (Hewstone and Brown 1986) each boast relatively large literatures. Besides such limited tests as that presented by Sigelman, Shockey, and Sigelman (1993), however, marginality and its theoretical relatives do not appear to have been seriously examined. Yet possible applications abound. One might try to determine if attitudes toward some marginalized groups are more susceptible to such effects than are views on other groups. Sigelman et al. (1993) suggest that, contrary to marginality theory, American blacks are multivariately *more* anti-Semitic than white American gentiles. Thus, must the respondent *perceive* the groups as outsiders for underdog solidarity to take place (here, blacks might have simply categorized all whites as "insiders" regardless of religious affiliation)? How well would marginality theory explain attitudes toward indigenous peoples, Roma ("Gypsies"), or the elderly, just to name a few oppressed or discriminated-against groups? One might also test the explanation on international relations. After one corrects for economic resources, would less powerful or relatively "insignificant" nations tend to contribute disproportionately to famine relief or economic development, accept proportionately more asylum seekers, or support the concerns of developing countries more often in the United Nations? Finally, legislative studies might prove another fruitful area. Would lawmakers who are themselves somehow marginalized or who come from economically disadvantaged or other types of "outsider" districts tend to oppose legislative attacks on certain outsiders (e.g., dispossessing Native American Indian tribes of their land, enacting Jim Crow laws, and outlawing the wearing of a *ḥijāb* or yarmulke in public schools)?

Yet confirmation of marginality theory does not necessarily mean that all outsiders in society will unite to fight attacks on disadvantaged groups. In the aftermath of Proposition 187, some Latino and African American leaders did join forces to oppose assaults on immigrant rights and affirmative action (Womack 1995). Because the "outsider-solidarity" model is multivariate, however, the centrifugal forces of low education might also nullify the centripetal effects of belonging to a minority. So while cooperation among highly educated, elite members of ethnic minorities seems likely, achieving interethnic solidarity among the more poorly educated rank and file might prove less tractable.

Ways to Reduce Nativism

Education about Immigration's Economic and Cultural Effects

The research in this book may, however, suggest less political ways to combat nativism. Good economic times in themselves should help, but educators and the media might also contribute immeasurably by dispelling popular misconceptions about immigrants and immigration. Scholars such as Simon (1989) have attempted to show that immigration usually helps rather than harms the overall economy, and Buttler (1992:161–166, 218–231) has illustrated how immigration might help solve Germany's looming social-security crisis. Further efforts might continue to examine critically the simpleminded notion that "one more immigrant equals one more unemployed native." But educators and the media should not restrict themselves to myths about the economics of immigration. As this book has shown, culture plays at least as large a role in nativism. Here, helpful educational efforts might focus on how the use of a "foreign language" almost invariably declines or disappears among the children and grandchildren of immigrants (that many first-generation immigrants speak languages other than English is unfortunately a selling point for many isolationist nativists in the United Sates),[4] on how most Muslim immigrants in Europe support religious tolerance (see Hofmann 1992:97–102), and perhaps on how immigrant and native birthrates converge across generations of immigrants (Tribalat 1991:141–171).

Education about Persecution of One's Group

Marginality theory might suggest yet another way to reduce hostility to immigrants and other disadvantaged groups. Because this explanation holds that the experience of being oppressed oneself creates sympathy for other persecuted groups, educators within particular religious or ethnic traditions might emphasize those periods in their own group's history in which they themselves faced persecution. Jewish adults, for instance, should continue to teach younger generations about the Holocaust via such events as *Yom ha-Sho'ah* (Imber 1994). By discussing stories from the *Martyrs' Mirror* (van Braght 1972; Jackson and Jackson 1989; Lowry 1997), Mennonites might similarly persist in educating Anabaptist youth about the persecutions endured by their genealogical or spiritual ancestors. Not only might such instruction help prevent future generations from forgetting their heritage, but instilling a sense of potential vulnerability might also help create sympathy for oppressed people of other ethnic or religious backgrounds.[5]

Abolition of the Concept of "Foreigner"

The very long-term solution to xenophobia may well lie elsewhere, however. Persuading natives that most immigrant groups are usually good for the economy and will eventually lose their mother tongue should increase tolerance for newcomers in the United States and western Europe. At least in the first generation, however, immigrants will continue to be perceived as "foreigners." Yet perhaps a better strategy would be to attack the concept of "foreigner" itself. Perhaps the best way to end antiforeigner or anti-immigrant sentiment is to make it conceptually impossible for "foreigners" to "immigrate" to a "foreign country."

The idea might not be as utopian as it sounds. For as Wihtol de Wenden (1988:276–379), Soysal (1994), and Jacobson (1996; see also Hollifield 1997) contend, not only are the conceptual and political differences between "citizens" and "noncitizens" or between "natives" and "foreigners" slowly eroding, but the disparity between the rights accorded to nationals as opposed to nonnationals seems to be gradually diminishing. The Évian Accords of 1962 declare that, except for "political rights" (i.e., voting, holding public office), Algerian citizens living in France possess the same rights as French nationals (Wihtol de Wenden 1988:137–138). German citizens living in France have even been granted certain political rights (see Wihtol de Wenden 1988:330, 344; Bauböck 1994:131–132). And Proposition 187 notwithstanding, the relative sociopolitical advantages of being a U.S.-born Chicana instead of a Mexican "green-carder" have become less and less significant (Jacobson 1996:65).

At the interpersonal level, moreover, anti-foreigner sentiment can only exist so long as the "native" recognizes the "nonnative" as a "foreign other." When natives instead view objective immigrants as essentially indistinguishable from nationals, xenophobia must disappear. Germans' relatively warm reception of the *Vertriebene* and *Übersiedler* probably arose from West Germans' great difficulty in even recognizing these ethnic Germans as foreigners. A similar logic might apply to late-twentieth-century Americans' high tolerance for Anglophone and even Francophone Canadian immigrants. Because most Americans cannot even detect an English-speaking Canadian's accent, they do not have a chance to develop antiforeigner hostility to her or him.

And some evidence suggests that this perception of "foreign otherness" is not rigid. The circle of those perceived as "like us," in other words, can expand or contract (Tajfel 1970; Varenne 1993; Inglehart, Nevitte, and Basañez 1996:158–162). Perhaps a personal anecdote will help illustrate this point. While I was attending a seminar at the Friedrich Ebert Foundation in Bonn, a German acquaintance who works as a journalist related that he had just returned from an information-gathering trip to Paris. One day he needed to enter the parliament building to interview a French legislator. As he was going through security, the gendarme asked, "Are you a foreigner?" "No," the German journalist replied, "I'm a European." While Franco-German relations could still stand improvement, this incident may well symbolize the shape of things to come. As the sense of being French or German or Spanish gives way to the feeling of being "European," and as the European Union expands to include much of eastern Europe, the kind of prejudice that once pitted French "natives" against Italian "immigrants" or German "nationals" against Polish "nonnationals" is bound to decline.

The Future of Nativism

Although transforming the countries of the North American Free Trade Agreement (NAFTA) into a North American Union seems farther off,[6] the same dynamic may well occur on the other side of the Atlantic. As the United States becomes more and more ethnically heterogenous and, especially, more and more Latino, the distinction between ethnic Mexicans on either side of the Rio Grande/*Río Bravo* is bound to strike Americans in general – not just those living in the Southwest's "borderlands" – as increasingly artificial and pointless. And, as noted, the distinction between ethnic Europeans on either side of the U.S.-Canadian border already seems to be viewed in this light.

At least for the United States, my long-term forecast for the particular prejudices studied in this book is bright. The children or grandchildren or great-grandchildren of today's Americans may well live to view the late twentieth century's anti-Mexican prejudice with the same disdain that we view the nineteenth century's anti-Irish or anti-German hysteria.[7] France and especially Germany are probably at an earlier stage in their immigration experience. Yet they too should eventually be able to claim their immigration history as a success story. The only requirement is that their behavior parallel America's relatively decent treatment of its European immigrants instead of its savage repression of its African ones.

APPENDIX 1

Demographic, Economic, and Political Data

Table A1.1. *Foreign-Born Population and Unemployment Rate in the United States, 1880–1997*

Year	Foreign-Born (%)[a]	Source	Unemployment Rate (%)[a]	Source
1880	13.3	HS (1989:14)	4.0[b]	L (1964:189)
1881			4.0[b]	L (1964:189)
1882			4.0[b]	L (1964:189)
1883			4.0[b]	L (1964:189)
1884			4.0[b]	L (1964:189)
1885			7.0[b]	L (1964:187)
1886			4.0[b]	L (1964:189)
1887			4.0[b]	L (1964:189)
1888			4.0[b]	L (1964:189)
1889			4.0[b]	L (1964:189)
1890	15.7	HS (1989:14)	4.0	HS (1989:135)
1891			5.4	HS (1989:135)
1892			3.0	HS (1989:135)
1893			11.7	HS (1989:135)
1894			18.4	HS (1989:135)
1895			13.7	HS (1989:135)
1896			14.4	HS (1989:135)
1897			14.5	HS (1989:135)
1898			12.4	HS (1989:135)
1899			6.5	HS (1989:135)
1900	14.5	HS (1989:14)	5.0	HS (1989:135)
1901			4.0	HS (1989:135)
1902			3.7	HS (1989:135)
1903			3.9	HS (1989:135)
1904			5.4	HS (1989:135)

Table A1.1. *(cont.)*

Year	Foreign-Born (%)[a]	Source	Unemployment Rate (%)[a]	Source
1905			4.3	HS (1989:135)
1906			1.7	HS (1989:135)
1907			2.8	HS (1989:135)
1908			8.0	HS (1989:135)
1909			5.1	HS (1989:135)
1910	16.2	HS (1989:14)	5.9	HS (1989:135)
1911			6.7	HS (1989:135)
1912			4.6	HS (1989:135)
1913			4.3	HS (1989:135)
1914			7.9	HS (1989:135)
1915			8.5	HS (1989:135)
1916			5.1	HS (1989:135)
1917			4.6	HS (1989:135)
1918			1.4	HS (1989:135)
1919			1.4	HS (1989:135)
1920	13.2	SA (1993:50)	5.2	HS (1989:135)
1921			11.7	HS (1989:135)
1922			6.7	HS (1989:135)
1923			2.4	HS (1989:135)
1924			5.0	HS (1989:135)
1925			3.2	HS (1989:135)
1926			1.8	HS (1989:135)
1927			3.3	HS (1989:135)
1928			4.2	HS (1989:135)
1929			3.2	HS (1989:135)
1930	11.6	SA (1993:50)	8.7	HS (1989:135)
1931			15.9	HS (1989:135)
1932			23.6	HS (1989:135)
1933			24.9	HS (1989:135)
1934			21.7	HS (1989:135)
1935			20.1	HS (1989:135)
1936			16.9	HS (1989:135)
1937			14.3	HS (1989:135)
1938			19.0	HS (1989:135)
1939			17.2	HS (1989:135)
1940	8.8	SA (1993:50)	14.6	HS (1989:135)
1941			9.9	HS (1989:135)
1942			4.7	HS (1989:135)
1943			1.9	HS (1989:135)
1944			1.2	HS (1989:135)

Table A1.1. *(cont.)*

Year	Foreign-Born (%)[a]	Source	Unemployment Rate (%)[a]	Source
1945			1.9	HS (1989:135)
1946			3.9	HS (1989:135)
1947			3.9	HS (1989:135)
1948			3.8	HS (1989:135)
1949			5.9	HS (1989:135)
1950	6.9	SA (1993:50)	5.2	SA (1993:393)
1951			3.3	HS (1989:135)
1952			3.0	HS (1989:135)
1953			2.9	HS (1989:135)
1954			5.5	HS (1989:135)
1955			4.4	HS (1989:135)
1956			4.1	HS (1989:135)
1957			4.3	HS (1989:135)
1958			6.8	HS (1989:135)
1959			5.5	HS (1989:135)
1960	5.4	SA (1993:50)	5.5	SA (1976:361)
1961			6.7	HS (1989:135)
1962			5.5	HS (1989:135)
1963			5.7	HS (1989:135)
1964			5.2	HS (1989:135)
1965			4.5	SA (1976:361)
1966			3.8	HS (1989:135)
1967			3.8	HS (1989:135)
1968			3.6	HS (1989:135)
1969			3.5	HS (1989:135)
1970	4.7	SA (1993:50)	4.9	SA (1976:361)
1971			5.9	SA (1976:361)
1972			5.6	SA (1976:361)
1973			4.9	SA (1976:361)
1974			5.6	SA (1976:361)
1975			8.5	SA (1976:361)
1976			7.7	SA (1984:422)
1977			7.1	SA (1984:422)
1978			6.1	SA (1984:422)
1979			5.8	SA (1984:422)
1980	6.2	SA (1993:50)	7.1	SA (1984:422)
1981			7.6	SA (1984:422)
1982			9.7	SA (1984:422)
1983			9.5	SA (1993:393)
1984			7.4	SA (1993:393)

Table A1.1. *(cont.)*

Year	Foreign-Born (%)[a]	Source	Unemployment Rate (%)[a]	Source
1985			7.1	SA (1993:393)
1986			6.9	SA (1993:393)
1987			6.1	SA (1993:393)
1988			5.4	SA (1993:393)
1989			5.3	EE (1998:9)
1990	7.9	SA (1993:50)	5.6	EE (1998:9)
1991			6.8	EE (1998:9)
1992			7.5	EE (1998:9)
1993			6.9	EE (1998:9)
1994	8.7	SR (1998)	6.1	EE (1998:9)
1995	9.3	SR (1998)	5.6	EE (1998:9)
1996	9.3	SR (1998)	5.4	EE (1998:9)
1997	9.7	SR (1998)	4.9	EE (1998:9)

Notes: EE = Bureau of Labor Statistics, *Employment and Earnings (January).*
HS = Bureau of the Census, *Historical Statistics of the United States.* L =
Lebergott 1964. SA = Bureau of the Census, *Statistical Abstract of the United
States.* SR = Schmidley and Robinson 1998.
[a] Territory included and definition of unemployment rate vary over time; see
original sources for details.
[b] Estimate.

Table A1.2. *Foreign-Born Population and
Unemployment Rate in France, 1888–1997*

Year	Foreign-Born (%)[a]	Source	Unemployment Rate (%)[a]	Source
1888	3.3[b]	Weil (1991:556)	3.5[c]	Bonin (1988:20–22)
1889			3.5[c]	Bonin (1988:20–22)
1890			3.5[c]	Bonin (1988:20–22)
1891	3.4	Weil (1991:556)	3.5[c]	Bonin (1988:20–23)
1892			3.5[c]	Bonin (1988:20–23)
1893			3.5[c]	Bonin (1988:20–23)
1894			3.5	V (1993:463)
1895			2.1	V (1993:463)
1896	3.3	Weil (1991:556)	1.5	V (1993:463)
1897			1.5	V (1993:463)
1898			1.5	V (1993:463)

Table A1.2. *(cont.)*

Year	Foreign-Born (%)[a]	Source	Unemployment Rate (%)[a]	Source
1899			1.5	V (1993:463–464)
1900			1.6	V (1993:464)
1901	3.3	Weil (1991:556)	1.3	V (1993:464)
1902			1.5	V (1993:464)
1903			1.7	V (1993:464)
1904			1.6	V (1993:464)
1905			1.4	V (1993:464–465)
1906	3.3	Weil (1991:557)	1.1	V (1993:465)
1907			1.2	V (1993:465)
1908			1.3	V (1993:465)
1909			1.1	V (1993:465)
1910			1.1	V (1993:465)
1911	3.6	Weil (1991:557)	1.1	V (1993:466)
1912			.9	V (1993:466)
1913			.8	V (1993:466)
1914			.7	V (1993:466)
1915			.5[c]	A (1995a:47); V (1993:325)
1916			.2[c]	A (1995a:47); V (1993:325)
1917			.0[c]	V (1993:325)
1918			.0[c]	V (1993:325)
1919			1.2	V (1993:449)
1920			1.4	V (1993:449)
1921	4.6	Weil (1991:557)	2.3	V (1993:449)
1922			1.4	V (1993:449)
1923			1.2	V (1993:449)
1924			1.2	V (1993:449)
1925			1.3	V (1993:449)
1926	6.6	Weil (1991:557)	1.2	V (1993:449)
1927			2.1	V (1993:449)
1928			1.3	V (1993:449)
1929			1.2	V (1993:449)
1930			1.2	V (1993:449)
1931	7.5	Weil (1991:557)	2.4	V (1993:449)
1932			3.7	V (1993:449)
1933			3.7	V (1993:449)
1934			4.1	V (1993:449)
1935			4.6	V (1993:449)
1936	7.0	Weil (1991:557)	4.7	V (1993:449)

Table A1.2. *(cont.)*

Year	Foreign-Born (%)[a]	Source	Unemployment Rate (%)[a]	Source
1937			4.1	V (1993:449)
1938			4.2	V (1993:449)
1939			4.0	V (1993:449)
1940			7.4[c]	I (1961:92); V (1993:449, 491)
1941			3.8[c]	I (1961:92); V (1993:449, 491)
1942			2.1[c]	I (1961:92); V (1993:449, 491)
1943			1.6[c]	I (1961:92); V (1993:449, 491)
1944			.8[c]	I (1961:92); V (1993:449, 491)
1945			1.8[c]	I (1961:92); V (1993:449, 491)
1946	6.5	Weil (1991:558)	1.7	V (1993:491); T (1975:122)
1947			1.7	V (1993:491)
1948			1.7	V (1993:491)
1949			1.7	V (1993:491)
1950			1.7	V (1993:491)
1951			1.7	V (1993:491)
1952			1.7	V (1993:491)
1953			1.7	V (1993:491)
1954	6.6	Weil (1991:558)	1.7	V (1993:491); T (1975:122)
1955			1.7	I (1990:72)
1956			1.2	I (1990:72)
1957			.9	I (1990:72)
1958			1.0	I (1990:72)
1959			1.5	I (1990:72)
1960			1.4	I (1990:72)
1961			1.2	I (1990:72)
1962	7.4	Weil (1991:558)	1.4	I (1990:72); T (1975:122)
1963			1.5	I (1990:72)
1964			1.2	I (1990:72)
1965			1.5	I (1990:72)
1966			1.6	I (1990:72)
1967			2.1	I (1990:72)

Table A1.2. *(cont.)*

Year	Foreign-Born (%)[a]	Source	Unemployment Rate (%)[a]	Source
1968	7.9	Weil (1991:558)	2.7	I (1990:72); T (1975:122)
1969			2.3	I (1990:72)
1970			2.5	I (1990:72)
1971			2.7	I (1990:72)
1972			2.8	I (1990:72)
1973			2.7	I (1990:72)
1974			2.8	I (1990:72)
1975	9.2	D (1988b:461)	4.0	I (1990:72)
1976			4.4	I (1990:72)
1977			5.0	I (1990:72)
1978			5.2	I (1990:72)
1979			5.9	I (1990:72)
1980			6.3	I (1990:72)
1981			7.4	I (1990:72)
1982	9.1	D (1988b:461)	8.1	I (1990:72)
1983			8.3	I (1990:72)
1984			9.7	I (1990:72)
1985			10.2	I (1990:72)
1986			10.4	I (1990:72)
1987			10.5	I (1990:72)
1988			10.1	I (1990:72)
1989			9.4	I (1994:121)
1990	9.4	D (1988b:461)	8.9	I (1994:121)
1991			9.4	I (1994:121)
1992			10.3	I (1994:121)
1993			11.6	I (1994:121)
1994			12.3	I (1997:126)
1995			11.6	I (1997:126)
1996			12.3	SD (1998:124)
1997			12.5	SD (1998:124)

Notes: A = Asselain 1995a. D = Dupâquier 1988b. I = INSEE. SD = Statistics Directorate 1998. T = Tapinos 1975. V = Villa (© 1993 by CNRS éditions of Paris, France).

[a] Foreign-born includes noncitizens or naturalized French citizens. Territory included and definition of unemployment rate vary over time; see original sources for details.

[b] Interpolation.

[c] Estimate.

Table A1.3. *Foreigners and Unemployment Rate in Germany,*
1880–1997

Year	Foreign (%)[a]	Source	Unemployment Rate (%)[a]	Source
1880	.6	SB (1994a:11)	15.0[b]	see Kitchen (1978: 156); Bade (1983b:17–22)
1885	.8	SB (1994a:11)		
1890	.9	SB (1994a:11)		
1895	.9	SB (1994a:11)	1.3	KSA (1897:3, 300)
1900	1.4	SB (1994a:11)		
1904			2.1	SR (1922:445)
1905	1.7	SB (1994a:11)	1.6	SR (1922:445)
1906			1.1	SR (1922:445)
1907			1.6	SR (1922:445)
1908			2.9	SR (1922:445)
1909			2.8	SR (1922:445)
1910	1.9	SB (1994a:11)	1.9	SR (1922:445)
1911			1.9	SR (1922:445)
1912			2.0	SR (1922:445)
1913			2.9	SR (1922:445)
1914			7.2	SR (1922:445)
1915			3.2	SR (1922:445)
1916	3.2[c]	Herbert (1990: 91, 108)	2.2	SR (1922:445)
1917			1.0	SR (1922:445)
1918			1.2	SR (1922:445)
1919			3.7	SR (1922:445)
1920			3.8	SR (1926:304)
1921			2.8	SR (1926:304)
1922			1.5	SR (1926:304)
1923			9.6	SR (1926:304)
1924			13.5	SR (1926:304)
1925	1.5	SB (1994a:11)	6.7	SR (1926:304)
1928			8.7[b]	LAB (1949:475, 484)
1929			11.5[b]	LAB (1949:475, 484)
1931			23.3	LAB (1949:484)
1932			30.3	SR (1933:290–291)
1933	1.2	SB (1994a:11)	26.3	LAB (1949:484)
1934			15.0	LAB (1949:484)
1935			11.6	LAB (1949:484)
1936			8.3	LAB (1949:484)
1937			4.6	LAB (1949:484)

Table A1.3. *(cont.)*

Year	Foreign (%)[a]	Source	Unemployment Rate (%)[a]	Source
1938			2.1	LAB (1949:484)
1939	1.3	SR (1942:28)	.6	LAB (1949:475, 484)
1940	1.7[c]	Herbert (1990:154)	.3	LAB (1949:475, 484)
1941	4.4[c]	Herbert (1990:154)	.0	LAB (1949:484); SR (1942:410)
1942	6.1[c]	Herbert (1990:154)	.0[b]	See Herbert (1985)
1943	9.5[c]	Herbert (1990:154)	.0[b]	See Herbert (1985)
1944	10.5[c]	Herbert (1990:154)	.0[b]	See Herbert (1985)
1945	9.7[c]	Jacobmeyer (1992)		
1946	2.6[c]	Jacobmeyer (1992)		
1950			11.0	SB (1972:148)
1951	1.0	SB (1994a:11)	10.4	SB (1972:148)
1952			9.5	SB (1972:148)
1953			8.4	SB (1972:148)
1954			7.6	SB (1972:148)
1955			5.6	SB (1972:148)
1956			4.4	SB (1972:148)
1957			3.7	SB (1972:148)
1958			3.7	SB (1972:148)
1959			2.6	SB (1972:148)
1960			1.3	SB (1972:148)
1961	1.2	SB (1994a:11)	.8	SB (1972:148)
1962			.7	SB (1972:148)
1963			.8	SB (1972:148)
1964			.8	SB (1972:148)
1965			.7	SB (1972:148)
1966			.7	SB (1972:148)
1967	3.0	SB (1994a:11)	2.1	SB (1972:148)
1968	3.2	SB (1994a:11)	1.5	SB (1972:148)
1969	3.9	SB (1994a:11)	.9	SB (1972:148)
1970	4.3	SB (1994a:11)	.7	SB (1972:148)
1971	5.6	SB (1994a:11)	.9	SB (1972:148)
1972	5.7	SB (1994a:11)	1.1	SB (1981:108)
1973	6.4	SB (1994a:11)	1.2	SB (1981:108)

Table A1.3. *(cont.)*

Year	Foreign (%)[a]	Source	Unemployment Rate (%)[a]	Source
1974	6.7	SB (1994a:11)	2.6	SB (1981:108)
1975	6.6	SB (1994a:11)	4.7	SB (1981:108)
1976	6.4	SB (1994a:11)	4.6	SB (1981:108)
1977	6.4	SB (1994a:11)	4.5	SB (1981:108)
1978	6.5	SB (1994a:11)	4.3	SB (1981:108)
1979	6.7	SB (1994a:11)	3.8	SB (1981:108)
1980	7.2	SB (1994a:11)	3.8	SB (1994b:128)
1981	7.5	SB (1994a:11)	5.5	SB (1988:111)
1982	7.6	SB (1994a:11)	7.5	SB (1994b:128)
1983	7.4	SB (1994a:11)	9.1	SB (1988:111)
1984	7.1	SB (1994a:11)	9.1	SB (1994b:128)
1985	7.2	SB (1994a:11)	9.3	SB (1988:111)
1986	7.4	SB (1994a:11)	9.0	SB (1994b:128)
1987	6.9	SB (1994a:11)	8.9	SB (1994b:128)
1988	7.3	SB (1994a:11)	8.7	SB (1994b:128)
1989	7.7	SB (1994a:11)	7.9	SB (1994b:128)
1990	8.4	SB (1994a:11)	7.2	SB (1994b:128)
1991	7.3	SB (1994a:11)	6.3	SB (1994b:128)
1992	8.0	SB (1994a:11)	6.6	SB (1994b:128)
1993	8.5	SB (1994a:11)	8.9	SD (1997:132)
1994	8.6	SB (1996:20)	9.6	SD (1998:132)
1995	8.8	SB (1996:20)	9.4	SD (1998:132)
1996	8.9	SB (1998a:66)	10.4	SD (1998:132)
1997	9.0	SB (1998a:66)	11.5	SD (1998:132)

Notes: KSA = Kaiserliches Statistisches Amt. LAB = Länderrat des Amerikanischen Besatzungsgebiet. SB = Statistisches Bundesamt. SD = Statistics Directorate. "SR" = Statistisches Reichsamt.

[a] Foreign at least in the view of the German government; many of these "foreigners" were born in Germany. Territory included and definition of unemployment rate vary over time; see original sources for details.

[b] Estimates.

[c] Estimate. Figures for total population are from SB (1972:90–91), interpolating where necessary.

Table A1.4. *Time-Series Data for the United States*

Year	Opposition to Immigration (%)	Immigration Rate (%)	Unemployment Rate (%)	Foreign-Born Population (%)	Change in Disposable Income (%)
1952		1.7	2.7	6.6[a]	
1953	43.8	1.5	2.9	6.4[a]	3.15
1954		1.5	5.5	6.3[a]	−.42
1955		2.0	4.4	6.2[a]	6.29
1956		2.3	4.1	6.0[a]	3.36
1957		1.6	4.3	5.8[a]	−.07
1958		1.7	6.8	5.7[a]	−1.35
1959		1.6	5.5	5.6[a]	6.24
1960		1.8	5.5	5.4	.23
1961		2.0	6.7	5.3[a]	1.70
1962		1.9	5.5	5.3[a]	3.22
1963		1.9	5.7	5.2[a]	2.20
1964		1.7	5.2	5.1[a]	5.72
1965	41.2	1.9	4.5	5.0[a]	4.88
1966		2.3	3.8	5.0[a]	3.91
1967		2.1	3.8	4.9[a]	3.01
1968		2.0	3.6	4.8[a]	3.24
1969		2.2	3.5	4.8[a]	.96
1970		2.1	4.9	4.7	1.55
1971		1.9	5.9	4.8[a]	2.82
1972		1.6	5.6	5.0[a]	3.71
1973		1.6	4.9	5.2[a]	5.30
1974		1.5	5.6	5.3[a]	−2.45
1975		2.1	8.5	5.4[a]	.21
1976		1.6	7.7	5.6[a]	2.80
1977	48.8	1.8	7.1	5.8[a]	2.27
1978		2.3	6.1	5.9[a]	3.58
1979		2.4	5.8	6.0[a]	−.39
1980		3.5	7.1	6.2	−3.04
1981	70.6	2.8	7.6	6.4[a]	−.37
1982	71.0	2.4	9.7	6.5[a]	−.41
1983		2.3	9.5	6.7[a]	3.24
1984		2.2	7.4	6.9[a]	5.09
1985		2.4	7.1	7.0[a]	2.08
1986	53.8	2.5	6.9	7.2[a]	3.73
1987		2.5	6.1	7.4[a]	.35
1988	57.0	2.6	5.4	7.6[a]	2.75
1989		2.5[b]	5.3	7.7[a]	.90
1990		2.6[b]	5.6	7.9	.64
1991		2.8[b]	6.8	8.1[a]	−1.47
1992		3.2[b]	7.5	8.3[a]	1.17
1993	64.5	3.4[b]	6.9	8.5[a]	1.46
1994		3.1[b]	6.1	8.7	1.17

Table A1.4. *(cont.)*

Year	Opposition to Immigration (%)	Immigration Rate (%)	Unemployment Rate (%)	Foreign- Born Population (%)	Change in Disposable Income (%)
1995	60.0	2.7[b]	5.6	9.3	1.71
1996		3.4[b]	5.4	9.3	.77
1997	48.0	3.4[a,b]	4.9	9.7	1.78

Notes: Data sources are as follows: opposition to immigration (Simon and Alexander 1993:41; Espenshade and Hempstead 1995; Hastings and Hastings 1997:191; Page 1997); immigration rate, measured as legal immigrants admitted per 1,000 persons in total U.S. population (Bureau of the Census 1956:5, 93; 1961:10–11; 1971:10; 1977:10; 1981:6; 1986:7; 1992:10, 14; 1995:10; 1996:10; 1997:8, 10, 15; Immigration and Naturalization Service 1997); unemployment rate (Bureau of the Census 1956:197; 1976:361; 1984:422; 1989:135; 1993:393; 1994b:395; Bureau of Labor Statistics 1998:9); and foreign-born population (Bureau of the Census 1993:50; Schmidley and Robinson 1998). Change in real disposable income per capita based on Bureau of the Census (1956:297; 1962a:314; 1992:431; 1993:449; 1994b:455; 1996:454, 481) and Clinton (1998:317, 349). Exact wording of questions measuring opposition to immigration varies slightly over time; see original sources for details.
[a] Interpolated/extrapolated datum.
[b] Excludes persons legalized under the Immigration Reform and Control Act of 1986.

Table A1.5. *Time-Series Data for France*

Month/ Year	Pro- FN (%)	Pro– Le Pen (%)	Unemployment Rate (%)	Gross Immigration	Change in Real Hourly Wage (%)
12/83	12.7	9			
01/84	14.1	12	9.36	4,949[a]	−.218[a]
02/84	17.3	16	9.38	6,188	−.188
03/84	18.4	15	9.33	7,427[a]	−.158
04/84	18.2	14	9.27	8,666[a]	−.116
05/84	16.4	14	8.99	9,905	.122
06/84	21.2	19	8.90	11,134[a]	.219
07/84	19.4[a]	19[a]	9.05	12,363[a]	−.018
08/84	17.5	19	9.29	13,592	−.164
09/84	16.4	17	10.01	15,260[a]	−.146
10/84	15.8	16	10.42	16,929[a]	−.231
11/84	15.5	14	10.46	18,597	.171
12/84	15.5	14	10.46	14,088[a]	.359
01/85	17.6	19	10.52	9,580[a]	.030

Month/ Year	Pro- FN (%)	Pro– Le Pen (%)	Unemployment Rate (%)	Gross Immigration	Change in Real Hourly Wage (%)
02/85	15.3	16	10.28	5,071	−.048
03/85	15.3	13	10.01	6,310[a]	−.273
04/85	14.0	12	9.67	7,550[a]	−.236
05/85	12.9	12	9.44	8,789	.000
06/85	14.4	14	9.25	11,054[a]	.122
07/85	13.9[a]	14[a]	9.34	13,319[a]	.116
08/85	13.4	14	9.54	15,584	.298
09/85	16.7	14	10.06	14,971[a]	.291
10/85	16.3	18	10.36	14,358[a]	.103
11/85	13.1	15	10.29	13,745	.157
12/85	12.8	12	10.04	10,734[a]	.175
01/86	12.5	12	10.28	7,723[a]	.227
02/86	15.9	14	10.03	4,712	.547
03/86	19.1	20	9.86	6,093[a]	.090
04/86	18.4	17	9.76	7,475[a]	−.078
05/86	15.9	16	9.53	8,856	.084
06/86	13.5	15	9.32	9,566[a]	−.012
07/86	12.4[a]	14[a]	9.52	10,275[a]	.209
08/86	11.4	13	9.75	10,985	.131
09/86	15.7	15	10.34	12,467[a]	−.113
10/86	14.0	14	10.95	13,950[a]	.012
11/86	16.1	15	10.97	15,432	.060
12/86	12.5	14	11.03	11,795[a]	.060
01/87	14.6	15	11.19	8,157[a]	−.726
02/87	14.9	15	11.06	4,520	.144
03/87	14.8	13	10.97	5,808[a]	.239
04/87	16.3	17	10.61	7,095[a]	−.215
05/87	14.8	16	10.32	8,383	.108
06/87	15.7	16	10.06	8,958[a]	.102
07/87	15.8[a]	16[a]	10.17	9,532[a]	.048
08/87	15.9	17	10.52	10,107	.048
09/87	9.1	10	10.92	11,914[a]	.191
10/87	11.2	12	11.02	13,721[a]	.042
11/87	11.1	12	10.90	15,529	.167
12/87	11.5	13	10.93	11,954[a]	.184
01/88	15.9	16	10.97	8,378[a]	.107
02/88	12.8	14	10.75	4,803	.160
03/88	10.0	13	10.39	6,106[a]	−.047
04/88	14.9	18	10.10	7,408[a]	−.320
05/88	14.0[a]	16	9.91	8,711	.077
06/88	13.2	14	9.78	9,054[a]	−.012
07/88	12.7[a]	14[a]	10.06	9,396[a]	−.042
08/88	12.2	14	10.38	9,739	−.012

Table A1.5. *(cont.)*

Month/ Year	Pro- FN (%)	Pro– Le Pen (%)	Unemployment Rate (%)	Gross Immigration	Change in Real Hourly Wage (%)
09/88	8.9	10	10.71	11,461[a]	.006
10/88	10.0	8	10.79	13,183[a]	.042
11/88	11.1	11	10.63	14,905	.196
12/88	8.9	9	10.74	11,767[a]	.101
01/89	11.4	12	10.80	8,629[a]	−.094
02/89	11.1	10	10.53	5,491	.118
03/89	13.3	13	10.32	6,743[a]	.154
04/89	12.1	12	10.07	7,995[a]	−.224
05/89	15.2	17	9.76	9,247	−.059
06/89	18.0	19	9.61	10,620[a]	.183
07/89	15.6[a]	16[a]	9.86	11,994[a]	.053
08/89	13.3	13	10.17	13,367	.165
09/89	12.4	12	10.45	12,333[a]	.071
10/89	15.4	16	10.49	11,298[a]	−.118
11/89	14.4	16	10.40	10,264	.195
12/89	17.6	19	10.43	9,044[a]	.282
01/90	15.4	15	10.49	7,824[a]	.076
02/90	13.6	14	10.29	6,604	.328
03/90	13.5	17	10.15	7,532[a]	.251
04/90	15.1[b]	18	9.99	8,461[a]	.157
05/90	12.1	14	9.53	9,389	.198
06/90	15.6	13	9.47	11,483[a]	.279
07/90	15.8[a]	15[a]	9.69	13,576[a]	.139
08/90	15.9	16	9.99	15,670	−.284
09/90	13.2	14	10.26	13,380[a]	−.255
10/90	11.1	13	10.39	11,091[a]	−.227
11/90	12.2	13	10.36	8,801	.571
12/90	13.3	15	10.47	8,011[a]	.429
01/91	12.1	13	10.61	7,222[a]	−.029
02/91	11.2	13	10.58	6,432	.144
03/91	8.8	12	10.49	7,521[a]	.236
04/91	11.1	12	10.28	8,609[a]	−.017
05/91	12.4	14	10.20	9,698	.253
06/91	14.8	18	10.20	9,776[a]	.339
07/91	16.3[a]	18[a]	10.65	9,854[a]	.143
08/91	17.8	18	11.00	9,932	.029
09/91	15.6	10	11.31	11,156[a]	.000
10/91	13.2	15	11.47	12,381[a]	−.177
11/91	14.1	15	11.50	13,605	.006
12/91	11.1	13	11.65	11,558[a]	.290
01/92	13.2	12	11.83	9,512[a]	.006
02/92	13.0	13	11.72	7,465	.320
03/92	16.1	16	11.47	7,313[a]	.216

Month/ Year	Pro- FN (%)	Pro– Le Pen (%)	Unemployment Rate (%)	Gross Immigration	Change in Real Hourly Wage (%)
04/92	10.9	11	11.26	7,162[a]	.182
05/92	12.0	13	11.04	7,010	.034
06/92	12.1	13	10.97	6,858[a]	.187
07/92	12.6[a]	13[a]			.034
08/92	13.0	13			.181
09/92	10.9	11			.153
10/92	12.1	12			−.028
11/92	10.9	12			.203
12/92	12.9	12			.225
01/93	11.8	12			−.280
02/93	12.9	12			−.236
03/93	12.0	12			−.310
04/93	12.1	13			.042
05/93	14.1	15			.130
06/93	11.8	12			.333
07/93	12.4[a]	14[a]			.236
08/93	13.0	15			.225
09/93	11.0	13			−.360
10/93	11.0	12			.022
11/93	12.9	13			.090
12/93	13.0	13			.163
01/94	10.6	11			−.011
02/94	12.0	14			−.073
03/94	12.9	14			.045
04/94	10.6	12			−.078
05/94	12.9	12			.000
06/94	16.1	16			.168
07/94	16.0	17			.190
08/94	15.6	18			.223
09/94	14.1	16			.900
10/94	12.9	15			−.078
11/94	13.0	15			.084
12/94	12.9	16			.206
01/95	15.2	17			−.090
02/95	12.9	15			
03/95	18.1	20			
04/95	25.0[b]	31			
05/95	19.4	21			
06/95	19.4	20			
07/95	20.4	21			
08/95	17.2	18			
09/95	21.5	22			
10/95	20.7	22			

Month/ Year	Pro- FN (%)	Pro– Le Pen (%)	Unemployment Rate (%)	Gross Immigration	Change in Real Hourly Wage (%)
11/95	18.5	20			
12/95	17.4	17			
01/96	16.0	18			
02/96	15.0	16			
03/96	16.0	18			
04/96	17.2	17			
05/96	14.7	15			
06/96	12.9	14			
07/96	14.6[b]	14			
08/96	16.3	19			
09/96	16.1	18			
10/96	16.3	17			
11/96	16.3	16			
12/96	15.2	16			
01/97	16.2[a]	15			
02/97	17.2	18			
03/97	15.0	15			
04/97	12.9	17			
05/97	12.9[a]	15			
06/97	12.9	14			
07/97	14.0	16			
08/97	13.0	14			
09/97	15.1	15			
10/97	11.8	13			
11/97	11.8	12			
12/97	10.9	13			

Notes: Data sources are as follows: Support for the Front national and Approval of Le Pen (SOFRES 1989:155, 157 [© 1989 by Éditions du Seuil]; *Le Figaro Magazine*, various issues [© 1988–1998 by *Le Figaro Magazine*]); unemployment rate, calculated from absolute number of unemployed per month and the mean annual economically active population, interpolated into monthly data (INSEE, *Bulletin mensuel de statistique*, various issues); gross immigration (INSEE, *Bulletin mensuel de statistique*, various issues, sum of "primo-immigration" divided by 3); percent change in real hourly wage, calculated from quarterly index of workers' hourly wages, interpolated into monthly data, and the monthly consumer price index (INSEE, *Bulletin mensuel de statistique*, various issues). Dates of *Le Figaro Magazine* surveys reflect month survey was conducted, not month of publication. Unfortunately, INSEE appears to have stopped publishing gross immigration figures after May 1992.
[a] Interpolated datum.
[b] Estimated datum.

Table A1.6. *Time-Series Data for Germany*

Month/Year	Opposition to Foreigners (%)	Intended Vote for Republikaner (%)	Unemployment Rate (%)	Foreign Population (%)	Change in Disposable Income (%)
01/89		.5	9.0	7.51[a]	−3.29
02/89		4.5	8.9	7.55[a]	−2.88
03/89		5.5	8.4	7.60	−2.65
04/89		9.7	7.9	7.65[a]	−1.05
05/89		5.8	7.6	7.69[a]	−.66
06/89		5.5	7.4	7.74	−.57
07/89		5.4[a]	7.7	7.79[a]	−.05
08/89		5.4	7.5	7.85[a]	−.37
09/89		5.6	7.3	7.90	−.50
10/89		2.5	7.3	7.93[a]	4.56
11/89		6.1	7.6	7.96[a]	4.42
12/89		4.6	8.0	7.99	4.09
01/90		2.5	8.4	8.03[a]	−1.98
02/90		2.2	8.2	8.06[a]	−1.80
03/90		1.1	7.7	8.10	−1.55
04/90		2.3	7.3	8.15[a]	−.51
05/90		1.1	7.0	8.21[a]	−.51
06/90		.6	6.9	8.26	−.42
07/90		.4[a]	7.1	8.32[a]	−.14
08/90		.2	6.9	8.39[a]	−.24
09/90		.1	6.6	8.45	−.42
10/90		1.4	6.5	8.48[a]	4.12
11/90		1.4	6.4	8.52[a]	4.83
12/90		.7	6.8	8.55	4.19
01/91		.5	7.0	8.58[a]	−2.11
02/91		2.2	7.0	8.62[a]	−1.76
03/91		1.1	6.5	8.65	−1.42
04/91		.8	6.2	8.70[a]	−.50
05/91		.9	6.0	8.75[a]	−.41
06/91		1.1	5.9	8.80	−.59
07/91		1.0[a]	6.3	8.87[a]	−1.41
08/91	50.3	.9	6.2	8.94[a]	−.52
09/91	50.5	1.9	6.0	9.01	−.70
10/91	34.2	2.2	6.0	9.07[a]	4.14
11/91	33.1	1.4	6.0	9.12[a]	3.76
12/91	32.5	2.2	6.5	9.18	3.96
01/92	31.6	2.2	6.9	9.23[a]	−2.59
02/92	33.6	1.5	6.8	9.27[a]	−2.80
03/92	33.8	1.6	6.5	9.32	−2.59
04/92	40.4	8.3	6.4	9.41[a]	−.76
05/92	36.3	5.7	6.2	9.49[a]	−.94
06/92	39.1	6.4	6.3	9.58	−.68
07/92	39.2	8.9	6.7	9.66[a]	.16

Table A1.6. *(cont.)*

Month/Year	Opposition to Foreigners (%)	Intended Vote for Republikaner (%)	Unemployment Rate (%)	Foreign Population (%)	Change in Disposable Income (%)
08/92	37.8[a]	7.9[a]	6.7	9.75[a]	−.01
09/92	36.3	6.9	6.5	9.83	−.10
10/92	35.2	6.5	6.7	9.85[a]	4.18
11/92	30.1	6.2	6.7	9.88[a]	3.79
12/92	22.4	6.4	7.4	9.90	4.05
01/93	22.8	4.8	8.1	9.95[a]	−4.16
02/93	21.5	6.0	8.3	9.99	−3.60
03/93	26.1	6.8	8.0	10.04	−3.62
04/93	29.9	6.2	7.9	10.08[a]	−.85
05/93	30.5	7.0	7.8	10.13[a]	−.85
06/93	26.0	3.2	7.8	10.17	−.68
07/93	26.3	4.3	8.4	10.19[a]	.03
08/93		4.2[a]	8.4	10.20[a]	.19
09/93		4.1	8.3	10.23	.11
10/93		5.0	8.5	10.23[a]	3.93
11/93		3.1	8.7	10.24[a]	3.76
12/93		2.3	9.1	10.24	3.69
01/94		3.1	9.8	10.25[a]	
02/94		2.3	9.9	10.27[a]	
03/94		3.0	9.5	10.28	
04/94		1.6	9.3	10.29[a]	
05/94		3.1	9.0	10.31[a]	
06/94		1.7	8.9	10.32	
07/94		1.0	9.3	10.34[a]	
08/94		1.7	9.1	10.35[a]	
09/94		1.8	8.8	10.37	
10/94		.5	8.8	10.37[a]	
11/94		.6	8.8	10.37[a]	
12/94		1.2	9.2	10.37	
01/95		3.1	9.9	10.40[a]	
02/95		2.3	9.8	10.44[a]	
03/95		3.0	9.4	10.47	
04/95		1.6	9.3	10.50[a]	
05/95		3.1	8.9	10.52[a]	
06/95		1.7	8.9	10.55	
07/95		1.0	9.2	10.57[a]	
08/95		1.8	9.2	10.60[a]	
09/95		1.8	9.0	10.62	
10/95		.5	9.0	10.61[a]	
11/95		.6	9.2	10.60[a]	
12/95		1.2	9.7	10.59	
01/96		1.7	10.5	10.61[a]	
02/96		1.1	10.7	10.62[a]	

Table A1.6. *(cont.)*

Month/ Year	Opposition to Foreigners (%)	Intended Vote for Republikaner (%)	Unemployment Rate (%)	Foreign Population (%)	Change in Disposable Income (%)
03/96	1.0	10.4	10.64		
04/96	1.8	10.1	10.66[a]		
05/96	.8	9.8	10.69[a]		
06/96	1.2	9.7	10.71		
07/96	1.6[a]	10.1	10.72[a]		
08/96	1.9	10.1	10.72[a]		
09/96	1.8	10.0	10.73		
10/96	1.7	10.1	10.73[a]		
11/96	.8	10.3	10.74[a]		
12/96	1.5	10.8	10.74		

Notes: Data sources are as follows: opposition to foreigners and intended vote for the Republikaner (Politbarometer West); unemployment rate (Bundesanstalt für Arbeit 1994:43; and Statistisches Bundesamt, *Wirtschaft und Statistik*, various issues); foreign population (Statistisches Bundesamt 1995b; 1998b); change in real disposable income per capita calculated based on the quarterly figures (monthly values were interpolated where necessary) for disposable nominal income in Statistisches Bundesamt (1994c:297), the monthly price index ("Preisindex für die Lebenshaltung – Alle privaten Haushalte") in Statistisches Bundesamt (1990:27; 1991:38; 1992a:53; 1993a:58; 1993b:795; 1995a:69), and the quarterly (interpolated into monthly figures) population totals from the Statistisches Bundesamt (1995b; 1998b).
[a] Interpolated datum.

Model Specifications

Chapter 5

Table 5.1

The original versions of the unemployment rate and immigration rate needed to be differenced once to become stationary. The percent foreign-born remained nonstationary after differencing once. Because 90% of this series consisted of inter-census-year interpolations, however, further differencing would probably have not yielded meaningful data. The percent change in real disposable income per capita was already stationary in its original form.

Probably because the usable sample was so small (t = 10), controlling for all three other possible causes at the same time produced statistically insignificant results for all four hypothesized causes. The only "regressor" that came at all close to statistical significance was real income (b = −.609, p = .147). The "partial r" column represents the most statistically significant result for a particular "independent variable" if one tries all possible combinations of two-variable controls (e.g., the partial correlation between real income and opposition to immigration after controls for the immigration rate and the percent foreign-born). This "optimum" set of controls consisted of the immigration rate and unemployment rate for real income, the immigration rate and percent foreign-born for the unemployment rate, the unemployment rate and percent foreign-born for the immigration rate, and the immigration rate and unemployment rate for the percent foreign-born. That none of the other "regressors" achieved its best results after a control for real income should make us all the more confident about the significance of this latter variable. The partial correlation between nativism and real income also remained statistically significant at the .05 or .10 level for the other two combinations of controls. Simply relying on the bivariate correlations in the first column of Table 5.1 entails the same inferential hazards as relying on bivariate regression instead of multivariate analysis.

Table 5.2

The Augmented Dickey-Fuller test (Cromwell, Labys, and Terraza 1994:16–19) and visual inspection of the data suggested the nonseasonal differencing indicated in Table 5.2. Inspection of the autocorrelation function (ACF) plots indicated the need for seasonal differencing (at lag = 12). Heteroskedasticity in the unemployment and immigration variables necessitated the natural-log transformations. The ACF and partial autocorrelation function (PACF) plots of the regression residuals indicated the need for the two autoregression terms. All transfer functions came from inspection of cross-correlation function (CCF) plots of the two relevant, prewhitened series.

The CCF plots for wages versus the two forms of nativism both indicated lead-2 processes. This puzzling two-month lead probably resulted from a one-month delay in reporting of the actual wage figures as well as *Le Figaro*'s practice of doing most interviewing at the end of a given month. Barring the invention of a functional time machine, we must assume the future cannot cause the past.

Because monthly immigration figures have been interpolated from quarterly ones, I smoothed this monthly series with a one-month moving average (i.e., with the mean of the current and previous months). In order to verify that this interpolation and smoothing did not change the substantive results, I also ran parallel "traditional time-series" models using quarterly data (and averages for the data reported monthly). In no such quarterly model did immigration achieve statistical significance. Unemployment also failed to yield any statistically significant effects in any of the quarterly models, perhaps suggesting that the results for unemployment in Table 5.2 are relatively fragile. (But, of course, statistical significance is inherently harder to achieve in the shorter, quarterly models; t = 31 for the Front model and 32 for the Le Pen model.)

If one differenced the immigration variable once, higher wages decreased support for the Front national (b = −5.171, SE = 2.448, percent change = −28.6, p ≤ .05). Wages were not statistically significant (at least at the .05 level) in the quarterly Le Pen model, however. As for all French time-series models, maximum likelihood provided the estimates.

Table 5.3

Opposition to foreigners required differencing once to remove nonstationarity. (Though traditional time-series regression does not necessarily require stationarity of all variables, I nonetheless tried to make the variables as stationary as possible to avoid spurious results.) Examination of bivariate cross-correlations determined lag lengths.

Other German Time-Series Models

In the ARIMA model of support for the Republikaner, I needed to difference the square root of the original Republikaner variable to achieve stationarity and reasonably homoskedastic errors. Unemployment also needed to be differenced once to eliminate its original nonstationarity. The univariate analysis of real disposable income per capita required an ARIMA $(0,0,2)(1,0,0)_{12}$ model to remove various trends. After prewhitening, cross-correlations revealed no reasonable, statistically significant effects of either economic variable on support for the Republikaner.

Except for simply differencing the Republikaner variable once, the traditional time-series model of support for the Republikaner was similar to the corresponding ARIMA model. Percent foreign was also differenced once to achieve stationarity.

Because these Republikaner models used data only through 1993, the results should not be significantly affected by the 1993 revision to the asylum provisions of the German constitution (see Chapter 4). This revision likely further reduced support for the Republikaner, and so models using post-1993 data may not be comparable to those using prerevision figures.

Chapter 6

Table 6.2

In order to maximize across-survey and across-country comparability and to avoid problems of nonlinearity, all regressors in this main regression table are dummies. This strategy may have thus reduced the amount of variance the models explain.

Because the dependent variables for affect and policy are finely graduated (range for affect from 0 to 200; range for policy from 4 to 12), this table uses ordinary least-squares for these response variables. The dichotomous dependent variable for Proposition 187, however, necessitated logit.

Although the *Los Angeles Times* poll contained a question on whether the respondent was "Native American," I chose to exclude such respondents because they were not necessarily American Indians. Susan Pinkus (1997), director of the poll, told me about problems with the Native American question and advised me not to use it. Respondents would say, "Sure, I'm a Native American – I was born in America," even though they apparently had no American Indian ancestors. Native American activists confirmed Pinkus's suspicions. According to Ron Andrade (1997), executive director of the Los Angeles City/County Native American Indian Commission, the indigenous people of California – especially those along the U.S.-Mexican border – were "very much opposed" to Proposition 187. The Kumeyaay tribe, of which Andrade is a member, has villages throughout Baja California, Mexico, and feared the measure would force them to discriminate against their tribal brethren who live south of the "international" border. Andrade even filed a complaint opposing the initiative with the U.S. federal government. Finally, he noted that the actual distribution of American Indians in California does not correspond at all to the distribution of supposedly "Native American" respondents in the *Los Angeles Times* poll.

Experiments in AMOS suggested that the dependent variable for affect contained significant nonrandom measurement error from the two "feeling thermometers" (see Green and Citrin 1994). Unfortunately, however, a confirmatory factor analysis model allowing for such error did not achieve identification. In theory one could have achieved identification by adding a third feeling thermometer (e.g., toward Asians in addition to those for immigrants in general and for Latinos), but then the affect variable would no longer be comparable with those for France and Germany. In the European analyses, an indicator for affect toward immigrants in general and one for the major immigrant group in each country (i.e., North Africans in France and Turks in Germany) constitute the corresponding dependent variable. Experiments also suggested that such a three-indicator model would not converge because of the many dummy regressors. Converting the dummies back into ordinal variables might have permitted convergence but destroyed cross-national comparability. At any rate, this possible contamination of the dependent variable with nonrandom measurement error renders the resulting estimates provisional.

Models for Cultural and Economic Threat

Ideally, one would have corrected for simultaneity between the various nativism variables and perceived cultural or economic threat. Experiments produced no suitable instruments for either form of threat, however. Most every potential instrument that was highly correlated with threat could plausibly have been influenced by nativism (e.g., liberalism, partisanship) or was already a regressor. The estimates for the effect of threat on the various forms of nativism thus indicate the *maximum* possible effect; correction for simultaneity may well reduce these effects to insignificance.

Models for Contact

The simultaneous-equations model for contact and affect uses the percent foreign-born in the county in 1960 and the quality of the respondent's housing in 1992 as primary instruments for the percent foreign-born in the county in 1990. This analysis thus assumes that the respondent's feelings toward immigrants in 1992 had no effect on the quality of her or his housing that year or on the number of immigrants in her or his county thirty-two years earlier. Standard two-stage least-squares (TSLS) provided the estimates. As usual, the TSLS also included all exogenous regressors (i.e., all regressors other than the percent foreign-born) as instruments in addition to the two primary instrumental variables (IVs).

Experiments with the policy model failed to produce any satisfactory instruments for personal contact or proximity in the community. As for threat, the ordinary least-squares (OLS) estimate of the effect of personal contact probably represents the maximum possible effect for this regressor. Even with OLS, proximity in the community fails to achieve statistical significance. Correcting this second contact variable for simultaneity would likely not produce any different results.

The contact model for Proposition 187 uses as instruments the percent foreign-born in 1960 and the percent second-generation immigrants in 1960. This model thus assumes that a respondent's views on undocumented immigrants in 1994 had no influence on the number of immigrants living in the respondent's region thirty-four years previously. Because the dependent variable takes on only two values, the analysis used maximum likelihood in EViews to estimate simultaneous-Logit coefficients. The model converged after only five iterations.

Chapter 7

Table 7.2

Whereas the relatively graduated and well-behaved dependent variables in the French affect and policy models permitted OLS regression, the highly skewed measure of support for the Front national required Tobit analysis. Because close to 40% of the valid French respondents in the SOFRES French National Election Study received the minimum possible value (0) on the Front-support scale, I chose to treat this distribution as left-censored and so use maximum-likelihood Tobit. Arguably, some of these 0-value, anti-Front respondents might consider violence to stop Le Pen (giving them a hypothetical −10 value, for example), while others simply dislike his populist style. The SOFRES poll would give 0s to both types of opponents, however.

Models for Cultural Threat, Economic Threat, and Relative Economic Deprivation

Correction for any simultaneity between the dependent variable and perceived cultural threat, economic threat, or relative economic deprivation would have proved theoretically very useful. No potential instrumental variables appeared satisfactory, however. As often happens with psychological variables, almost all exogenous causes of, say, cultural threat (e.g., religious affiliation), were likewise potential causes of nativism and so already in the model as regressors. Any psychological variables highly correlated with cultural threat (e.g., liberalism) were also arguably influenced by nativism and thus useless as instruments. The estimated OLS coefficients for the effect of cultural threat, economic threat, and relative economic deprivation therefore represent the maximum possible influence on nativism. As in the U.S. models, correction for simultaneity may well make their influence vanish.

The French subsample of the Eurobarometer 30 used a split sample for the indicators of economic threat and relative deprivation (Reif and Melich 1991:181). Roughly half the sample answered questions about economic threat or deprivation caused by North Africans, while the rest of the interviewees responded to items about threat or deprivation by "Asians" (in France, mainly Southeast Asians). To control for any possible effects of this split ballot, the models for economic threat and relative deprivation therefore included a dummy variable for the immigrant group in the questionnaire (1 = North Africans) and an interaction term between this dummy and the threat or deprivation variable. Neither the interaction term nor the dummy variable achieved statistical significance (at least at the .05 level) in any of the regressions.

Models for Contact

Satisfactory instruments for proximity in the neighborhood or at the workplace do not appear to exist. Lagged and squared lagged values of regional proximity should suffice as instruments of current values of regional proximity. It is hard to argue, after all, that the present caused the past. In the affect and policy models of contact, the regional contact variable is the percentage of foreign nationals in one's *région* (a French administrative district composed of several *départements*) in 1990, the closest census year. Instruments included the percentage of foreign nationals in the same *région* in 1962, 1954, and 1946 as well as the square of the 1954 percentage. Two-stage least-squares provided the estimates. For the contact model of support for the Front national, the percentage of foreign nationals in one's *département* in 1990 (the closest available census year) served as the measure of regional proximity. Instruments included the proportion of foreign citizens in this same *département* in 1954, 1946, and 1936 as well as squares of these three latter percentages. Although estimation by simultaneous Tobit would have been ideal, I was unwilling to make the necessary fairly strong assumptions for such estimation and instead used simultaneous Logit (where the second equation in the system is roughly equivalent to a Logit version of the first stage of the Heckman two-step Tobit method). All respondents having given the minimum possible support for the Front received 0s for the dependent variable, while the remaining interviewees had the dependent variable recoded to 1.

Chapter 8

Table 8.2

The relatively graduated and well-behaved dependent variables in the German affect and policy models allowed for OLS regression. The very skewed measure of support for the Republikaner necessitated Tobit analysis, however (cf. the model for Front national support in Table 7.2). Because close to 40% of the valid German respondents in the German Election Panel Study registered the minimum possible score (3) on the Republikaner-support scale, I treated this distribution as left-censored and used maximum-likelihood Tobit.

Models for Cultural Threat, Economic Threat, and Relative Economic Deprivation

Correction for any simultaneity between the dependent variable and perceived cultural threat, economic threat, or relative economic deprivation proved impossible for lack of usable instruments. The estimated OLS coefficients for the effect of cultural threat, economic threat, and relative economic deprivation therefore indicate the maximum possible impact on xenophobia. As for the American and French models, correction for bidirectional causality may well make their effect disappear.

Models for Contact

Usable instruments for proximity in the neighborhood or at the workplace do not seem to exist. On the other hand, lagged and squared lagged values of the regional proximity to foreigners and *Vertriebene* should suffice as instruments of current values of regional proximity to foreigners. In all three models of regional contact, the regional proximity variable is the percentage of foreigners in one's *Land* (a German political district equivalent to a U.S. state) in 1987 (for the affect and policy models) or 1990 (for the Republikaner model). Instruments included the percentage of foreigners in the same *Land* in 1961, the percentage of *Vertriebene* in the *Land* in 1964, and the squares of both the 1961 and 1964 percentages. Two-stage least-squares yielded the estimates for the affect and policy models. For the contact model of support for the Front national, estimation by simultaneous Tobit would have been optimal. I hesitated to make the necessary strong assumptions for such estimation, however, and instead used simultaneous Logit (where the second equation in the system is roughly equivalent to a Logit version of the first stage of the Heckman two-step Tobit method). All interviewees who gave the minimum possible support for the Republikaner received 0s for the dependent variable, while the remaining respondents had the dependent variable recoded to 1.

Survey Characteristics

Chapter 5

United States: Various Polls on Immigration

The American data come from several nationally representative polls conducted by Gallup, CBS News/*New York Times*/Tokyo Broadcasting System, Princeton Survey Research Associates, and other firms from 1953 to 1997 (Simon and Alexander 1993:34–47; Espenshade and Hempstead 1995; Hastings and Hastings 1997:191; Page 1997). For technical details on a particular survey, see these same references.

France: SOFRES/Le Figaro Surveys

To obtain a monthly measure of French attitudes toward Le Pen and his National Front, SOFRES and *Le Figaro* selected one thousand respondents using stratification by region and urbanicity and quota sampling by gender, age, and occupation. Interviews appear to have been in person (*Le Figaro Magazine*, various issues).

Germany: Politbarometer West

The German time-series data represent monthly samples of the West German respondents included in the Forschungsgruppe Wahlen's Politbarometer from August 1991 to July 1993 (models for opposition to foreigners) or from January 1989 to December 1993 (models for support for the Republikaner). The relevant population was all eligible voters who lived in private households in western Germany (the *alte Bundesländer*) and had telephone connections. Although models of support for the Republikaner excluded respondents from West Berlin, the shorter time series for opposition to foreigners did include voters from this area. The Forschungsgruppe Wahlen then used random-digit dialing to select the approximately 1,000 respondents per month for telephone interviews (Forschungsgruppe Wahlen and Zentralarchiv für empirische Sozialforschung 1994:2).

Chapter 6

1990–1992 American National Election Study (Full Panel)

This dataset consists of four waves of a nationwide panel survey conducted by the Institute for Social Research at the University of Michigan. In Wave 1, investigators first used multistage area probability sampling to select 2,808 potential households of voting-age American citizens living in the coterminous United States. The researchers then conducted face-to-face interviews with 2,004 selected and cooperative respondents (for a response rate of 71%) in these households between November 7, 1990, and January 26, 1991. Wave 2 involved telephone reinterviews of 1,385 of the original Wave 1 respondents (for a reinterview rate of 69%) from June 4, 1991, to July 31, 1991. From September 1, 1992, to November 2, 1992 (Wave 3), investigators located and reinterviewed by telephone or in person 1,361 of the original 1990 respondents (reinterview rate = 68%). Wave 4, which occurred from November 4, 1992, to January 13, 1993, included 1,250 of the original 1990 respondents (reinterview rate = 62%). For further information, see Miller et al. (1993).

Because most of the questions analyzed in this chapter come from 1992, I included for possible analysis only those 1,250 panel respondents who had participated in the two waves from this year. The 1992 data also exist in an "enhanced" version (ICPSR 6067), which includes additional, cross-sectional respondents. I nonetheless wished to avoid any confounding effects that might have arisen from the different types of administration (e.g., "panel training").

1986 CBS News/New York Times National Survey

Using stratified random-digit dialing, CBS News and the *New York Times* attempted to select a nationally representative group of respondents as well as a smaller oversample of Latino interviewees. In the end the survey's organizers interviewed 1,618 respondents from June 19 to 23, 1986. Although most interviews took place in English, Spanish speakers also had the option of responding in their native language. For more details, see CBS News/*New York Times* (1988).

1994 Los Angeles Times Exit Poll

The *Los Angeles Times* conducted this exit poll on election day, November 8, 1994. Interviewers administered confidential questionnaires to 5,336 voters at eighty-five polling places across California. Turnout in past general elections determined which precincts to select. Sampling was not completely random, however, because the *Times* did not interview those who voted by absentee ballot or refused to participate (*Los Angeles Times* 1994). Furthermore, the survey included an oversample of 1,306 voters from Orange County (Martínez 1994). Though 5,336 respondents participated, incomplete answers reduced the usable sample to about 4,400.

Chapter 7

French Sample of 1988 Eurobarometer 30

The population for this poll, which was carried out in person from October 22 to November 10, 1988, was all residents of France (excluding Corsica and the overseas territories and *départements*) age fifteen and over. In the first stage of sampling, the Institut de Sondage Lavialle randomly chose a number of sampling points within this area. In the second stage, interviewers used quota sampling (by age, gender, and occupation) to select individual respondents from each sampling point. Although the total number for France was originally 1,001, the usable sample size was often smaller because of missing data (Reif and Melich 1991:iv–ix).

1995 SOFRES French National Election Study

Under the guidance of principal investigators Michael S. Lewis-Beck, Nonna Mayer, and Daniel Boy, SOFRES conducted its French National Election Study from May 8 to 23, 1995, just after the second round of the 1995 French presidential election. This poll targeted all French citizens age eighteen and over living in France (excluding Corsica and the overseas territories and *départements*) and registered on the electoral lists. From this population, SOFRES used quota sampling (by age, sex, and occupation of head of household) and regional stratification to select 4,078 individuals for the extensive in-person interviews (Boy and Mayer 1997:347–349).

Chapter 8

German Sample of 1988 Eurobarometer 30

The relevant population for the Eurobarometer 30, which was carried out in person from October 17 to November 9, 1988, was all residents of West Germany (FRG) aged fifteen and over. In the first stage of sampling, the Institut für Markt und Meinungsforschung (EMNID) randomly chose a number of sampling points within this area. In the second stage, interviewers used a "random route" technique, a combination of quota sampling (by age, gender, and occupation) and random selection from electoral lists or population registers, to choose individual respondents from each sampling point. Although the total number for West Germany was originally 1,051, the usable sample size was significantly smaller because of missing data (Reif and Melich 1991:iv–ix).

1990 German Election Panel Study (Wahlstudie 1990)

The first wave of this four-wave panel survey (this book only examines the first wave) took place during November and December 1989 and targeted West German (excluding residents of West Berlin), eligible voters age eighteen and older. The Forschungsgruppe Wahlen used stratified random sampling to choose 2,056 respondents for in-person interviews.

APPENDIX 4

Definition of Variables

Chapter 5

*United States: Gallup, CBS News/New York Times/
Tokyo Broadcasting System, and Princeton Survey
Research Associates for 1953–1997*

Opposition to Immigration. Variable constructed from percentage of respondents (excluding "don't know" responses) who thought immigration should be "decreased" (or "decreased or stopped altogether" in 1997) in a question asking whether immigration should be "kept at its present level, increased, or decreased" (or "decreased or stopped altogether" in 1997).

France: 1983–1997 SOFRES/Le Figaro Surveys

Support for Front national. Variable constructed from percentage of respondents (excluding "no opinion" responses) who said they had a "very good" or "somewhat good" opinion of the Front national.

Approval of Le Pen. Percentage of respondents who answered yes to question about whether they would like to see Jean-Marie Le Pen "play an important role in the months and years to come."

Germany: 1989–1993 Politbarometer West

Opposition to Foreigners. Variable constructed from monthly percentage of respondents (excluding nonresponses) who found it "not OK" (*nicht in Ordnung*) that "many foreigners live in Germany" (V106).[1]

Support for Republikaner. Percentage of valid (i.e., no nonresponses or probable nonvoters) respondents who said they would vote for the Republikaner if the Federal legislative elections (*Bundestagswahl*) were to be held the following Sunday (V5, V6).

Chapter 6

1990–1992 American National Election Study (Full Panel)

Affect toward Immigrants. Additive index of two "thermometer scales" on feelings toward Hispanic Americans (Q.B2m [VAR5327]) and immigrants (Q.B2w [VAR5336]).

Perceived Cultural Threat. Additive index of two items on whether Hispanics (Q.Q4a [VAR6236]) and Asians (Q.Q5a [VAR6239]) will improve American culture.

Catholic. Self-reported religious preference (Q.X4z [VAR3850]).

Jewish. Self-reported religious preference (Q.X4z [VAR3850]).

Other Religion. Self-reported religious preference, mainly including Orthodox, nontraditional Protestants, and non-Judeo-Christian religions (Q.X4z [VAR3850]).

No Religion. Self-reported religious preference (Q.X4z [VAR3850]).

Foreign Origin. Items on whether either of the respondent's parents was born outside the United States (Q.Y44 [VAR4120]).

Latino. Self-reported ethnicity (Q.Y46 [VAR4122]).

African American. Self-reported race (Q.Z2 [VAR4202]).

Asian American. Self-reported race (Q.Z2 [VAR4202]).

Native American. Self-reported race (Q.Z2 [VAR4202]).

Perceived Economic Threat. Additive index of extent to which respondent thinks that Hispanics (Q.Q4c [VAR6238]) and Asians (Q.Q5c [VAR6241]) will take jobs away from "people already here."

Poor. Whether respondent reported a 1991 gross household income of less than $10,000 (Q.Y40 [VAR4104]). Goal for this variable throughout the book was to include roughly the bottom 15% of income distribution.

Rich. Whether respondent reported a 1991 gross household income of $50,000 or more (Q.Y40 [VAR4104]). Goal for this variable throughout the book was to include roughly the top 15% of income distribution.

Finances Declined. Whether respondent reported a decline in her or his family's finances over the preceding year (Q.F1a/F1b [VAR3426]).

Finances Improved. Whether respondent reported an improvement in her or his family's finances over the preceding year (Q.F1a/F1b [VAR3426]).

Unemployed. Whether respondent reported being unemployed or temporarily laid off (Q.Y4 [VAR3914]).

Professional/Manager. Whether respondent reported working as a professional or manager (e.g., medical doctor, lawyer, CEO; Q.Y5x1 [VAR3922]).

Manual Laborer. Whether respondent reported working as some type of manual laborer (e.g., farmer, fisher, construction worker; Q.Y5x1 [VAR3922]).

Nonpaid Worker. Whether respondent reported an occupation for which she or he is not usually paid directly (e.g., student, homemaker, retiree, unemployed; Q.Y4 [VAR3914]).

Perceived Decline in National Economy. Whether respondent perceived a decline in the nation's economy over the preceding year (Q.H4a/H4b [VAR3532]).

Perceived Improvement in National Economy. Whether respondent perceived an improvement in the nation's economy over the preceding year (Q.H4a/H4b [VAR3532]).

Percent Foreign/County (1990). Percentage of respondent's county listed as foreign-born in the 1990 census (Bureau of the Census 1994a).

Percent Foreign/County (1960). Percent of respondent's county listed as foreign-born in 1960 census (Bureau of the Census 1967).

Housing Quality. Observed quality of respondent's home (VAR3044), ranging from mobile home and rental apartment to detached single-family dwelling.

Secondary School Graduate. Whether respondent reported having earned a high school diploma but not a four-year college degree (Q.Y3x [VAR3908]).

University Graduate. Whether respondent reported having earned a degree from a four-year college or university (Q.Y3x [VAR3908]).

Female. Self-reported gender of respondent.

Age ≤ 30. Age in years less than or equal to thirty, based on self-reported date of birth (Q.Y1x [VAR3903]).

Age $\geq$ *60.* Age in years greater than fifty-nine, based on self-reported date of birth (Q.Y1x [VAR3903]).

South. Coded as southern if respondent was from Alabama, Arkansas, Florida, Georgia, Kentucky, Louisiana, Mississippi, North Carolina, South Carolina, Tennessee, or Virginia.

1986 CBS News/New York Times National Survey

Preferences on Immigration Policy. Additive index of questions on whether the level of immigration should be increased, decreased, or kept the same (Q.6), whether otherwise law-abiding "illegal aliens" should be deported (Q.26), whether the government should use the army to stop unauthorized immigration from Mexico (Q.27), and whether the United States should admit more, fewer, or the same number of political refugees (Q.37).

Catholic. Self-reported religious preference (Q.59).

Jewish. Self-reported religious preference (Q.59).

Other Religion. Self-reported religious preference (Q.59).

No Religion. Self-reported religious preference (Q.59).

Foreign Origin. Whether respondent's ancestors first came to America after 1941 (Q.31).

Latino. Self-reported ethnicity (Q.60).

African American. Self-reported race (Q.63).

Other Race. Self-reported race (Q.63).

Perceived Economic Threat. Additive index based on whether respondent believes immigrants take Americans' jobs (Q.38) and whether she or he worries about immigrants competing with her or him for a job (Q.39).

Poor. Self-reported total family income in 1985 under $12,500 (Q.65).

Rich. Self-reported total family income in 1985 over $50,000 (Q.65).

Unemployed. Coded as "unemployed" if respondent reported being "not employed" (Q.57) and under age sixty-six (to eliminate retirees), was coded as male (to eliminate homemakers), and appeared old enough (Q.62), given the reported highest level of education completed (Q.61), no longer to be a student (i.e., age eighteen or more but not a high-school graduate, age twenty-three or more but not a college graduate, or age twenty-seven or more and a "college graduate and beyond"). Unfortunately, the questionnaire did not ask about unemployment directly.

Proximity/Neighborhood. Self-report on whether many immigrants live in one's community (Q.45).

Personal Contact. Self-report on whether respondent knows any immigrants (other than family members) personally (Q.44) and, if so, how well (Q.44a).

Secondary School Graduate. Whether respondent reported having earned a high school diploma but not a four-year college degree (Q.61).

University Graduate. Whether respondent reported having earned a degree from a four-year college or university (Q.61).

Female. Observed gender of respondent.

Age ≤ 30. Self-reported age in years less than or equal to thirty (Q.62).

Age ≥ 60. Self-reported age in years greater than fifty-nine (Q.62).

South. Coded as southern if respondent was from Alabama, Arkansas, Florida, Georgia, Kentucky, Louisiana, Mississippi, North Carolina, South Carolina, Tennessee, or Virginia.

1994 Los Angeles Times Exit Poll

Support for Proposition 187. Self-reported vote on Proposition 187 (Q.QJ [VOTE187]).

Catholic. Self-reported religious preference (Q.QHH [FAITH]).

Other Christian. Self-reported religious preference (Q.QHH [FAITH]).

Jewish. Self-reported religious preference (Q.QHH [FAITH]).

Other Religion. Self-reported religious preference (Q.QHH [FAITH]).

No Religion. Self-reported religious preference (Q.QHH [FAITH]).

Foreign Origin. Whether respondent's parents born outside the United States (Q.QBB [WHERBORN]).

Latino. Self-reported ethnicity (Q.QFF [RESRACE]).

African American. Self-reported race (Q.QFF [RESRACE]).

Asian American. Self-reported race (Q.QFF [RESRACE]).

Other Race. Self-reported race (Q.QFF [RESRACE]).

Poor. Self-reported 1993 household income of less than $20,000 (Q.QHH [INCOME]).

Rich. Self-reported 1993 household income of more than $75,000 (Q.QHH [INCOME]).

Finances Declined. Whether respondent reported a decline in her or his finances over the preceding four years (Q.QW [PERSFIN]).

Finances Improved. Whether respondent reported an improvement in her or his finances over the preceding four years (Q.QW [PERSFIN]).

Percent Foreign/Region (1990). Percentage of respondent's *Los Angeles Times* regional break (according to Pinkus [1997], defined as Los Angeles County [including the San Fernando Valley], Orange County, San Diego County, Kern County, the rest of southern California [San Bernadino, Ventura, Santa Barbara, San Luis Obispo, Riverside, and Imperial Counties], the Bay area [Marin, San Mateo, Alameda, Contra Costa, and San Francisco Counties], the Central Valley [Shasta, Tehama, Glenn, Butte, Colusa, Sutter, Yolo, Sacramento, Solano, San Joaquín, Stanislas, Merced, Madera, Fresno, Kings, and Tulare Counties], and the rest of northern California [Alpine, Amador, Calaveras, Del Norte, El Dorado, Humboldt, Inyo, Lake, Lassen, Mariposa, Mendocino, Modoc, Mono, Monterey, Napa, Nevada, Placer, Plumas, San Benito, Santa Clara, Santa Cruz, Sierra, Siskiyou, Sonoma, Trinity, Tuolumne, and Yuba Counties]) that was foreign-born according the U.S. census of 1990 (Slater and Hall 1993:88, 102).

Percent Foreign/Region (1960). Percentage of respondent's *Los Angeles Times* region that was foreign-born according to the U.S. census of 1960 (Bureau of the Census 1962b:32, 42).

Percent Second-Generation Immigrants/Region (1960). Percentage of respondent's *Los Angeles Times* region that was native-born with at least one foreign-born parent according to the U.S. census of 1960 (Bureau of the Census 1962b:32, 42).

Secondary School Graduate. Whether respondent reported having earned a high school diploma but not a four-year college degree (Q.QEE [EDUC]).

University Graduate. Whether respondent reported having earned a degree from a four-year college or university (Q.QEE [EDUC]).

Female. Self-reported gender (Q.QCC [GENDER]).

Age ≤ 30. Self-reported age in years less than or equal to twenty-nine (Q.QDD [AGE]). Note that the label of this variable is not literally accurate.

Age ≥ 60. Self-reported age in years greater than fifty-nine (Q.QDD [AGE]).

Chapter 7

French Sample of 1988 Eurobarometer 30

Affect toward Immigrants. Additive index of "thermometer scale" on feelings toward North Africans (Q.331/330(2) [VAR0458]) and item about whether the respondent finds people of another nationality disturbing (*gênante*) (Q.223/225(a) [VAR0236]).

Preferences on Immigration Policy. Additive index of items on right to asylum (Q.166/168(7) [VAR0129]), rights of non–European Community citizens living in France (Q.272 [VAR0438]), and facilitating naturalization for foreigners (Q.274/276(7) [VAR0446]).

Perceived Cultural Threat. Additive index of items on whether foreigners' customs are difficult to understand (Q.238(a) [VAR0270]) and on the advisability of learning foreigners' language (Q.274/276(4) [VAR0443]) or getting to know their customs (Q.274/276(5) [VAR0444]).

Non-Catholic. Self-reported religious identification (Q.559 [VAR0715]). The survey did not include enough people from other religious backgrounds to evaluate separately.

Foreign Origin. Self-reported non-French ethnic roots of respondent's family (Q.334 [VAR0471]), although no persons of North African origin are included in the analysis in Table 7.2.

Perceived Economic Threat. Item on whether North Africans or Asians have jobs that French people should have (Q.339/351 [VAR0476]).

Poor. Having a monthly gross household income of less than 5,000 French francs (Q.540 [VAR0694]).

Rich. Having a monthly gross household income of 15,000 French francs or more (Q.540 [VAR0694]).

Unemployed. Self-reported employment status (Q.541/542 [VAR0696]).

Finances Declined. Self-reported decline in one's household finances during the previous year (Q.117 [VAR0016]).

Finances Improved. Self-reported improvement in one's household finances during the previous year (Q.117 [VAR0016]).

Professional/Manager. Whether respondent reported working as a professional or manager (e.g., lawyer, accountant, general management; Q.541–Q.543 [VAR0696]).

Manual Laborer. Whether respondent reported working as some type of manual laborer (e.g., farmer, fisher, "skilled manual worker"; Q.541–Q.543 [VAR0696]).

Nonpaid Worker. Whether respondent reported an occupation for which she or he is not usually paid directly (e.g., student, homemaker, retiree, military service, unemployed; Q.541–Q.543 [VAR0696]).

Perceived Decline in National Economy. Perceived downturn in France's "general economic situation" over the previous twelve months (Q.116 [VAR0015]).

Perceived Improvement in National Economy. Perceived improvement in France's "general economic situation" over the previous twelve months (Q.116 [VAR0015]).

Perceived Relative Economic Deprivation. How respondent thinks people like her or him have fared economically over the previous five years compared with most of the North African or Asian immigrants living in France (Q.353 [VAR0495]).

Proximity/Region (1990). Percentage of noncitizens living in the respondent's *région* in 1990 according to INSEE (1992:erratum for p. 18).

Proximity/Region (1962). Percentage of noncitizens living in the respondent's *région* in 1962 according to INSEE (1992:17).

Proximity/Region (1954). Percentage of noncitizens living in the respondent's *région* in 1954 according to INSEE (1992:17).

Proximity/Region (1946). Percentage of noncitizens living in the respondent's *région* in 1946 according to INSEE (1992:17).

Proximity/Region (1954), squared. Square of *Proximity/Region (1954)*.

Proximity/Neighborhood. Self-reported number of people of another nationality living in one's neighborhood ("*quartier*") (Q.226/228(1) [VAR0241]).

Proximity/Work. Self-reported number of people of another nationality at one's workplace (Q.232/235(1) [VAR0251]).

Secondary School Graduate. Whether respondent reported being a student or having completed her or his education while between ages nineteen and twenty-one (Q.528 [VAR0685], Q.536/537 [VAR0690]).

University Graduate. Whether respondent reported being a student or having completed her or his education while age twenty-two or older (Q.528 [VAR0685], Q.536/537 [VAR0690]).

Female. Self-reported gender (Q.535 [VAR0689]).

Age ≤ 30. Self-reported age in years of thirty or younger (Q.536/537 [VAR0690]).

Age ≥ 60. Self-reported age in years of sixty or older (Q.536/537 [VAR0690]).

1995 SOFRES French National Election Study

Support for Front National. Additive index of a feeling thermometer for Le Pen (Q26a8) and items on how likely Le Pen was to solve various problems (Q11), on the respondent's actual (Q5a2) and second-choice (Q15) vote in the first round of the 1995 presidential elections, and on her or his vote in the 1994 European elections (Q16) and 1993 legislative elections (Q17).

Non-Catholic. Self-reported religious identification (RS21). The survey did not include enough non-Catholics for extensive separate analysis.

Poor. Having a monthly gross household income of 5,000 French francs or below (RS5).

Rich. Having a monthly gross household income of more than 20,000 french Francs (RS5).

Unemployed. Self-reported employment status (RS8a1).

Finances Declined. Self-reported decline in one's personal finances during the previous year (Q2a1).

Finances Improved. Self-reported improvement in one's personal finances during the previous year (Q2a1).

Professional/Manager. Whether respondent reported working as a professional or manager (e.g., lawyer, engineer, large business owner, professor; RS8a1, RS10a2).

Manual Laborer. Whether respondent reported working as some type of manual laborer (e.g., farmer, fisher, laborer; RS8a1, RS10a2).

Nonpaid Worker. Whether respondent reported an occupation for which she or he is not usually paid directly (e.g., student, homemaker, retiree, military service, unemployed; RS8a1, RS10a2).

Perceived Decline in National Economy. Perceived downturn in France's economy over the previous twelve months (Q2a2).

Perceived Improvement in National Economy. Perceived improvement in France's economy over the previous twelve months (Q2a2).

Proximity/Region (1990). Percentage of noncitizens living in the respondent's *département* in 1990 according to INSEE (1992:94–95).

Proximity/Region (1954). Percentage of noncitizens living in the respondent's *département* in 1954 according to INSEE (1956: 294–297).

Proximity/Region (1946). Percentage of noncitizens living in the respondent's *département* in 1946 according to INSEE (1956: 294–297).

Proximity/Region (1936). Percentage of noncitizens living in the respondent's *département* in 1936 according to INSEE (1956: 294–297).

Proximity/Region (1954), squared. Square of *Proximity/Region (1954).*

Proximity/Region (1946), squared. Square of *Proximity/Region (1946).*

Proximity/Region (1936), squared. Square of *Proximity/Region (1936).*

Secondary School Graduate. Whether respondent reported the *bac* as highest degree (RS6).

University Graduate. Whether respondent reported at least *bac* + 2 as highest degree (RS6).

Female. Observed gender (RS2).

Age ≤ 30. Self-reported age in years of thirty or younger (RS1).

Age ≥ 60. Self-reported age in years of sixty or older (RS1).

Chapter 8

German Sample of Eurobarometer 30

Affect toward Immigrants. Additive index of "thermometer scale" on feelings toward Turks (Q.331/330(3) [VAR0459]) and item about whether the respondent finds people of another nationality disturbing (*störend*) (Q.223/225(a) [VAR0236]).

Preferences on Immigration Policy. Additive index of items on right to asylum (Q.166/168(7) [VAR0129]), rights of non–European

Community citizens living in Germany (Q.272 [VAR0438]), and facilitating naturalization for foreigners (Q.274/276(7) [VAR0446]).

Perceived Cultural Threat. Additive index of items on whether foreigners' customs are difficult to understand (Q.238(a) [VAR0270]) and on the advisability of learning foreigners' language (Q.274/276(4) [VAR0443]) or getting to know their customs (Q.274/276(5) [VAR0444]).

Catholic. Self-reported religious identification (Q.559 [VAR0715]). Because the survey did not include enough people from other religious backgrounds to evaluate (one "orthodoxe Kirche" [probably a Free Church Protestant], six "other religion," and five "no religion"), all respondents who were neither Catholic nor *evangelische* were eliminated from the analysis.

Foreign Origin. Self-reported non-German ethnic roots of respondent's family (Q.334 [VAR0471]), although no persons of Turkish origin are included in the analysis.

Perceived Economic Threat. Whether Turks have jobs that German people should have (Q.339/351 [VAR0476]).

Poor. Having a monthly gross household income of less than 1,750 German marks (Q.540 [VAR0694]).

Rich. Having a monthly gross household income of 5,000 German marks or more (Q.540 [VAR0694]).

Unemployed. Self-reported employment status (Q.541/542 [VAR0696]).

Finances Declined. Self-reported decline in one's household finances during the previous year (Q.117 [VAR0016]).

Finances Improved. Self-reported improvement in one's household finances during the previous year (Q.117 [VAR0016]).

Professional/Manager. Whether respondent reported working as a professional or manager (e.g., lawyer, accountant, general management; Q.541–Q.543 [VAR0696]).

Manual Laborer. Whether respondent reported working as some type of manual laborer (e.g., farmer, fisher, "skilled manual worker"; Q.541–Q.543 [VAR0696]).

Nonpaid Worker. Whether respondent reported an occupation for which she or he is not usually paid directly (e.g., student, homemaker, retiree, military service, unemployed; Q.541–Q.543 [VAR0696]).

Perceived Decline in National Economy. Perceived downturn in

West Germany's "general economic situation" over the previous twelve months (Q.116 [VAR0015]).

Perceived Improvement in National Economy. Perceived improvement in West Germany's "general economic situation" over the previous twelve months (Q.116 [VAR0015]).

Perceived Relative Economic Deprivation. How respondent thinks people like her or him have fared economically over the previous five years compared with most of the Turkish immigrants living in West Germany (Q.353 [VAR0495]).

Proximity/Region (1987). Percentage of foreigners living in the respondent's *Land* at the end of 1987 (the closest year of available data) according to Statistisches Bundesamt (1989:32–33).

Proximity/Region (1961). Percentage of foreigners living in the respondent's *Land* in 1961 according to Statistisches Bundesamt (1965:31, 55).

Proximity (Vertriebene)/Region (1964). Percentage of *Vertriebene* living in the respondent's *Land* in 1964 according to Statistisches Bundesamt (1967:45).

Proximity/Region (1961), Squared. Square of *Proximity/Region (1961).*

Proximity (Vertriebene)/Region (1964), Squared. Square of *Proximity (Vertriebene)/Region (1964).*

Proximity/Neighborhood. Self-reported number of people of another nationality living in one's neighborhood (*Nachbarschaft*) (Q.226/228(1) [VAR0241]).

Proximity/Work. Self-reported number of people of another nationality at one's workplace (Q.232/235(1) [VAR0251]).

Secondary School Graduate. Whether respondent reported being a student or having completed her or his education while between ages nineteen and twenty-one (Q.528 [VAR0685], Q.536/537 [VAR0690]).

University Graduate. Whether respondent reported being a student or having completed her or his education while age twenty-two or older (Q.528 [VAR0685], Q.536/537 [VAR0690]).

Female. Self-reported gender (Q.535 [VAR0689]).

Age ≤ 30. Self-reported age in years of thirty or younger (Q.536/537 [VAR0690]).

Age ≥ 60. Self-reported age in years of sixty or older (Q.536/537 [VAR0690]).

1990 German Election Panel Study (Wahlstudie 1990)

Support for Republikaner. Additive index of "feeling thermometers" for the Republikaner (F.I-8(f) [V18]) and Schönhuber (F.I-14(j) [V40]) as well as one's ranking of the Republikaner as compared with the other five parties (F.I-15 [V42–V47]).

Catholic. Self-reported religious identification (S.I-G [V143]).

Other Religion. Self-reported religious identification (S.I-G [V143]).

No Religion. Self-reported religious identification (S.I-G [V143]).

Unemployed. Self-reported employment status (S.I-N [V149]).

Finances Declined. Self-reported "poor" state of one's finances (F.I-18 [V50]).

Finances Improved. Self-reported "good" state of one's finances (F.I-18 [V50]).

Professional/Manager. Whether respondent reported working as a professional or manager (e.g., general management, upper-level civil servant; S.I-N [V149], S.I-O [V151]).

Manual Laborer. Whether respondent reported working as some type of manual laborer (e.g., farmer, "unskilled" worker; S.I-N [V149], S.I-O [V151]).

Nonpaid Worker. Whether respondent reported an occupation for which she or he is not usually paid directly (e.g., student, homemaker, retiree, military service, unemployed; S.I-N [V149], S.I-O [V151]).

Perceived Decline in National Economy. Perceived "poor" state of Germany's economy (F.I-16 [V48]).

Perceived Improvement in National Economy. Perceived "good" state of Germany's economy (F.I-16 [V48]).

Proximity/Region (1990). Percentage of foreigners living in the respondent's *Land* in 1990 according to Statistisches Bundesamt (1992b:26–27).

Proximity/Region (1961). Percentage of foreigners living in the respondent's *Land* in 1961 according to Statistisches Bundesamt (1965:31, 55).

Proximity (Vertriebene)/Region (1964). Percentage of *Vertriebene* living in the respondent's *Land* in 1964 according to Statistisches Bundesamt (1967:45).

Proximity/Region (1961), Squared. Square of *Proximity/Region (1961).*

Proximity (Vertriebene)/Region (1964), Squared. Square of *Proximity (Vertriebene)/Region (1964).*

Secondary School Graduate. Whether respondent has an *Abitur, Hochschulreife,* or *Fachhochschulreife* (V145) but no *Staatsexamen, Diplom,* or similar credential (V147).

University Graduate. Whether respondent has a *Staatsexamen, Diplom,* or similar credential (V147).

Female. Self-reported gender (V136).

Age ≤ 30. Self-reported year of birth (S.I-C [V137]), recoded to age in years (V139) of thirty or younger.

Age ≥ 60. Self-reported year of birth (S.I-C [V137]), recoded to age in years (V139) of sixty or older.

Notes

Chapter 1. Marginality, Economic Self-Interest, and Contact

1. While examining a few cases of pro-immigrant sentiment, this book primarily concentrates on *negative* attitudes toward immigration and the foreign-born. Responsible policy makers are usually more concerned with reducing the xenophobia that leads to anti-immigrant violence than with attenuating any "excessively" warm feelings toward newcomers. At least in the short term, the human rights of immigrants are probably violated more often because of significantly negative feelings than because of a lack of particularly positive ones. Nonetheless, the search for ways of reducing very negative views will likely yield new methods for making relatively tolerant individuals even more pro-immigrant.

2. Note, however, that this explanation by Espenshade and Calhoun would not necessarily predict pro-immigrant attitudes where the native comes from a minority but unrelated culture (e.g., a native-born or "Nisei" Japanese American giving her views on immigration from Mexico). As formulated later in this chapter, marginality theory indeed makes such a prediction.

    For a classic statement of cultural-similarity theory, see Bogardus (1928:78–81).

3. As discussed later, other economic theorists point more to immigrants' use of taxpayer-funded services instead of to foreign-born workers' effects on the labor market.

4. A *département* roughly equals the size of a U.S. county, though its role in French politics is closer to that of an American state.

5. Unless otherwise noted, all translations into English are the author's.

6. For examples of how such "solidarity of the marginalized" occurs in the individual, see Takaki (1989:350) and Rasmussen (1998). Saxton (1971:x, 222–223) may well provide a third example.

7. Although marginality theory primarily acts multivariately, its definition of a "marginalized group" (i.e., a group whose members all have the same marginality-producing characteristic) does not deviate very much from

Louis Wirth's classic definition (1945) of a "minority": "We may define a minority as a group of people who, because of their physical or cultural characteristics, are singled out from the others in the society in which they live for differential and unequal treatment, and who therefore regard themselves as objects of collective discrimination." Wirth also labels as "dominant" the group having the "mainstream" characteristic.

8. The marginalized individual shares her or his marginalization with other members of a *group*, all of whom have the same marginality-producing characteristic (e.g., ethnicity). In other words, marginalization affects each person in the group. This form of marginality differs from that experienced by Stonequist's "Marginal Man" (1961:2–3), who "finds himself on the margin of each [group] but a member of neither." A person experiencing Stonequist's marginalization thus might be the only "member" of the group affected by this condition.

9. During our telephone conversation (1997a), Holocaust survivor and scholar Nechama Tec greatly contributed to my thinking about marginality theory (not that she would necessarily agree with all the details of my formulation here, however). She nonetheless warned against thinking that the behavior of Holocaust era rescuers, for example, arose from being actively persecuted themselves. She instead focused on the rescuers' lack of constraint resulting from their society's norms. Elsewhere (1986:153), for example, Tec describes one rescuer, an unmarried foreign woman, who "for years had had an open love affair with a married doctor in the small town" and who "was said to have associated mainly with bohemians."

10. This multivariate prediction does not necessarily contradict the bivariate results or arguments in Williams (1947:60–61), Daniels and Kitano (1970:71–72), Daniels (1977:v), and McClain and Karnig (1990).

11. The major difference, of course, is that Marx's new members of the proletariat appear to have lost their group consciousness. Former shopkeepers, for example, would no longer think of themselves as a separate occupational group but rather as factory workers indistinguishable from the rest of the proletariat.

12. See Baltzell (1964:238; see also Myrdal 1994:1073–1078): "[F]rom Harriet Beecher Stowe to Eleanor Roosevelt, educated women have always identified with minorities who, like women themselves, have been discriminated against because of inherited physical characteristics." For a more recent example of such gender effects, see Betz (1994:100–101).

13. Using a different sample and more quantitative methods, however, Oliner and Oliner (1988:176, 306) find no correlation between marginality and being a rescuer.

14. As Tec explains further (1997b), "Being on the periphery of a community, whether one is aware of it or not, means being less affected by this community's expectations and controls. Therefore, with individuality come fewer social constraints and a higher level of independence. This, in turn, has other important implications. Freedom from social

constraints and a high level of independence offer an opportunity to act in accordance with personal values and moral precepts, even when these are in opposition to societal demands. Thus, to the extent that people are less controlled by their environment and are more independent, they are more likely to be guided by their own moral imperatives, regardless of whether or not these imperatives conform to societal expectations."

15. This is not to imply, however, that Jews' religious beliefs per se are irrelevant. Like Christians (see the subsequent discussion in text), Jews who support immigrants and other minorities are, of course, following the essence of their religion's ethical teachings. Leviticus 19:33–34, for example, reads, "And if a stranger sojourn with thee in your land, ye shall not vex him. But the stranger . . . shall be unto you as one born among you, and thou shalt love him as thyself; for ye were strangers in the land of Egypt." Once Jews (and Christians) are no longer marginalized or facing persecution, however, the temptation appears very great to ignore these humanitarian elements in their doctrine (for a similar argument, see Ellul 1986:113–136). From a sociological point of view, then, Jews' status as a religious minority best "explains" their views on other minorities.

16. For similar terminology if not identical empirical predictions, see Karst (1989:81–104). Minkenberg (1998) uses a relative of status politics to explain support for far-right parties in the United States, France, and Germany.

17. As a prominent Turkish-German politician suggests (Özdemir 1999: 195–262), however, Huntington's theory can serve as an excuse for oppressing immigrants, cultural minorities, and Muslims.

18. Of course, as Harris (1995:175) indicates, immigrants might also fill those "3-D" or undesirable jobs which the native-born are no longer willing to take. In such a two-tiered labor market, immigrants and natives would rarely if ever compete for the same positions. This possibility, however, seems to escape most members of the general public and especially the hard core of the nativist movements.

19. For a related theory, see Dollard et al. (1939).

20. Not all of the economic theories discussed in this chapter necessarily see self-interest as people's only motive. This book nonetheless generally uses "economic theory" and "economic self-interest" interchangeably because even relative-deprivation and sociotropic interpretations see a possible role for self-interest.

21. In his restatement of Allport's theory, Pettigrew (1971:333, n. 55) seems more willing to consider more "casual" contacts as prejudice-reducing.

22. For an effort in this direction, see the excellent focus-group study by Fairbank, Maslin, Maullin & Associates (1996). Participants voice concerns about immigration-induced cultural changes, competition with foreigners on the labor market, and immigrants' extensive use of public services.

23. Of course, voting for a neofascist party is not quite the same as voting

for Proposition 187. Analysis of these dependent variables therefore focuses primarily on whether the kinds of people who support one form of anti-immigrant politics are similar to those who cast their votes for the other.

Chapter 2. History of Attitudes toward Immigration in the United States

1. Cohen (1995) probably represents the best single-volume introduction to the history of migration throughout the world.
2. For a brief introduction to immigration history and politics in the United States, France, and Germany (albeit from a German, centrist perspective), see Knight and Kowalsky (1991).
3. Although the Chinese Exclusion Act of 1882 supposedly halted further Chinese immigration, the ploy of "paper sons," a technically fraudulent method of obtaining entry, actually allowed a trickle of immigration from China even after 1882 (Daniels 1988:96; 1990:246; Takaki 1989:234–239). Some undocumented Chinese immigrants probably also entered via the Caribbean and across the Mexican and Canadian borders (Daniels 1988:96), and immigration officials usually allowed the Chinese wives of Chinese merchants to join their husbands in the United States (Chan 1991). In addition, federal judges in San Francisco sometimes sided with Chinese litigants who challenged exclusion (Salyer 1995: 33–116).
4. Scholars in the United States usually label opposition to immigration as "nativism," while many of their colleagues in Europe prefer the term "xenophobia." While this book defers to the U.S. norm, one must acknowledge the term's irony in the North American context. Instead of referring to the immigration attitudes of North American Indians – the only people truly indigenous to that continent – U.S. scholars use "nativist" to describe the views of relatively recent immigrants (e.g., third- or fourth-generation "Americans") toward today's newcomers.

    This usage dates from at least 1845 (Simpson and Weiner 1989:238) and was perhaps a reaction to anti-immigrant and anti-Catholic groups of the era who styled themselves "Native Americans" (see Billington 1938:209–211). That these xenophobes likely did not consider American Indians or African Americans "Native Americans" as well shows all the more clearly how this use of the term was arbitrary and socially constructed. American Indians first came to be called "Native Americans" only in the 1950s (Simpson and Weiner 1989:237).
5. Opposition to European immigrants, at any rate, seems to have been low from 1880 to 1885 (see Handlin 1979:240). Chinese exclusion, moreover, might not have occurred in 1882 if California natives and their politicians had not agitated so vehemently against the Chinese at the national level (Sandmeyer 1991:88–95, 110–111).
6. The major exceptions to this pattern seem to have been the wave of

anti-Japanese hate crimes committed in California in 1906 and 1907 and the perhaps related anti-Japanese "Gentlemen's Agreement" of 1907 (Daniels 1977:32–34, 44).

7. Of course, Filipinos constituted an exception to the exclusion of Asians because the Philippines at the time were an American territory (Takaki 1989:315, 331).

8. Arizona, Idaho, Kansas, Louisiana, Minnesota, Missouri, Montana, Nebraska, New Mexico, Oregon, Texas, and Washington also enacted similar land laws about this time (Takaki 1989:206–207).

9. After the Tydings-McDuffie Act of 1934, even Filipinos were virtually excluded (the annual quota for the island was a minuscule fifty people; Takaki 1989:331–332; Daniels 1990:358).

10. Although the many ethnic African immigrants from the British West Indies did fall under the quota for Great Britain, this restriction does not seem to have significantly hindered Caribbean immigration. (The racist authors of the 1924 Immigration Act were undoubtedly thinking of whites from the British Isles rather than blacks from the British Caribbean when granting a generous quota for British citizens.)

11. Various *bracero* programs, for instance, continued intermittently through 1964 (Bau 1985:42–43; McWilliams 1990:311–317; Reimers 1992:37–48; Simon and Alexander 1993:15).

12. The old nativist residue still persisted, however, especially among well-to-do WASPs. Lucius Beebe, for instance, deplored the nomination of Kennedy, a "rich mick from the Boston lace curtain district," instead of the more "gentleman[ly]" Stevenson (Baltzell 1964:78–79).

13. The stock market crash of 1987 does not seem to have itself caused an immediate recession (Congressional Quarterly 1990:27–29).

14. See Higham (1988:24–25): "In the absence of other disturbing factors, Americans rated lowest the nationalities most conspicuously remote in culture and race. No variety of anti-European sentiment has ever approached the violent extremes to which anti-Chinese agitation went in the 1870's and 1880's." For a related argument about the racist origins of U.S. citizenship law, see Smith (1997).

15. Actually, Gompers was Jewish and had himself immigrated from England as a youth (Higham, 1988:71). He was thus not a complete cultural "insider." Compared with the Mexican American Lizarras, however, Gompers might as well have come over on the Mayflower. Treating him as a cultural insider therefore seems defensible.

16. Without Gompers's support, Lizarras's interethnic union soon foundered.

17. Of course, factors other than whites' minority or majority status may have been involved. The comparison between *haoles* and white Californians nevertheless appears useful even if not conclusive.

18. For a prominent counterexample, however, see Saxton (1971:279–282) and Smith (1997:353–356).

19. During the earlier anti-Chinese movement, for example, the *San*

Francisco Post opined that "Chinese, whether they profess Christianity or not, remain at heart worshipers of their ancestors. . . . Our opinion is that the time, money, and effort wasted on Chinese missions could be turned to very much better account among our own people" (Sandmeyer 1991:35–36).

20. The more rigorous analysis in Chapter 5 demonstrates that the unemployment rate itself does not seem to affect American or German nativism. Rather, time-series modeling suggests that changes in real disposable income cause over-time variations in opposition to immigrants. Reliable historical statistics on the change in real disposable income per capita are much harder to come by, however. But because real income and the unemployment rate are often correlated in annual data, plots of the unemployment rate in Figures 2.1, 3.1, and 4.1 should indicate the approximate state of the economy as a whole.

Chapter 3. History of Attitudes toward Immigration in France

1. The next year, the parliament also passed a law easing the acquisition of French nationality so as to increase the number of young men subject to military service (Decouflé 1992).

2. Mauco (1977:36) reports that a French general supervising the construction of one such concentration camp commented, "Either these red [Communist] refugees will die [from the malaria-carrying mosquitoes which infested the area] and we'll be rid of them, or it will be the mosquitoes who will croak [from biting the Spaniards] and the Languedoc [a region of southern France] will be free [of mosquitoes]."

3. Most of the remaining Spanish refugees, however, eventually found themselves in wartime work gangs instead of back in Franco's Spain (Weil 1995).

4. For more on the political economy of immigration into France during this period, see Hollifield (1992).

5. For the pre-1993 regime, see Brubaker (1992:81–82). French citizenship law shifted back to a more *jus soli* system in 1998 (Agence France Presse 1998). Weil (1998) compares French nationality policy to that of other European states.

6. Compare, for example, the anti-Italian hate crimes documented in Perrot (1960; 1974:1:170–173), Vertone (1977), and Milza (1979; 1981:1:275–284; 1981:2:815–829) with the anti–North African violence described in Jordi, Sayad, and Temime (1991:109–111) and Gastault (1993).

7. For a parallel view, see Noiriel (1988:273–274).

8. Mauco's *Les étrangers en France: Leur rôle dans l'activité économique* (1932) is indisputably the pioneer work in the field and reveals considerable sympathy for the plight of immigrants in France. Mauco's works nevertheless demand caution as they are often laced with veiled or blatant prejudice and anti-Semitism (see, for example, Mauco 1932:72; 1977: 215–239; Weil 1991:65–72; 1995). His anti-Semitic article in a 1942 issue

of *L'Ethnie française*, a journal edited by a prominent French "racial theorist" and war criminal later killed by the French Resistance, seems to have intellectually paved the way for the deportation of Jewish refugees to Nazi death camps (Weil 1991:65–72; 1995). During the formulation of postwar immigration policy, Mauco also championed the selection of immigrants according to explicitly racial, ethnic, and religious criteria (Weil 1995).

Chapter 4. History of Attitudes toward Immigration in Germany

1. Unfortunately, vast segments of the German populace still refuse to view Germany as a land of immigration ("Die Bundesrepublik Deutschland ist kein Einwanderungsland"), and so referring to German "immigration" is already to take a political position. By virtually all internationally recognized indicators, however, Germany has experienced large-scale immigration for at least the last century (see especially Heckman 1981; Bade 1992a:271–464; Cohn-Bendit and Schmid 1992; Leggewie 1993; Bade 1996; 1997). This chapter therefore refers to "immigration" and "immigrants" in Germany rather than restricting itself exclusively to "foreign workers," "guest workers," "migrant laborers," and the like.
2. Exactly what constitutes "Germany" has been a perennial theme of German history. Perhaps more than any other European nation, Germany has experienced dramatic expansions and contractions of its territory (Fulbrook 1990:35, 61, 81, 102, 116, 130, 162, 192, 196, 205). This book generally considers "Germany" to be those regions which were more or less internationally recognized as such at the time (e.g., East Prussia was part of Germany in 1910 but not in 1990).
3. By and large, this nationality policy remained in effect until it was replaced by the Schröder reforms in January 2000 (Brubaker 1992:165; Deutsche Presse Agentur 1999).
4. For more on the political economy of immigration into Germany during this period, see Hollifield (1992).
5. Some observers might argue that the post–Cold War rise of the global economy and a multicultural youth culture in the affluent West indicate or are causing a decline in overall nativism. This argument does seem valid for some sectors of the U.S., French, and German populations. Texas industry – as opposed to that in California – has apparently learned that being perceived as tolerant toward Mexican immigrants pays financial dividends when one deals with Mexican firms (Katz 1995; see also Lowenthal and Burgess 1993). The many young, western European aficionados of traditional African drum music whom I encountered at a concert in Swabia in 1994 were probably less opposed to African immigration than were some of their less "multicultural" elders. Some forms of "multiculturalism" or "cosmopolitanism" are compatible with nativism, however. One relatively young German woman interviewed in Gedmin (1995), for example, had been married to an American, had lived

in the United States, and worked in the international music business – at the very heart of the multicultural, global economy. But while this German citizen welcomed interaction with U.S. and some European cultures and companies, she nonetheless complained bitterly about immigrants: "I don't like going to Frankfurt and all I hear is some different, strange language, but definitely not German. And . . . yeah, I get upset. It's like [expletive deleted], this is my own country!" Some individuals might thus embrace the cultures of rich, predominantly Christian nations (e.g., the United States, Sweden, or the United Kingdom), but still despise the traditions of poorer, predominantly Muslim countries (e.g., Turkey or Algeria; for a related critique of certain forms of cosmopolitanism, see Brennen 1997).

6. Many German skinheads (especially the "SHARP [Skin Heads against Racial Prejudice] Skins"), however, oppose racism and attacks on immigrants (Farin and Seidel-Pielen 1993).

7. In this case, the ministers might not have been acting completely altruistically because they later appear to have tried to influence the way the mosque was run (Mucan 1999). For another example of German opposition to the building of a mosque, see Cohn-Bendit and Schmid (1992:306–309).

8. During the high-immigration periods of World War I and the 1980s and 1990s, the economy was ailing and/or the targets of xenophobic attacks came from cultures very different from Germany's.

Part II. Quantitative Analysis

1. Though ideally one might examine only attitudes toward the *admission* of immigrants in all three countries, the different political situations in the nations studied do not permit such strictly parallel analyses. The United States is a traditional country of immigration and hence has an explicit "immigration" policy. France and Germany, however, do not publicly bill themselves as settler societies. Asking French or German respondents whether "the immigration rate should increase, decrease, or stay the same," then, would be impossible. In Germany, psychological resistance to immigration is so strong that Germans normally speak of "Ausländerpolitik," literally "foreigner policy," instead of "immigration policy." The dependent variables for immigration policy therefore concentrate more on the admission of immigrants in the United States and on the postsettlement treatment of the foreign-born, or immigrant rights, in France and Germany.

Chapter 5. Over-Time Opposition to Immigration and Support for Nativist Political Movements

1. The basic methodological problem is that two series might be correlated merely because both have trends (e.g., nominal prices and the population

of a country). Instead of looking for correlated trends, we should instead demand that upward or downward "blips" in one time series correspond to upward or downward fluctuations in the other series. If one or both of the variables are detrended, any correlation between the two indicators should represent parallel "blips" instead of just a common trend. Testing causal hypotheses using detrended variables is therefore less likely to produce spurious results. For further methodological details, see McCleary and Hay (1980:36–45, 229) and Cromwell et al. (1994:v, 10). In the U.S. case, of course, the dependent variable has too many missing data to allow for detrending.

2. The French public-opinion data used in this chapter were collected and published by SOFRES and *Le Figaro* of Paris, France. Neither organization bears any responsibility for the analysis in this chapter.

3. For similar models of over-time levels of support for political parties or candidates, see Tufte (1978:105–136); Jacobson (1987:140–180); Norpoth, Lewis-Beck, and Lafay (1991); and Frey and Kirchgässner (1994:18).

4. This and several other variables have been mathematically transformed. See notes in Tables 5.2 and 5.3.

5. Throughout this book, "percent change" provides a more "user-friendly" statistic to indicate the relative power of a given cause of nativism. In general, this figure refers to the percent change in the observed range of the dependent variable that is associated with a 100% increase in the observed range of the particular independent variable. For later Logit models, percent change refers to the change in probability of "success" associated with a given regressor moving from its minimum observed to maximum observed value where all other regressors are set to 0. For the Tobit models in Chapters 7 and 8, percent change refers to changes in the latent dependent variable y^* (assuming the model is correct and given the particular observed values of the regressors). Since Logit, Tobit, and OLS models assume different underlying distributions of the error term, percent changes are not necessarily comparable across different types of regression techniques (e.g., Logit vs. OLS).

6. As with most time-series models, statistical significance of these parameter estimates has a different meaning than those from a properly executed cross-sectional analysis. Because standard ARIMA techniques, for example, constitute a form of "data dredging," this analysis partly violates some of the traditional assumptions of regression. In a strict sense, one cannot rely on the standard errors of parameter estimates because the asymptotic sampling distribution of estimates based on "datamining" is unknown. The reported regression estimates in this chapter should therefore be viewed more as exploratory indicators of which variables might be important determinants of immigration-related attitudes rather than as rigorous "tests" of the hypothesis that the independent variables have significant effects. Standard errors and significance tests also function more as rough suggestions of how far away from

zero the estimate is than as strict tests of statistical significance at the .05 level.

7. Data from the Politbarometer West 1989–1996 analyzed in this section were produced by the Forschungsgruppe Wahlen in Mannheim, Germany, and provided by the Zentralarchiv für Empirische Sozialforschung at the University of Cologne, Germany. Neither the producers nor distributors of these data are responsible for the analyses or interpretations in this chapter. The author gratefully acknowledges the permission of the Forschungsgruppe Wahlen to use their data.

8. As Falter (1994:162) documents, the general public in Germany does not think the Republikaner have much expertise in reducing unemployment.

9. This lack of effect for unemployment thus might confirm Chapin's (1997:78–85) results. Though the proportion of foreigners in the population did reach statistical significance for Chapin, he employed a *Land*-based panel model instead of a nationally based times-series one. My results for the percentage of foreigners therefore might not necessarily conflict with his.

10. Most of the attacks occurred toward the end of the month (*Der Spiegel* 1993): Hoyerswerda, September 17, 1991; Rostock, August 24, 1992; Mölln, November 23, 1992; and Solingen, May 29, 1993. Using data from the previous month would therefore seem to capture the peak effects of these hate crimes.

11. Since the series for opposition to foreigners is so short (usable t = 23), however, any findings from the model in this paragraph must be treated with caution.

Chapter 6. Recent Attitudes toward Immigration in the United States

1. Data from the 1986 CBS News/*New York Times* National Survey and the 1990–1992 American National Election Study (Full Panel) were provided by the Inter-university Consortium for Political and Social Research (ICPSR) in Ann Arbor, Michigan. The original collector of these data, ICPSR, and the relevant funding agency bear no responsibility for the uses of these data or for interpretations or inferences based upon such uses.

   This chapter also analyzes the 1994 *Los Angeles Times* exit poll, which was distributed by the Roper Center of Storrs, Connecticut. Neither the *Los Angeles Times* nor the Roper Center bears any responsibility for the use of these data or the views expressed in this book.

2. Marginality also predicts that education's egalitarian message would stimulate pro-immigration attitudes. This chapter does not discuss the effect of education extensively, however, because economic self-interest makes a similar empirical prediction.

3. To keep the analysis manageable, this chapter conflates attitudes on the admission of immigrants (immigration policy per se) with views on the treatment of immigrants already in the United States (immigrant rights or immigrant policy). Although these two strands of policy are usually highly intertwined, occasionally the determinants of the two forms differ slightly. Using the 1986 CBS/*New York Times* data, for example (see Appendix 3), I created one scale for admission policy (for refugees and immigrants in general) and another for postsettlement policy (on employer sanctions and deportation of *indocumentados*). After correction in AMOS for random measurement error, the two traits correlated at a relatively high .55. Estimating parallel regression equations yielded mostly comparable coefficients. The estimate for being Latino was a major exception, however, strongly reducing support for anti-immigrant postsettlement policies (percent change = −17.0, p < .001) but failing to achieve statistical significance for admissions. Latinos may thus be more concerned about protecting ethnic Latin Americans already in the United States than about allowing more of their ethnic cousins to enter the country.

4. Unfortunately, the lack of suitable indicators of cultural threat prevented a parallel analysis for opposition to immigration and support for Proposition 187.

5. Of course, the suggestion that the United States has a single culture or, indeed, any culture at all amuses many Europeans.

6. Or at least according to economic self-interest theory. For studies questioning the empirical assumptions behind this model, see Simon (1989:296–300), Cornelius (1998), and Marcelli (in press).

7. Unfortunately, these data do not permit correction for the possibility that people rationalize their already existent anti-immigrant affect or opposition to immigration by claiming that immigrants will take their jobs ("reciprocal causation"). The paths in this paragraph between economic threat and nativism thus represent the *maximum* possible effect of such threat.

8. A parallel model for anti-immigrant affect indicated that education did directly affect nativism even after controlling for perceived economic threat (b = −15.185 and SE = 3.890 for university graduate; b = −8.395 and SE = 2.977 for secondary school graduate).

9. Here again, correction for bidirectional causality did not appear practicable.

Chapter 7. Recent Attitudes toward Immigration in France

1. For a methodological critique of the early social-science literature on the Front national, see Husbands (1991).

2. Most of the "Antilleans" in Table 7.1 are probably French citizens from French *départements* in the Caribbean and so not technically immigrants.

U.S. law treats Puerto Ricans living on the American mainland similarly. Data for Table 7.1 come from Hastings and Hastings (1987:494).

3. Data from the Eurobarometer 30 analyzed in this chapter were provided by the Inter-university Consortium for Political and Social Research (ICPSR) in Ann Arbor, Michigan. The original collector of these data, ICPSR, and the relevant funding agency bear no responsibility for the uses of these data or for interpretations or inferences based upon such uses.

   Data from the 1995 SOFRES French National Election Study were provided by the Banque de Données Socio-Politiques in Saint Martin d'Hères, France. Neither the producers nor distributors of these data are responsible for the analysis or interpretations in this chapter.

4. Because the third set of estimates in Table 7.2 came from Tobit, one cannot simply divide the coefficient for non-Catholic by the total observed range of the dependent variable. In theory one should instead use the range of the latent dependent variable y^*, which unfortunately is not observed (or, more precisely, the maximum value is observed, but the minimum value has been left-censored to 0). As a substitute, one could presumably use the maximum observed value for y (29) and the minimum possible value for y^* (−8.02) given the Tobit coefficients in Table 7.2. The resulting range then approximates 37, but this estimate might not be completely comparable with the observed range for the dependent variables in the regressions for affect and policy.

5. For a contrary finding based on earlier data, see Lewis-Beck and Mitchell (1993).

6. This result remains provisional because correction for bidirectional causation proved impracticable.

7. Unfortunately, the SOFRES survey on support for the National Front contained no satisfactory measures of perceived cultural threat.

8. Because correcting for bidirectional causation did not prove feasible, these results remain provisional.

9. The 1995 SOFRES survey contained no usable measures of perceived relative economic deprivation.

10. These paths are tentative because opposition to immigration might have some (uncorrected-for) effect on perceived economic threat.

11. In contrast to the U.S. results, having a French university degree produces no greater reduction in perceived economic threat than does possessing only a secondary school degree. Once again, the system of higher education in France may not be doing much to combat the questionable economic claims of Le Pen and his allies. Or, alternatively, a French university degree may provide much less advantage on the job market than does an American equivalent.

12. Results uncorrected for any bidirectional causality. Unfortunately, the SOFRES survey on the National Front contained no questions on contact with immigrants at the workplace or in the neighborhood.

Chapter 8. Recent Attitudes toward Immigration in Germany

1. Data from the Eurobarometer 30 and 1990 German Election Panel Study (Wahlstudie) analyzed in this chapter were provided by the Inter-university Consortium for Political and Social Research (ICPSR) in Ann Arbor, Michigan. The original collectors of these data, ICPSR, and the relevant funding agencies bear no responsibility for the uses of these data or for interpretations or inferences based upon such uses.

   Data from the surveys Einstellungen zu aktuellen Fragen der Innen-politik and Einstellungen gegenüber Juden und anderen Minderheiten were distributed by the Zentralarchiv für Empirische Sozialforschung at the University of Cologne, Germany. Neither the producers nor distrib-utors of these data are responsible for the analyses or interpretations in this chapter.

2. The major surveys analyzed in this chapter include only respondents from the pre-unification Federal Republic of Germany or "old Federal states." East (and eastern) German attitudes toward immigration originate in such a different economic, political, and social context that conflating them with West German opinion probably raises too many inferential hazards. For studies of immigration-related attitudes in the "new Federal states," see Breuer (1990), Ireland (1997), and Watts (1997).

3. The German Election Panel Study contained no measure of foreign origin, making parallel analysis of the Republikaner model impossible. All ethnic Turks were excluded from the Eurobarometer models.

4. This cross-national comparison appears especially valid because both the German and the French data come from the same survey (Eurobarometer 30).

5. An anecdote from my field work in southwestern Germany may support this interpretation. Some middle-aged, relatively well educated German acquaintances and I were discussing German immigrants to the United States who had later "made it big." At one point someone mentioned Heinz (a.k.a. Henry) Kissinger as yet another notable German American. "Yes, but I was thinking more of real Germans. Kissinger had other origins," one man replied. The appalling (especially given the context) anti-Semitism aside, this remark suggests that many Germans refuse to regard as a "true German" anyone with the slightest hint of any "non-German" ancestry. Whether one carries a German passport (as did a Turkish-born journalist I knew) is apparently beside the point. In the late 1990s, at least, only "German blood" made the "German." Popular German attitudes may or may not follow the shift to a more *jus soli* policy in January 2000 (Deutsche Presse Agentur 1999).

6. As throughout this book, the estimated effect of cultural threat on nativism remains tentative because correction for bidirectional causation proved impossible.

7. Of course, originating in an immigrant family also decreases cultural

threat in the United States (see Table 6.1), another traditional country of immigration, but one cannot compare the weak effect of this variable in the United States (percent change = −3.5) to the very substantial influence of "foreign origin" in Germany (percent change = −15.1).

8. I am grateful to Herbert Kitschelt for suggesting the possible role of political elites.

9. Or, "Foreigners are our misfortune." During the 1930s, German Nazis scapegoated Jews with the phrase "Die Juden sind unser Unglück."

10. This "finances declined" variable uses a less dynamic wording (finances "poor" or "very poor" instead of "got worse" or "declined") than the other corresponding variables in this book; see Appendix 4 for further details.

11. These paths remain provisional because opposition to immigration might have some (uncorrected-for) effect on perceived economic threat.

12. For similar results with German data, see Krauth and Porst (1984).

13. Correction for any bidirectional causality proved impossible. Unfortunately, the German Election Panel Study of support for the Republikaner included no questions on contact with immigrants at the workplace or in the neighborhood.

14. My experience growing up in the Washington, D.C., suburbs, moreover, suggests a similar pattern of relatively superficial relations with one's next-door neighbors.

15. All of the German models of *Land*-level proximity are corrected for bidirectional causality (see Appendix 2).

Chapter 9. Culture, Nationality, and the Future of Nativism

1. This American exception may stem from the more diverse backgrounds of its immigrants and its longer historical experience with immigration. In France and Germany, the relevant "data" may simply be too few for any trend to appear.

2. That is, Table 9.3 "drops" minority findings across countries and types of dependent variables and instead reports only the "majority opinion." Where the evidence was evenly split, Table 9.3 favored the nonzero results.

3. That contact – even on the evidence of Allport and Pettigrew – only increases tolerance under relatively restricted and perhaps unlikely conditions nonetheless suggests that this variable cannot play a large role in improving attitudes toward immigrants and immigration.

4. For evidence that nativism and isolationism are linked, see McClosky (1967); Espenshade and Hempstead (1996). For data on the loss of ethnic languages among second- and third-generation immigrants in France, see Tribalat (1995:48–53). Skerry (1993) likewise examines the linguistic and cultural integration of Mexican Americans.

5. As the 1999 war in Kosovo suggests, however, a sense of belonging to a group that was once persecuted might not increase one's sympathy for

oppressed outsiders if one's group constitutes a majority or controls the government in a given nation-state.

6. For evidence that North American publics do not find political union as preposterous as one might suppose, see Inglehart, Nevitte, and Besañez (1996:135–164).

7. For a similar empirical prediction, see Portes and Rumbaut (1996:300).

Appendix 4. Definition of Variables

1. Variable denotations refer to the way they are listed in the relevant codebook.

Glossary of Non-English Terms

Arbeiternot (Ger.)	Critical lack of industrial workers in western Germany of the late 1800s and early 1900s.
Asylbewerber (Ger.)	Asylum seekers in Germany.
Aussiedler (Ger.)	Ethnic Germans whose ancestors had originally settled in Russia under the czars but who have been returning to Germany since the end of the Cold War.
braceros (Span.)	From 1940s to 1960s, Mexican workers recruited by American government and employers to work temporarily in the United States.
commune (Fr.)	Relatively small administrative unit in the French system of regional government. In urban areas, similar to a U.S. city ward.
département (Fr.)	Subnational governmental division in France. About the same size as a U.S. county but serves a political role similar to a U.S. state.
Evangelische (Ger.)	Members of the largest, state-supported Protestant denomination in Germany. Similar to U.S. Lutherans or Reformed believers.
français de souche (Fr.)	French person whose ancestry is "ethnically French" back through recorded time.
Fremdarbeiter (Ger.)	"Foreign workers" during the Nazi era in Germany. Many had been forcibly rounded up in their home countries and deported to work as slaves in the Third Reich.
Gastarbeiter (Ger.)	"Guest workers" in Germany, many of whom have lived in the country since the 1950s or 1960s.

Gymnasium (Ger.)	Elite German secondary school. Roughly equivalent to a combined U.S. high school and junior college.
haoles (Hawaiian)	Ethnic Europeans living in Hawaiian Islands.
harkis (Arab.)	Ethnically Arabic or Berber Algerians who sided with the French government during the Algerian War and fled to France after the French defeat.
ḥijāb (Arab.):	Scarf-like head-covering worn by orthodox Muslim women.
indocumentados (Span.)	Undocumented immigrants.
jus sanguinis (Lat.)	Literally, "law of the blood." System under which one becomes a citizen by being born to someone of the ethnic group dominant in a certain country (e.g., being born to ethnic Germans in Germany).
jus soli (Lat.)	Literally, "law of the soil." System under which one becomes a citizen by being born within the boundaries of a certain country (e.g., being born in the United States regardless of one's ethnicity).
Kaiserreich (Ger.)	German empire under the German *Kaisers*, or emperors.
Kulturkampf (Ger.)	Literally, "cultural struggle." Anti-Catholic campaign waged by German Chancellor Otto von Bismarck in late nineteenth century.
Land/Länder (Ger.)	Subnational governmental division(s) in Germany. About the same size as a U.S. county but serves a political role similar to a U.S. state under federalism.
Languedoc (Fr.)	Region of southern France historically known for its particular dialect of proto-French.
Leutenot (Ger.)	Critical lack of agricultural workers in eastern Prussia during the late 1800s and early 1900s.
lycée (Fr.)	Elite French secondary school. Roughly equivalent to a combined U.S. high school and junior college.
Nachbarn (Ger.)	Close (e.g., next-door) neighbors.
Nachbarschaft (Ger.)	All those who live in dwellings immediately next to one's own, or close neighbors one knows personally or by sight.

Nisei (Japan.)	Literally, "second generation." U.S.-born Japanese Americans whose parents were born in Japan.
pieds-noirs (Fr.)	Literally, "black feet." Ethnically European colonists in Algeria who fled to France after the French defeat in the Algerian War.
quartier (Fr.)	City "quarter" in France. Roughly equivalent to a U.S. city ward.
région (Fr.)	Relatively large administrative unit in French system of regional government. Usually composed of several *départements*. Roughly equivalent to a small U.S. state.
Roma (Romany)	Historically nomadic, ethnic southern Asians also known as Romany or "Gypsies."
Ruhrpolen (Ger.)	Ethnically Polish industrial workers in the *Ruhr* region of northwestern Germany.
Sinti (Ger.)	Name Roma living in German-speaking areas of Europe normally call themselves.
Trente Glorieuses (Fr.)	Literally, "thirty glorious ones." Thirty-year period of economic expansion in France from end of World War II until early 1970s.
Übersiedler (Ger.)	East Germans who escaped to West Germany during the Cold War.
Überfremdung (Ger.)	"Foreign infiltration" or excessive foreign influence supposedly caused by immigration. Term frequently used by German nativists.
Volkstum (Ger.)	German national traditions, culture, or character.
Wirtschaftswunder (Ger.)	"Economic miracle," or dramatic economic recovery, of post–World War II Germany.
yarmulke (Yiddish)	Small, round, cap-like headcovering worn by some Jewish males.
Yom ha-Sho'ah (Hebr.)	Jewish day of remembrance for the victims of the Holocaust.
Vertriebene (Ger.)	Ethnic Germans expelled from eastern Europe following Hitler's defeat in World War II.

Bibliography

Data Sources

American National Election Study, Full Panel Survey, 1990–1992. ICPSR no. 6230. Archived at the Inter-university Consortium for Political and Social Research, Ann Arbor, MI.

American National Election Study, Pre- and Post-Election Survey, 1992. Enhanced with 1990 and 1991 data. ICPSR no. 6067. Archived at the Inter-university Consortium for Political and Social Research, Ann Arbor, MI.

CBS News/New York Times *National Survey, Part 7*, June 19–23, 1986. ICPSR no. 8695. Archived at the Inter-university Consortium for Political and Social Research, Ann Arbor, MI.

CBS News/New York Times/*Tokyo Broadcasting System Japan Poll and Call-Back*, June 21–27, 1993. ICPSR no. 6206. Reported in Espenshade and Hempstead (1995; 1996) and archived at the Inter-university Consortium for Political and Social Research, Ann Arbor, MI.

Einstellungen gegenüber Juden und anderen Minderheiten Survey, January 1994. ZA no. 2418. Archived at the Zentralarchiv für Empirische Sozialforschung, Cologne, Germany.

Eurobarometer 30: Immigrants and Out-Groups in Western Europe, October–November 1988. ICPSR no. 9321. Archived at the Inter-university Consortium for Political and Social Research, Ann Arbor, MI.

Gallup Polls, various years. Reported in Simon and Alexander (1993:41) and archived at the Roper Center, Storrs, CT.

German Election Panel Study/Wahlstudie (Panel), 1990. ICPSR no. 6192. ZA no. 1919. Archived at the Inter-university Consortium for Political and Social Research, Ann Arbor, MI, and at the Zentralarchiv für Empirische Sozialforschung, Cologne, Germany.

INSEE Employment, Immigration, and Inflation Data, various months. Reported in INSEE (Institut national de la statistique et des études économiques), *Bulletin mensuel de statistique*, various issues.

Institut Français d'Opinion Publique "Racism" Survey, April 1985. Privately held data. Reported in Hastings and Hastings (1987:494) and produced by Institut Français d'Opinion Publique, Paris, France.

Institut für praxisorientierte Sozialforschung "Einstellungen zu aktuellen Fragen der Innenpolitik" Poll, May 1992. ZA no. 2288. Archived at the Zentralarchiv für Empirische Sozialforschung, Cologne, Germany.

Los Angeles Times *California General Election Exit Poll*, November 8, 1994. Roper no. USLAT94-350. Archived at the Roper Center, Storrs, CT.

Politbarometer West, 1989–1996. ZA nos. 1779, 1920, 2102, 2275, 2378, 2546, 2765, and 2894. Archived at the Zentralarchiv für Empirische Sozialforschung, Cologne, Germany.

Princeton Survey Research Associates "Looking for America" Poll, July 31–August 17, 1997. Roper no. USPSRA1997-COLUMBUS. Reported in Page (1997) and archived at the Roper Center, Storrs, CT.

SOFRES French National Election Study/Enquête postélectorale – CEVIPOF, May 8–23, 1995. ICPSR no. 6806. BDSP no. Q0891. Archived at the Inter-university Consortium for Political and Social Research, Ann Arbor, MI, and at the Banque de Données Socio-Politiques, Saint Martin d'Hères, France.

SOFRES/Le Figaro Monthly *"baromètre" Surveys*, various dates. Reported in SOFRES (1989:155, 157) and *Le Figaro Magazine*, various issues.

Other Sources

Agence France Press. 1998. "New Softer French Citizenship Laws Enforced." Agence France Press wire service, September 2.

Ageron, Charles-Robert. 1985. "L'immigration maghrébine en France: Un survol historique." *Vingtième siècle: Revue d'histoire*, no. 7 (July–September), pp. 59–70.

Allinsmith, Wesley, and Beverly Allinsmith. 1948. "Religious Affiliation and Politico-Economic Attitude: A Study of Eight Major U.S. Religious Groups." *Public Opinion Quarterly* 12:377–389.

Allport, Gordon. 1979. *The Nature of Prejudice*. 25th anniversary ed. Reading, MA: Addison-Wesley.

Anderson, Mark M., ed. 1998. *Hitler's Exiles: Personal Stories of the Flight from Nazi Germany to America*. New York: New Press.

Andrade, Ron. 1997. Telephone conversation with author, August 5.

Asselain, Jean-Charles. 1984a. *Histoire économique de la France du XVIIIᵉ siècle à nos jours: 1. De l'Ancien Régime à la Première Guerre mondiale*. Paris: Éditions du Seuil.

1984b. *Histoire économique de la France du XVIIIᵉ siècle à nos jours: 2. De 1919 à la fin des années 1970*. Paris: Éditions du Seuil.

1995a. *Histoire économique du XXᵉ siècle*. Vol. 1, *La montée de l'État (1914–1939)*. Paris: Presses de la Fondation nationale des sciences politiques & Dalloz.

1995b. *Histoire économique du XXᵉ siècle*. Vol. 2, *La réouverture des économies nationales (1939 aux années 1980).* Paris: Presses de la Fondation nationale des sciences politiques & Dalloz.

Assouline, David, and Mehdi Lallaoui. 1996a. *Un siècle d'immigrations en France, première période: De la mine au champ de bataille, 1851/1918.* Paris: Syros & Au nom de la mémoire.

1996b. *Un siècle d'immigrations en France, deuxième période: De l'usine au maquis, 1919/1945.* Paris: Syros & Au nom de la mémoire.

Axt, Heinz-Jürgen. 1997. "The Impact of German Policy on Refugee Flows from Former Yugoslavia." Pp. 1–33 in Rainer Münz and Myron Weiner, eds., *Migrants, Refugees, and Foreign Policy: U.S. and German Policies toward Countries of Origin.* Providence, RI: Berghahn Books.

Bacon, Francis. [1625] 1994. "Of Goodness, and Goodness of Nature." Pp. 32–33 in Michael J. Hawkins, ed., *Essays/Francis Bacon.* London: Everyman.

Bade, Klaus J. 1980. "Arbeitsmarkt, Bevölkerung und Wanderung in der Weimarer Republik." Pp. 160–187 in Michael Stürmer, ed., *Die Weimarer Republik: Belagerte Civitas.* Königstein/Ts.: Verlagsgruppe Athenäum, Hain, Scriptor, Hanstein.

1983a. "'Kulturkampf' auf dem Arbeitsmarkt: Bismarcks 'Polenpolitik' 1885–1890." Pp. 121–142 in Otto Pflanze, ed., *Innenpolitische Probleme des Bismarck-Reiches.* Munich: R. Oldenbourg Verlag.

1983b. *Vom Auswanderungsland zum Einwanderungsland? Deutschland 1880–1980.* Berlin: Colloquium Verlag.

1990. "Aussiedler – Rückwanderer über Generationen hinweg." Pp. 128–149 in Klaus J. Bade, ed., *Neue Heimat im Westen: Vertriebene, Flüchtlinge, Aussiedler.* Münster: Westfälischer Heimatbund.

ed. 1992a. *Deutsche im Ausland – Fremde in Deutschland: Migration in Geschichte und Gegenwart.* Munich: Beck.

1992b. "'Billig und Willig' – die 'ausländischen Wanderarbeiter' im kaiserlichen Deutschland." Pp. 311–324 in Klaus J. Bade, ed., *Deutsche im Ausland – Fremde in Deutschland: Migration in Geschichte und Gegenwart.* Munich: Beck.

1992c. "Fremde Deutsche: 'Republikflüchtlinge' – Übersiedler – Aussiedler." Pp. 401–410 in Klaus J. Bade, ed., *Deutsche im Ausland – Fremde in Deutschland: Migration in Geschichte und Gegenwart.* Munich: Beck.

1992d. "'Politisch Verfolgte genießen . . .': Asyl bei den Deutschen – Idee und Wirklichkeit." Pp. 411–422 in Klaus J. Bade, ed., *Deutsche im Ausland – Fremde in Deutschland: Migration in Geschichte und Gegenwart.* Munich: Beck.

1992e. "Einheimische Ausländer: 'Gastarbeiter' – Dauergäste – Einwanderer." Pp. 393–401 in Klaus J. Bade, ed., *Deutsche im Ausland – Fremde in Deutschland: Migration in Geschichte und Gegenwart.* Munich: Beck.

1994a. *Ausländer – Aussiedler – Asyl: Eine Bestandsaufnahme.* Munich: Beck.

ed. 1994b. *Das Manifest der 60: Deutschland und die Einwanderung.* Munich: Beck.

1996. "Einwanderung und Gesellschaftspolitik in Deutschland – quo vadis Bundesrepublik?" Pp. 230–253 in Klaus J. Bade, ed., *Die multikulturelle Herausforderung: Menschen über Grenzen – Grenzen über Menschen.* Munich: Beck.

1997. "From Emigration to Immigration: The German Experience in the Nineteenth and Twentieth Centuries." Pp. 1–37 in Klaus J. Bade and Myron Weiner, eds., *Migration Past, Migration Future: Germany and the United States.* Providence, RI: Berghahn.

Bade, Klaus J., Hans-Bernd Meier, and Bernhard Parisius, eds. 1997. *Zeitzeugen im Interview: Flüchtlinge und Vertriebene im Raum Osnabrück nach 1945.* Osnabrück: Universitätsverlag Rasch.

Baltzell, E. Digby. 1964. *The Protestant Establishment: Aristocracy and Caste in America.* New Haven: Yale University Press.

Barkan, Elliott Robert. 1996. *And Still They Come: Immigrants and American Society, 1920 to the 1990s.* Wheeling, IL: Harlan Davidson.

Barnett, George Ramsey, III. 1991. "Excluding the Japanese: The Politics of Diplomacy, 1908–1924." Ph.D. dissertation, University of Pennsylvania.

Bau, Ignatius. 1985. *This Ground Is Holy: Church Sanctuary and Central American Refugees.* Mahwah, NJ: Paulist Press.

Bauböck, Rainer. 1994. *Transnational Citizenship: Membership and Rights in International Migration.* Aldershot, England: Edward Elgar.

Becker, Jules. 1991. *The Course of Exclusion, 1882–1924: San Francisco Newspaper Coverage of the Chinese and Japanese in the United States.* San Francisco: Mellen Research University Press.

Bédarida, Renée. 1991. "Les catholiques français et les refugiés espagnols." Pp. 193–196 in Pierre Milza and Denis Peschanski, eds., *Italiens et Espagnols en France, 1938–1946.* Paris: Centre National de la Recherche Scientifique.

Ben Jelloun, Tahar. 1984. *Hospitalité française.* Paris: Éditions du Seuil.

Bennassar, Bartolomé, and Marie-Line Montbroussous. 1991. "De l'immigration à l'intégration: Les Espagnols dans le bassin houiller de l'Aveyron 1926–1954." Pp. 87–115 in CNRS (Centre National de la Recherche Scientifique), *Exil politique et migration économique: Espagnols et Français aux XIXe–XXe siècles.* Paris: CNRS.

Bennett, David H. 1995. *The Party of Fear: The American Far Right from Nativism to the Militia Movement.* 2d ed. New York: Vintage.

Benz, Wolfgang. 1992. "Fremde in der Heimat: Flucht – Vertreibung – Integration." Pp. 374–386 in Klaus J. Bade, ed., *Deutsche im Ausland – Fremde in Deutschland: Migration in Geschichte und Gegenwart.* Munich: Beck.

Berelson, Bernard R., Paul F. Lazarsfeld, and William N. McPhee. 1954. *Voting: A Study of Opinion Formation in a Presidential Campaign.* Chicago: University of Chicago Press.

Berger, Joseph. 1999. "Fleshing Out Stories of Ship Denied Refuge from Hitler." *New York Times,* March 31, p. B1.

Betz, Hans-Georg. 1994. *Radical Right-Wing Populism in Western Europe.* New York: St. Martin's Press.

Billington, Ray Allen. 1938. *The Protestant Crusade, 1800–1860: A Study of the Origins of American Nativism*. New York: Macmillan.

Blank, Inge. 1992. "'. . . nirgends eine Heimat, aber Gräber auf jedem Friedhof': Ostjuden in Kaiserreich und Weimarer Republik." Pp. 324–332 in Klaus J. Bade, ed., *Deutsche im Ausland – Fremde in Deutschland: Migration in Geschichte und Gegenwart*. Munich: Beck.

Bœgner, Marc. 1989. "Le combat de l'Église à Vichy." Pp. 9–28 in Émile C. Fabre, ed., *Les clandestins de Dieu: CIMADE 1939–1945*. Geneva: Labor et Fides.

Bogardus, Emory S. 1928. *Immigration and Race Attitudes*. Boston: D. C. Heath.

Bonin, Hubert. 1988. *Histoire économique de la France depuis 1880*. Paris: Masson.

Bork, Robert H. 1996. *Slouching towards Gomorrah: Modern Liberalism and American Decline*. New York: Regan Books.

Borras, José. 1991. "Les migrations d'Espagnols en France après la Guerre Civile (1939–1945)." Pp. 159–173 in CNRS (Centre National de la Recherche Scientifique), *Exil politique et migration économique: Espagnols et Français aux XIXᵉ–XXᵉ siècles*. Paris: CNRS.

Bosc, Alain. 1995. Interview with author. Comité inter-mouvements auprès des évacués (CIMADE), Paris, July 25.

Boy, Daniel, and Nonna Mayer. 1997. *L'électeur a ses raisons*. Paris: Presses de la Fondation nationale des sciences politiques.

Branigin, William. 1995. "Report to Clinton Urges Global Attack on Growing Trade in Alien-Smuggling." *Washington Post*, December 28, p. A1.

Brault, Gerard J. 1986. *The French-Canadian Heritage in New England*. Hanover and Montreal: University Press of New England and McGill/Queen's University Press.

Braun, Hans-Joachim. 1990. *The German Economy in the Twentieth Century: The German Reich and the Federal Republic*. London: Routledge.

Breitman, Richard, and Alan M. Kraut. 1987. *American Refugee Policy and European Jewry, 1933–1945*. Bloomington: Indiana University Press.

Brennen, Timothy. 1997. *At Home in the World: Cosmopolitanism Now*. Cambridge, MA: Harvard University Press.

Bretting, Agnes, Horst Rößler, Christiane Harzig, Monika Blaschke, and Karen Schniedewind. 1992. "Deutsche in den USA." Pp. 135–185 in Klaus J. Bade, ed., *Deutsche im Ausland – Fremde in Deutschland: Migration in Geschichte und Gegenwart*. Munich: Beck.

Breuer, Wilhelm. 1990. *Ausländerfeindlichkeit in der ehemaligen DDR*. Bonn: Der Bundesminister für Arbeit und Sozialordnung.

Brinton, Crane. 1958. *The Anatomy of Revolution*. Rev. ed. New York: Vintage Books.

Brownlee, W. Eliot. 1979. *Dynamics of Ascent: A History of the American Economy*. 2d ed. New York: Knopf.

Brubaker, Rogers. 1992. *Citizenship and Nationhood in France and Germany.* Cambridge, MA: Harvard University Press.

Bundesanstalt für Arbeit. 1994. *Amtliche Nachrichten der Bundesanstalt für Arbeit: Arbeitsstatistik 1993 – Jahreszahlen.* Vol. 41, Special ed., July 25.

Bundesministerium des Innern. 1993. *Verfassungsschutzbericht 1992.* Bonn: Bundesministerium des Innern.

Bureau of Labor Statistics. 1998. *Employment and Earnings (January).* Washington, DC: U.S. Department of Labor.

Bureau of the Census. 1956. *Statistical Abstract of the United States, 1956.* Washington, DC: U.S. Department of Commerce.

1961. *Statistical Abstract of the United States, 1961.* Washington, DC: U.S. Department of Commerce.

1962a. *Statistical Abstract of the United States, 1962.* Washington, DC: U.S. Department of Commerce.

1962b. *County and City Data Book, 1962: A Statistical Abstract Supplement.* Washington, DC: U.S. Department of Commerce.

1967. *County and City Data Book, 1967.* Washington, DC: U.S. Department of Commerce.

1971. *Statistical Abstract of the United States, 1971.* Washington, DC: U.S. Department of Commerce.

1976. *Statistical Abstract of the United States, 1976.* Washington, DC: U.S. Department of Commerce.

1977. *Statistical Abstract of the United States, 1977.* Washington, DC: U.S. Department of Commerce.

1981. *Statistical Abstract of the United States, 1981.* Washington, DC: U.S. Department of Commerce.

1984. *Statistical Abstract of the United States, 1984.* Washington, DC: U.S. Department of Commerce.

1986. *Statistical Abstract of the United States, 1986.* Washington, DC: U.S. Department of Commerce.

1989. *Historical Statistics of the United States: Colonial Times to 1970.* White Plains, NY: Kraus International Publications.

1992. *Statistical Abstract of the United States, 1992.* Washington, DC: U.S. Department of Commerce.

1993. *Statistical Abstract of the United States, 1993.* Washington, DC: U.S. Department of Commerce.

1994a. *County and City Data Book, 1994.* Washington, DC: U.S. Department of Commerce.

1994b. *Statistical Abstract of the United States, 1994.* Washington, DC: U.S. Department of Commerce.

1995. *Statistical Abstract of the United States, 1995.* Washington, DC: U.S. Department of Commerce.

1996. *Statistical Abstract of the United States, 1996.* Washington, DC: U.S. Department of Commerce.

1997. *Statistical Abstract of the United States, 1997.* Washington, DC: U.S. Department of Commerce.

Buttler, Günter. 1992. *Der gefährdete Wohlstand: Deutschlands Wirtschaft braucht die Einwanderer.* Frankfurt a.M.: Fischer.

Calavita, Kitty. 1984. *U.S. Immigration Law and the Control of Labor: 1820–1924.* Orlando, FL: Academic Press.

Campbell, Angus, Philip E. Converse, Warren E. Miller, and Donald E. Stokes. 1960. *The American Voter.* Chicago: University of Chicago Press.

Camus, Jean-Yves. 1996. "Origine et formation du Front national (1972–1981)." Pp. 17–36 in Nonna Mayer and Pascal Perrineau, eds., *Le Front national à découvert.* Paris: Presses de la Fondation nationale des sciences politiques.

Caron, François. 1979. *An Economic History of Modern France.* Barbara Bray, trans. New York: Columbia University Press.

CBS News/*New York Times.* 1988. *CBS News*/New York Times *National Surveys, 1986.* ICPSR no. 8695. Codebook. First ICPSR edition. Ann Arbor, MI: ICPSR.

Centro de Estudios Puertorriqueños. 1979. *Labor Migration under Capitalism: The Puerto Rican Experience.* New York: Monthly Review Press.

Chan, Sucheng. 1991. "The Exclusion of Chinese Women, 1870–1943." Pp. 94–146 in Sucheng Chan, ed., *Entry Denied: Exclusion and the Chinese Community in America, 1882–1943.* Philadelphia: Temple University Press.

Chapin, Wesley D. 1997. *Germany for the Germans?: The Political Effects of International Migration.* Westport, CT: Greenwood Press.

Charbit, Yves, and Marie-Laurence Lamy. 1975. "Attitudes à l'égard des étrangers et seuils de tolérance: Les enquêtes de l'I.N.E.D." *Sociologie du Sud-Est,* no. 5, pp. 85–99.

Charlot, Monica. 1986. "L'émergence du Front national." *Revue française de science politique* 36 (1):30–45.

Citrin, Jack, Donald P. Green, Christopher Muste, and Cara Wong. 1997. "Public Opinion toward Immigration Reform: The Role of Economic Motivations." *Journal of Politics* 59:858–881.

Clinton, William J. 1998. *Economic Report of the President.* Washington, DC: Government Printing Office.

Cohen, David Steven, ed. 1990. *America, the Dream of My Life: Selections from the Federal Writers' Project's New Jersey Ethnic Survey.* New Brunswick, NJ: Rutgers University Press.

Cohen, Robin. 1995. *The Cambridge Survey of World Migration.* Cambridge: Cambridge University Press.

Cohn-Bendit, Daniel, and Thomas Schmid. 1992. *Heimat Babylon: Das Wagnis der multikulturellen Demokratie.* Hamburg: Hoffmann und Campe.

Commission nationale consultative des droits de l'homme (CNCDH). 1994. *La lutte contre le racisme et la xénophobie.* Paris: La documentation française.

Congressional Quarterly. 1969. *Congress and the Nation.* Vol. 2, *1965–1968: A*

Review of Government and Politics during the Johnson Years. Washington, DC: Congressional Quarterly.

1973. *Congress and the Nation.* Vol. 3, *1969–1972: A Review of Government and Politics during Nixon's First Term.* Washington, DC: Congressional Quarterly.

1977. *Congress and the Nation.* Vol. 4, *1973–1976: A Review of Government and Politics.* Washington, DC: Congressional Quarterly.

1981. *Congress and the Nation.* Vol. 5, *1977–1980: A Review of Government and Politics.* Washington, DC: Congressional Quarterly.

1985. *Congress and the Nation.* Vol. 6, *1981–1984: A Review of Government and Politics.* Washington, DC: Congressional Quarterly.

1990. *Congress and the Nation.* Vol. 7, *1985–1988: A Review of Government and Politics.* Washington, DC: Congressional Quarterly.

1993. *Congress and the Nation.* Vol. 8, *1989–1992: A Review of Government and Politics.* Washington, DC: Congressional Quarterly.

Cornelius, Wayne A. 1982. *America in the Era of Limits: Migrants, Nativists, and the Future of U.S.-Mexican Relations.* San Diego: Center for U.S.-Mexican Studies.

1998. *The Role of Immigrant Labor in the U.S. and Japanese Economies: A Comparative Study of San Diego and Hamamatsu, Japan.* With the assistance of Yasuo Kuwahara. San Diego: Center for U.S.-Mexican Studies.

Cromwell, Jeff B., Walter C. Labys, and Michel Terraza. 1994. *Univariate Tests for Time Series Models.* Thousand Oaks, CA: Sage.

Cross, Gary S. 1983. *Immigrant Workers in Industrial France: The Making of a New Laboring Class.* Philadelphia: Temple University Press.

Daniels, Roger. 1977. *The Politics of Prejudice: The Anti-Japanese Movement in California and the Struggle for Japanese Exclusion.* Berkeley: University of California Press.

1981. *Concentration Camps: North America: Japanese in the United States and Canada during World War II.* Malabar, FL: Robert E. Krieger.

1988. *Asian America: Chinese and Japanese in the United States since 1850.* Seattle: University of Washington Press.

1990. *Coming to America: A History of Immigration and Ethnicity in American Life.* New York: Harper-Collins.

1996. "The Immigrant Experience in the Gilded Age." Pp. 63–89 in Charles W. Calhoun, ed., *The Gilded Age: Essays on the Origins of Modern America.* Wilmington, DE: Scholarly Resources.

1997. *Not Like Us: Immigrants and Minorities in America, 1890–1924.* Chicago: Ivan R. Dee.

Daniels, Roger, and Harry H. L. Kitano. 1970. *American Racism: Exploration of the Nature of Prejudice.* Englewood Cliffs, NJ: Prentice-Hall.

Daniels, Roger, Sandra C. Taylor, and Harry H. L. Kitano, eds. 1991. *Japanese Americans: From Relocation to Redress.* Rev. ed. Seattle: University of Washington Press.

Decouflé, André-Clément. 1992. "Historic Elements of the Politics of Nationality in France (1889–1989)." Pp. 357–367 in Donald L.

Horowitz and Gérard Noiriel, eds., *Immigrants in Two Democracies: French and American Experience*. New York: New York University Press.

Deutsche Presse Agentur. 1999. "Bundesrat billigt neues Staatsbürgerschafts-recht." *Berliner Zeitung*, no. 117 (May 22–23), p. 6.

de Zayas, Alfred-Maurice. 1994. *A Terrible Revenge: The Ethnic Cleansing of the East European Germans, 1944–1950*. John A. Koehler, trans. New York: St. Martin's Press.

Dohse, Knuth. 1985. *Ausländische Arbeiter und bürgerlicher Staat: Genese und Funktion von staatlicher Ausländerpolitik und Ausländerrech vom Kaiserreich bis zur Bundesrepublik Deutschland*. Berlin: EXpress Edition.

Dollard, John, Leonard W. Doob, Neal E. Miller, O. H. Mowrer, and Robert R. Sears. 1939. *Frustration and Aggression*. New Haven: Yale University Press.

Downs, Anthony. 1957. *An Economic Theory of Democracy*. New York: Harper.

Drosdowski, Günther, ed. 1989. *DUDEN Deutsches Universalwörterbuch*. 2d ed. Mannheim: DUDEN.

Dupâquier, Jacques, ed. 1988a. *Histoire de la population française*. Vol. 3, *De 1789 à 1914*. Paris: Presses Universitaires de France.

1988b. *Histoire de la population française*. Vol. 4, *De 1914 à nos jours*. First "Quadrige" edition, May 1995. Paris: Presses Universitaires de France.

Ebersole, Luke. 1960. "Religion and Politics." *Annals of the American Academy of Political and Social Sciences* 332:101–111.

Ellul, Jacques. 1986. *The Subversion of Christianity*. Geoffrey W. Bromiley, trans. Grand Rapids, MI: Eerdmans.

EMNID. 1988. *Fragebogen für Eurobarometer 30: Befragung-Nr. 841411*. Questionnaire. Bielfeld, Germany: EMNID-Institut GmbH & Co.

Enzensberger, Hans Magnus. 1992. *Die große Wanderung: Dreiunddreißig Markierungen, mit einer Fußnote "Über einige Besonderheiten bei der Menschenjagd."* Frankfurt: Suhrkamp.

Erikson, Robert S., Norman R. Luttbeg, and Kent L. Tedin. 1991. *American Public Opinion: Its Origins, Content, and Impact*. 4th ed. New York: Macmillan.

Espenshade, Thomas J., and Charles A. Calhoun. 1993. "An Analysis of Public Opinion toward Undocumented Immigration." *Population Research and Policy Review* 12:189–224.

Espenshade, Thomas J., and Katherine Hempstead. 1995. "Contemporary American Attitudes toward U.S. Immigration." Office of Population Research, Princeton. Unpublished manuscript.

1996. "Contemporary American Attitudes toward U.S. Immigration." *International Migration Review* 30 (2):535–570.

Fabre, Émile C., ed. 1989. *Les clandestins de Dieu: CIMADE 1939–1945*. Geneva: Labor et Fides.

Fairbank, Maslin, Maullin & Associates. 1996. "Immigration at the End of the 20th Century: A Summary Report on Two Focus Groups." Prepared on behalf of the Center for National Policy. Los Angeles: Fairbank, Maslin, Maullin & Associates.

Falter, Jürgen W. 1994. *Wer wählt rechts? Die Wähler und Anhänger rechtsextremistischer Parteien im vereinigten Deutschland.* Munich: C. H. Beck.

Farin, Klaus, and Eberhard Seidel-Pielen. 1993. *Skinheads.* Munich: Beck.

Federal News Service. 1995. "Remarks by Patrick Buchanan, 1996 Republican Presidential Candidate, at United We Stand America National Conference." Major leader special transcript. August 12. Washington, DC: Federal Information Systems Corporation.

Fein, Leonard. 1988. *Where Are We? The Inner Life of America's Jews.* New York: Harper and Row.

Fetzer, Joel. 1989. *Selective Prosecution of Religiously Motivated Offenders in America.* Lewiston, NY: Edwin Mellen.

Fineman, Mark. 1994. "California Election; Mexico Assails State's Passage of Prop. 187." *Los Angeles Times,* November 10, p. A28.

Forschungsgruppe Wahlen and Zentralarchiv für empirische Sozialforschung. 1994. *Partielle Kumulation der Politbarometer West 1977 bis 1993.* Machine-readable codebook. ZA no. S2391. Cologne: Zentralarchiv für Empirische Sozialforschung.

Frey, Bruno S., and Gebhard Kirchgässner. 1994. *Demokratische Wirtschaftspolitik: Theorie und Anwendung.* 2d ed. Munich: Verlag Franz Vahlen.

Fuchs, Laurence. 1956. *The Political Behavior of American Jews.* Glencoe, IL: Free Press.

Fulbrook, Mary. 1990. *A Concise History of Germany.* Cambridge: Cambridge University Press.

García, Mario T. 1981. *Desert Immigrants: The Mexicans of El Paso, 1880–1920.* New Haven: Yale University Press.

Gaspard, Françoise, and Farhad Khosrokhavar. 1995. *Le foulard et la République.* Paris: La Découverte.

Gastault, Yvan. 1993. "La flambée raciste de 1973 en France." *Revue européenne des migrations internationales* 9 (2):61–75.

——— 1994. "1973, 1983, 1993: Les chrétiens en première ligne pour soutenir les immigrés." *Migrations et société* 6 (33–34):9–27.

Gedmin, Jeffrey. 1995. *The Germans: Portrait of a New Nation.* Videorecording. Princeton: Films for the Humanities & Sciences.

Gilens, Martin. 1999. *Why Americans Hate Welfare: Race, Media, and the Politics of Antipoverty Policy.* Chicago: University of Chicago Press.

Girard, Alain. 1977. "Opinion publique, immigration et immigrés." *Ethnologie française* 7 (3):219–228.

Glazer, Nathan, and Daniel P. Moynihan. 1970. *Beyond the Melting Pot: The Negroes, Puerto Ricans, Jews, Italians, and Irish of New York City.* 2d ed. Cambridge, MA: MIT Press.

Golden, Renny, and Michael McConnell. 1986. *Sanctuary: The New Underground Railroad.* Maryknoll, NY: Orbis.

Green, Donald Philip, and Jack Citrin. 1994. "Measurement Error and the Structure of Attitudes: Are Positive and Negative Judgments Opposites?" *American Journal of Political Science* 38 (1):256–281.

Green, Donald P., and Ian Shapiro. 1994. *Pathologies of Rational Choice Theory: A Critique of Applications in Political Science.* New Haven: Yale University Press.

Guerin-Gonzáles, Camille. 1985. "Repatriación de familias inmigrantes mexicanas durante la Gran Depresión." *Historia mexicana* 35:241–274.

———. 1994. *Mexican Workers and American Dreams: Immigration, Repatriation, and California Farm Labor, 1900–1939.* New Brunswick, NJ: Rutgers University Press.

Gurr, Ted Robert. 1970. *Why Men Rebel.* Princeton: Princeton University Press.

Gusfield, Joseph R. 1963. *Symbolic Crusade: Status Politics and the American Temperance Movement.* Urbana: University of Illinois Press.

Hallie, Phillip. 1979. *Lest Innocent Blood Be Shed: The Story of Le Chambon-sur-Lignon and How Goodness Happened There.* New York: Harper & Row.

Handlin, Oscar. 1979. *The Uprooted: The Epic Story of the Great Migrations That Made the American People.* 2d ed. Boston: Little, Brown.

Harenberg, Bodo. 1993. *Aktuell '94: Das Lexikon der Gegenwart.* Dortmund: Harenberg Lexikon-Verlag.

Harris, Nigel. 1995. *The New Untouchables: Immigration and the New World Worker.* London: Penguin.

Harwood, Edwin. 1983. "Alienation: American Attitudes toward Immigration." *Public Opinion* 6 (3):49–51.

———. 1986. "American Public Opinion and U.S. Immigration Policy." *Annals of the American Academy of Political and Social Science* 487:201–212.

Hastings, Elizabeth Hann, and Philip K. Hastings, eds. 1987. *Index to International Public Opinion, 1985–1986.* Westport, CT: Greenwood.

———. 1997. *Index to International Public Opinion, 1995–1996.* Westport, CT: Greenwood.

Heckmann, Friedrich. 1981. *Die Bundesrepublik: Ein Einwanderungsland? Zur Soziologie der Gastarbeiterbevölkerung als Einwandererminorität.* Stuttgart: Klett-Cotta.

Heer, David M. 1990. *Undocumented Mexicans in the United States.* Cambridge: Cambridge University Press.

Henning, Friedrich-Wilhelm. 1978. *Das Industrialisierte Deutschland 1914 bis 1976.* Paderborn: UTB/Verlag Ferdinand Schöningh.

Herbert, Ulrich. 1985. *Fremdarbeiter: Politik und Praxis des "Ausländer-Einsatzes" in der Kriegswirtschaft des Dritten Reiches.* Berlin: Dietz.

———. 1990. *A History of Foreign Labor in Germany, 1880–1980.* William Templer, trans. Ann Arbor: University of Michigan Press.

Hernes, Gudmund, and Knud Knudsen. 1989. "Over grensen: Om holdninger til innvandrere og asylsøkere." *Tidsskrift for samfunnsforskning* 30:27–60.

———. 1992. "Norwegians' Attitudes toward New Immigrants." *Acta Sociologica* 35:123–139.

Hewstone, Miles, and Rupert Brown, eds. 1986. *Contact and Conflict in Intergroup Encounters.* Oxford: Basil Blackwell.

Higham, John. 1988. *Strangers in the Land: Patterns of American Nativism, 1860–1925*. New Brunswick, NJ: Rutgers University Press.

Hoffman, Abraham. 1974. *Unwanted Mexican Americans in the Great Depression: Repatriation Pressures, 1929–1939*. Tucson: University of Arizona Press.

Hofmann, Murad Wilfried. 1992. *Der Islam als Alternative*. Munich: Eugen Diederichs Verlag.

Hollifield, James F. 1992. *Immigrants, Markets, and States: The Political Economy of Post-War Europe*. Cambridge, MA: Harvard University Press.

1997. *L'immigration et l'état-nation: À la recherche d'un modèle national*. Paris: L'Harmattan.

Holsti, Ole R. 1996. *Public Opinion and American Foreign Policy*. Ann Arbor: University of Michigan Press.

Homze, Edward L. 1967. *Foreign Labor in Nazi Germany*. Princeton: Princeton University Press.

Hoskin, Marilyn. 1991. *New Immigrants and Democratic Society: Minority Integration in Western Democracies*. New York: Praeger.

Houston, Jeanne Wakatsuki, and James D. Houston. 1974. *Farewell to Manzanar*. New York: Bantam.

Human Rights Watch. 1995. *"Germany for Germans": Xenophobia and Racist Violence in Germany*. New York: Human Rights Watch.

Huntington, Samuel P. 1993. "The Clash of Civilizations?" *Foreign Affairs* 72 (3):22–49.

Husbands, Christopher T. 1991. "The Support for the *Front national*: Analyses and Findings." *Ethnic and Racial Studies* 14 (3):382–416.

Imber, Shulamit. 1994. *To Bear Witness: An Educational Kit for Teaching the Holocaust and Observing Yom ha-Sho'ah*. 2d ed. Jerusalem: Yad Vashem, Pedagogic Resource Center – Education Department.

Immigration and Naturalization Service. 1997. *Statistical Yearbook of the Immigration and Naturalization Service, 1996*. Washington, DC: Government Printing Office.

Inglehart, Ronald, Neil Nevitte, and Miguel Basañez. 1996. *The North American Trajectory: Cultural, Economic, and Political Ties among the United States, Canada, and Mexico*. New York: Aldine de Gruyter.

INSEE (Institut national de la statistique et des études économiques). 1956. *Recensement générale de la population de mai 1954: Population légale (résultats statistiques)*. Paris: Imprimerie nationale & Presses Universitaires de France.

1961. *Annuaire statistique de la France. Rétrospectif*. Paris: Presses Universitaires de France.

1990. *Annuaire rétrospectif de la France: Séries longues 1948–1988*. Paris: INSEE.

1992. *Recensement de la population de 1990, nationalités: Résultats du sondage au quart*. Collection INSEE Résultats no. 217, Démographie-Société no. 21. Paris: INSEE.

1994. *Annuaire statistique de la France*. Paris: INSEE.

1997. *Annuaire statistique de la France*. Paris: INSEE.

Ireland, Patrick R. 1997. "Socialism, Unification Policy and the Rise of Racism in Eastern Germany." *International Migration Review* 31 (3): 541–568.

Jackson, Dave, and Neta Jackson. 1989. *On Fire for Christ: Stories of Anabaptist Martyrs Retold from* Martyrs Mirror. Scottdale, PA: Herald Press.

Jacobmeyer, Wolfgang. 1992. "Ortlos am Ende des Grauens: 'Displaced Persons' in der Nachkreigszeit." Pp. 367–373 in Klaus J. Bade, ed., *Deutsche im Ausland – Fremde in Deutschland: Migration in Geschichte und Gegenwart*. Munich: Beck.

Jacobson, David. 1996. *Rights across Borders: Immigration and the Decline of Citizenship*. Baltimore: Johns Hopkins University Press.

Jacobson, Gary C. 1987. *The Politics of Congressional Elections*. 2d ed. Washington, DC: Congressional Quarterly.

Jelen, Ted G., and Clyde Wilcox. 1998. "Context and Conscience: The Catholic Church as an Agent of Political Socialization in Western Europe." *Journal for the Scientific Study of Religion* 37 (1):28–40.

Johnson, Harry M. 1960. *Sociology: A Systematic Introduction*. New York: Harcourt, Brace.

Jordi, Jean-Jacques. 1995. *1962: L'arrivée des Pieds-Noirs*. Paris: Autrement.

Jordi, Jean-Jacques, Abdelmalek Sayad, and Émile Temime. 1991. *Migrance: Histoire des Migrations à Marseille*. Vol. 4, *Le choc de la décolonisation (1945–1990)*. Aix-en-Provence: Edusud.

Just, Wolf-Dieter. 1990. "Ausländer im Kaiserreich – Zur Haltung der Kirchen." Pp. 38–59 in Wolf-Dieter Just, ed., *Kirchen und Ausländerpolitik seit 1871: Theologische Voraussetzungen und Begründungen des Engagements*. Mülheim: Evangelische Akademie Mülheim.

———. ed. 1993. *Asyl von unten: Kirchenasyl und ziviler Ungehorsam – Ein Ratgeber*. Reinbek bei Hamburg: Rowohlt.

Kaiserliches Statisches Amt. 1897. *Berufsstatistik für das Reich im Ganzen*. Part I. *Statistik des Deutschen Reiches*, n.s., vol. 102. Berlin: Verlag von Puttkammer & Mühlbrecht.

Karst, Kenneth L. 1989. *Belonging to America: Equal Citizenship and the Constitution*. New Haven: Yale University Press.

Katz, Jesse. 1995. "Prop. 187 Gives Texas a Selling Point in Mexico." *Los Angeles Times*, February 6, p. A1.

Kennedy, John F. 1964. *A Nation of Immigrants*. Rev. and enl. ed. New York: Harper & Row.

Kennedy, Paul. 1993. *Preparing for the Twenty-First Century*. New York: Random House.

Kinder, Donald R., and D. Roderick Kiewiet. 1981. "Sociotropic Politics: The American Case." *British Journal of Political Science* 11 (2):129–161.

King, Gary, Robert O. Keohane, and Sidney Verba. 1994. *Designing Social Inquiry: Scientific Inference in Qualitative Research*. Princeton: Princeton University Press.

Kitchen, Martin. 1978. *The Political Economy of Germany, 1815–1914.* Montreal: McGill-Queens University Press.

Kitschelt, Herbert. 1995. *The Radical Right in Western Europe: A Comparative Analysis.* Ann Arbor: University of Michigan Press.

Kleinert, Uwe. 1990. "Die Flüchtlinge als Arbeitskräfte – zur Eingliederung der Flüchtlinge in Nordrhein-Westfalen nach 1945." Pp. 37–60 in Klaus J. Bade, ed., *Neue Heimat im Westen: Vertriebene, Flüchtlinge, Aussiedler.* Münster: Westfälischer Heimatbund.

Kleßmann, Christoph. 1978. *Polnische Bergarbeiter im Ruhrgebiet 1870–1945: Soziale Integration und nationale Subkultur einer Minderheit in der deutschen Industriegesellschaft.* Göttingen: Vandenhoeck & Ruprecht.

——— 1992. "Einwanderungsprobleme im Auswanderungsland: Das Beispiel der 'Ruhrpolen.'" Pp. 303–310 in Klaus J. Bade, ed., *Deutsche im Ausland – Fremde in Deutschland: Migration in Geschichte und Gegenwart.* Munich: Beck.

Knight, Ute, and Wolfgang Kowalsky. 1991. *Deutschland nur den Deutschen?: Die Ausländerfrage in Deutschland, Frankreich und den USA.* Erlangen: Straube.

Korman, Max O. 1998. "The Ill-Fated Steamship *St. Louis*." Pp. 185–191 in Mark M. Anderson, ed., *Hitler's Exiles: Personal Stories of the Flight from Nazi Germany to America.* New York: New Press.

Kramer, Gerald H. 1983. "The Ecological Fallacy Revisited: Aggregate-versus Individual-level Findings on Economics and Elections, and Sociotropic Voting." *American Political Science Review* 77:92–111.

Krauth, Cornelia, and Rolf Porst. 1984. "Sozioökonomische Determinanten von Einstellungen zu Gastarbeitern." Pp. 233–266 in Karl Ulrich Mayer and Peter Schmidt, eds., *Allgemeine Bevölkerungsumfrage der Sozialwissenschaften: Beiträge zu methodischen Problemen des ALLBUS 1980.* Frankfurt: Campus Verlag.

Krieger-Krynicki, Annie. 1985. *Les musulmans en France: Religion et culture.* Paris: Éditions Maisonneuve et Larose.

Kristol, Irving. 1995. *Neoconservatism: The Autobiography of an Idea.* New York: Free Press.

Kulczycki, John J. 1994. *The Foreign Worker and the German Labor Movement: Xenophobia and Solidarity in the Coal Fields of the Ruhr, 1871–1914.* Oxford: Berg.

Kulischer, Eugene M. 1948. *Europe on the Move: War and Population Changes, 1917–47.* New York: Columbia University Press.

Kürsat-Ahlers, Elçin. 1996. "The Turkish Minority in German Society." Pp. 113–135 in David Horrocks and Eva Kolinsky, eds., *Turkish Culture in German Society Today.* Providence, RI: Berghahn.

Kurthen, Hermann, Werner Bergmann, and Rainer Erb, eds. 1997. *Antisemitism and Xenophobia in Germany after Unification.* New York: Oxford University Press.

Lagarde, Eric. 1991. "Le camp de réfugiés de Bram, une vision de l'exode espagnol de 1939." Pp. 145–157 in CNRS (Centre National de la

Recherche Scientifique), *Exil politique et migration économique: Espagnols et Français aux XIXe–XXe siècles*. Paris: CNRS.

Länderrat des Amerikanischen Besatzungsgebiet. 1949. *Statistisches Jahrbuch für Deutschland 1928–1944*. Munich: Franz Ehrenwirth-Verlag.

Laster, Molly C., and Sabrina P. Ramet. 1998. "Xenophobia and Rightwing Extremism in Germany: The New *Bundesländer*." Pp. 75–92 in Patricia J. Smith, ed., *After the Wall: Eastern Germany since 1989*. Boulder, CO: Westview Press.

Lebergott, Stanley. 1964. *Manpower in Economic Growth: The American Record since 1800*. New York: McGraw-Hill.

Le Bras, Hervé. 1986. *Les trois France*. Paris: Éditions Odile Jacob.

Lee, Kenneth K. 1998. *Huddled Masses, Muddled Laws: Why Contemporary Immigration Policy Fails to Reflect Public Opinion*. Westport, CT: Praeger.

Lee, Patrick. 1994. "Elections '94: Impact on Business; Prop. 187's Passage Threatens to Disrupt Ties with Mexico." *Los Angeles Times*, November 10, p. D1.

Leggewie, Claus. 1990. *Die Republikaner: Ein Phantom nimmt Gestalt an*. Rev. ed. Berlin: Rotbuch.

———. 1992. "'Stolz, ein Deutscher zu sein...' – die neue Angst vor den Fremden." Pp. 423–430 in Klaus J. Bade, ed., *Deutsche im Ausland – Fremde in Deutschland: Migration in Geschichte und Gegenwart*. Munich: Verlag C. H. Beck.

———. 1993. *Multi Kulti: Spielregeln für die Vielvölkerrepublik*. Berlin: Rotbuch Verlag.

Lemberg, Eugen, and Friedrich Edding, eds. 1959. *Die Vertriebenen in Westdeutschland. Ihre Eingliederung und ihr Einfluß auf Gesellschaft, Wirtschaft, Politik und Geistesleben*. 3 vols. Kiel: Ferdinand Hirt.

Le Moigne, Guy. 1995. *L'immigration en France*. 3d ed. Collection "Que sais-je?" Paris: Presses Universitaires de France.

Lepszy, Norbert. 1989. "Die Republikaner: Ideologie – Programm – Organization. *Aus Politik und Zeitgeschichte* B41–42/89 (October 6):3–9.

Lequin, Yves, ed. 1988. *La mosaïque France: Histoire des étrangers et de l'immigration en France*. Paris: Larousse.

———. ed. 1992. *Histoire des étrangers et de l'immigration en France*. Paris: Références Larousse.

Levey, Geoffrey Brahm. 1996. "The Liberalism of American Jews: Has It Been Explained?" *British Journal of Political Science* 26:369–401.

Lewis-Beck, Michael S., and Glenn E. Mitchell II. 1993. "French Electoral Theory: The National Front Test." *Electoral Studies* 12:112–127.

Lipshultz, Robert J. 1971. *American Attitudes toward Mexican Immigration, 1924–1952*. San Francisco: R and E Research Associates.

Loch, Dietmar. 1990. *Der schnelle Aufstieg des Front National: Rechtsextremismus im Frankreich der 80er Jahre*. Munich: tuduv.

———. 1995. "Moi, Khaled Kelkal." *Le Monde*, October 7, pp. 10–12.

London, Perry. 1970. "The Rescuers: Motivational Hypotheses about Christians Who Saved Jews from the Nazis." Pp. 241–250 in Jacqueline R.

Macauley and Leonard Berkowitz, eds., *Altruism and Helping Behavior: Social Psychological Studies of Some Antecedents and Consequences*. New York: Academic Press.

Lookstein, Haskel. 1985. *Were We Our Brothers' Keepers? The Public Response of American Jews to the Holocaust, 1938–1944*. New York: Vintage.

Lopez, Renée, and Émile Temime. 1990. *Migrance: Histoire des migrations à Marseille*. Vol. 2, *L'expansion marseillaise et "L'invasion italienne" (1830–1918)*. Aix-en-Provence: Edisud.

Los Angeles Times. 1994. "*Times* Poll: A Look at the Electorate." *Los Angeles Times*, November 10, p. B2.

Los Angeles Times Staff. 1994. "Going against the Grain on Easier Trade." *Los Angeles Times*, November 25, p. D3.

Los Angeles Times Wire Service. 1994. "McDonald's in Mexico City Vandalized by Prop. 187 Foes." *Los Angeles Times*, November 9, p. A26.

———. 1997. "Germany: Soldiers Arrested after Racist Attack." *Los Angeles Times*, March 19, p. A8.

Lowenthal, Abraham F., and Katrina Burgess, eds. 1993. *The California-Mexico Connection*. Stanford: Stanford University Press.

Lowry, James W. 1997. *The Martyrs' Mirror Made Plain: A Study Guide and Further Studies*. Lagrange, IN: Pathway.

Luebke, Frederick C. 1990. *Germans in the New World: Essays in the History of Immigration*. Urbana: University of Illinois Press.

Luker, Kristin. 1984. *Abortion and the Politics of Motherhood*. Berkeley: University of California Press.

MacMaster, Neil. 1997. *Colonial Migrants and Racism: Algerians in France, 1900–1962*. London: Macmillan.

Marcelli, Enrico A. In press. *California in Denial: A Political Economy of Unauthorized Mexican Immigration*. Boulder, CO: Westview Press.

Martin, Philip. 1995. "Proposition 187 in California." *International Migration Review* 29 (1):255–263.

Martínez, Gebe. 1994. "*Los Angeles Times* Poll." *Los Angeles Times*, November 10, p. A35.

Martínez-Ebers, Valerie, and Zixian Deng. 1996. "Americans' Cultural Perspectives and Immigration Attitudes: A Structural Model." Paper presented at the annual meeting of the American Political Science Association, San Francisco, CA, August 29–September 1.

Massey, Douglas S., and Nancy A. Denton. 1993. *American Apartheid: Segregation and the Making of the Underclass*. Cambridge, MA: Harvard University Press.

Masud-Piloto, Felix Roberto. 1996. *From Welcomed Exiles to Illegal Immigrants: Cuban Migration to the U.S., 1959–1995*. Lanham, MD: Rowman & Littlefield.

Mauco, Georges. 1932. *Les étrangers en France: Leur rôle dans l'activité économique*. Paris: Armand Colin.

———. 1977. *Les étrangers en France et le problème du racisme*. Paris: La pensée universelle.

Mayer, Nonna. 1987. "De Passy à Barbès: Deux visages du vote Le Pen à Paris." *Revue française de science politique* 37 (6):891–906.

Mayer, Nonna, and Pascal Perrineau. 1993. "La puissance et le rejet ou le lepénisme dans l'opinion." Pp. 63–78 in Olivier Duhamel and Jérôme Jaffré, eds., *L'état de l'opinion 1993*. Paris: Éditions du Seuil.

Mazón, Mauricio. 1984. *The Zoot-Suit Riots: The Psychology of Symbolic Annihilation*. Austin: University of Texas Press.

McCaffrey, Lawrence J. 1984. *The Irish Diaspora in America*. Washington, DC: Catholic University of America Press.

McClain, Paula D., and Albert K. Karnig. 1990. "Black and Hispanic Socioeconomic and Political Competition." *American Political Science Review* 84:535–545.

McCleary, Richard, and Richard A. Hay Jr. 1980. *Applied Time Series Analysis for the Social Sciences*. Beverly Hills, CA: Sage.

McClosky, Herbert. 1967. "Personality and Attitude Correlates of Foreign Policy Orientation." Pp. 51–109 in James N. Rosenau, ed., *Domestic Sources of Foreign Policy*. New York: Free Press.

McDonnell, Patrick J. 1997. "Prop. 187 Found Unconstitutional by Federal Judge." *Los Angeles Times*, November 15, pp. A1, A24.

McWilliams, Carey. 1990. *North from Mexico: The Spanish-Speaking People of the United States*. Westport, CT: Praeger.

Mehrländer, Ursula. 1974. *Soziale Aspekte der Ausländerbeschäftigung*. Bonn-Bad Godesberg: Verlag Neue Gesellschaft.

Messinger, Heinz. 1988. *Langenscheidt's New College German Dictionary, German-English/English-German*. Berlin: Langenscheidt.

Miller, Kerby A. 1985. *Emigrants and Exiles: Ireland and the Irish Exodus to North America*. New York: Oxford University Press.

Miller, Warren E., Donald R. Kinder, Steven J. Rosenstone, and the National Election Studies. 1993. *American National Election Study, 1990–1992: Full Panel Survey*. ICPSR no. 6230. Codebook. First ICPSR Edition. Ann Arbor, MI: ICPSR.

Milza, Pierre. 1979. "Le racisme anti-italien en France: La 'tuerie d'Aigues-Mortes' (1893)." *L'Histoire*, 10 (March):23–31.

———. 1981. *Français et Italiens à la fin du XIXe siècle: Aux origines du rapprochement franco-italien de 1900–1902*. 2 vols. Rome: École française de Rome.

Minkenberg, Michael. 1998. *Die neue radikale Rechte im Vergleich: USA, Frankreich, Deutschland*. Wiesbaden: Westdeutscher Verlag.

Modell, John, ed. 1973. *The Kikuchi Diary: Chronicle from an American Concentration Camp*. Urbana: University of Illinois Press.

Le Monde. 1993. "M. Pasqua contre une société 'pluriculturelle.'" *Le Monde*, March 22, section "politique."

Moore, Stephen, and Julian L. Simon. 1989. "Views of Economists and Other Social Scientists toward Immigration." Pp. 357–361 in Julian L. Simon, *The Economic Consequences of Immigration*. Cambridge: Basil Blackwell and the Cato Institute.

Morales, Patricia. 1989. *Indocumentados mexicanos: Causas y razones de la migración laboral.* 2d ed. Mexico City: Grijalbo.

Morris, Nomi. 1993. "Turks in Germany Fight Back against Racism." *San Francisco Chronicle*, June 11, p. A13.

Morrison, Joan, and Charlotte Fox Zabusky. 1980. *American Mosaic: The Immigrant Experience in the Words of Those Who Lived It.* Pittsburgh: University of Pittsburgh Press.

Morse, Arthur D. 1968. *While Six Million Died: A Chronicle of American Apathy.* Woodstock, NY: Overlook Press.

Mucan, Asım [President, Dachverband Mannheimer Muslime]. 1999. E-mail message of June 29 to author.

Muller, Thomas, and Thomas J. Espenshade. 1985. *The Fourth Wave: California's Newest Immigrants.* Washington, DC: Urban Institute Press.

Myrdal, Gunnar. 1944. *An American Dilemma: The Negro Problem and Modern Democracy.* New York: Harper & Brothers.

Neubach, Helmut. 1967. *Die Ausweisungen von Polen und Juden aus Preußen 1885/86: Ein Beitrag zu Bismarcks Polenpolitik und zur Geschichte des deutsch-polnischen Verhältnisses.* Wiesbaden: Otto Harrassowitz.

Niebuhr, H. Richard. 1957. *The Social Sources of Denominationalism.* New York: Meridian.

Nieves, Evelyn. 1999. "California Calls Off Effort to Carry Out Immigrant Measure." *New York Times*, July 30, p. A1.

Nieves Falcón, Luis. 1987. *El emigrante puertorriqueño.* Rio Piedras, Puerto Rico: Ediciones EDIL.

Noiriel, Gérard. 1988. *Le creuset français: Histoire de l'immigration XIXᵉ–XXᵉ siècles.* Paris: Éditions du Seuil.

   1996. *The French Melting Pot: Immigration, Citizenship, and National Identity.* Geoffroy de Laforcade, trans. Minneapolis: University of Minnesota Press.

Norpoth, Helmut, Michael S. Lewis-Beck, and Jean-Dominique Lafay, eds. 1991. *Economics and Politics: The Calculus of Support.* Ann Arbor: University of Michigan Press.

O'Connor, Anne-Marie. 1997. "The Sum of Unequal Parts: In His Latest Work, Novelist Carlos Fuentes Uses the U.S.-Mexican Border to Explore the Love-Hate Relationship between Americans and Immigrants." *Los Angeles Times*, October 24, p. E1.

O'Hanlon, Ray. 1998. *The New Irish Americans.* Niwot, CO: Roberts Rinehart.

Oliner, Samuel P., and Pearl M. Oliner. 1988. *The Altruistic Personality: Rescuers of Jews in Nazi Europe.* New York: Free Press.

Özdemir, Cem. 1999. *Currywurst und Döner: Integration in Deutschland.* Bergisch Gladbach: Gustav Lübbe Verlag.

Page, Susan. 1997. "Poll: Fear of Immigration Eases." *USA Today*, October 13, p. 1A.

Perrineau, Pascal. 1985. "Le Front National: Un électorat autoritaire." *Revue politique et parlementaire*, 87 (916–917):24–31.

1996. "Les étapes d'une implantation électorale (1972–1988)." Pp. 37–62 in Nonna Mayer and Pascal Perrineau, eds., *Le Front national à découvert*. Paris: Presses de la Fondation nationale des sciences politiques.

Perrot, Michelle. 1960. "Les rapports entre ouvriers français et ouvriers étrangers (1871–1893)." *Bulletin de la Société d'histoire moderne*, no. 12, 58ᵉ année, pp. 4–9. Supplement to the *Revue d'histoire moderne et contemporaine*, no. 1.

———. 1974. *Les ouvriers en grève: France 1871–1890*. 2 vols. Paris: Mouton.

Pettigrew, Thomas F. 1971. *Racially Separate or Together?* New York: McGraw-Hill.

———. 1986. "The Intergroup Contact Hypothesis Reconsidered." Pp. 169–195 in Miles Hewstone and Rupert Brown, eds., *Contact and Conflict in Intergroup Encounters*. Oxford: Basil Blackwell.

Pinkus, Susan. 1997. Telephone conversation with author, August 5.

Ponty, Janine. 1988. *Polonais méconnus: Histoire des travailleurs immigrés en France dans l'entre-deux-guerres*. Paris: Publications de la Sorbonne.

Portes, Alejandro, and Rubén G. Rumbaut. 1996. *Immigrant America: A Portrait*. 2d ed. Berkeley: University of California Press.

Rasmussen, Cecilia. 1998. "A Teenager's Courage Remembered." *Los Angeles Times* (San Fernando Valley edition), April 8, p. B9.

Ravenstein, E. G. 1889. "The Laws of Migration." *Journal of the Royal Statistical Society* 52:241–305.

Reid, Ira De Augustine. 1968. *The Negro Immigrant: His Background, Characteristics and Social Adjustment, 1899–1937*. New York: AMS Press.

Reif, Karlheinz, and Anna Melich. 1991. *Eurobarometer 30: Immigrants and Out-Groups in Western Europe, October–November 1988*. ICPSR no. 9321. Codebook. Ann Arbor: Inter-University Consortium for Political and Social Research.

Reimers, David M. 1992. *Still the Golden Door: The Third World Comes to America*. 2d ed. New York: Columbia University Press.

———. 1998. *Unwelcome Strangers: American Identity and the Turn against Immigration*. New York: Columbia University Press.

Republikaner. 1990. *Die Republikaner: Parteiprogramm*. Bonn: Der Bundesgesellschäftsstelle der Republikaner.

Robert, Paul, ed. 1986. *Le Petit Robert 1: Dictionnaire alphabétique et analogique de la langue française*. Paris: Le Robert.

Robert, Paul, and Jan Collins, eds. 1978. *Robert-Collins Dictionaire Français-Anglais/Anglais-Français*. Paris: Société du Nouveau Littré.

Röder, Werner. 1992. "Die Emigration aus dem nationalsozialistischen Deutschland." Pp. 345–353 in Klaus J. Bade, ed., *Deutsche im Ausland – Fremde in Deutschland: Migration in Geschichte und Gegenwart*. Munich: Beck.

Rößler, Horst. 1992. "Massenexodus: Die Neue Welt des 19. Jahrhunderts." Pp. 148–157 in Klaus J. Bade, ed., *Deutsche im Ausland – Fremde in Deutschland: Migration in Geschichte und Gegenwart*. Munich: Beck.

Roth, Dieter. 1989. "Sind die Republikaner die fünfte Partei? Sozial- und

Meinungsstruktur der Wähler der Republikaner." *Aus Politik und Zeitgeschichte* B41–42/89 (October 6):10–20.

1990. "Die Republikaner: Schneller Aufstieg und tiefer Fall einer Protestpartei am rechten Rand." *Aus Politik und Zeitgeschichte* B37–38/90 (September 14):27–39.

Rothenberg, Daniel. 1998. *With These Hands: The Hidden World of Migrant Farmworkers Today*. New York: Harcourt Brace.

Rovan, Joseph. 1983. "Des Français contre les immigrés." *L'Histoire* 57 (June):6–17.

Runge, Irene. 1995. *"Ich bin kein Russe": Jüdische Zuwanderung zwischen 1989 und 1994*. Berlin: Dietz Verlag.

Salgas, Emannuelle. 1991. "Une population face à l'exil espagnol: Représentations et opinion. Le cas des Pyrénées-Orientales, Janvier–Septembre 1939." Pp. 277–284 in Pierre Milza and Denis Peschanski, eds., *Italiens et Espagnols en France 1938–1946*. Paris: Centre National de la Recherche Scientifique.

Salyer, Lucy E. 1995. *Laws Harsh as Tigers: Chinese Immigrants and the Shaping of Modern Immigration Law*. Chapel Hill: University of North Carolina Press.

Sandmeyer, Elmer Clarence. 1991. *The Anti-Chinese Movement in California*. Urbana, IL: University of Illinois Press.

Saxton, Alexander. 1971. *The Indispensable Enemy: Labor and the Anti-Chinese Movement in California*. Berkeley: University of California Press.

Schain, Martin A. 1987. "The National Front in France and the Construction of Political Legitimacy." *West European Politics* 10 (2):229–252.

Scheiber, Harry N., Harold G. Vatter, and Harold Underwood Faulkner. 1976. *American Economic History*. 9th ed. New York: Harper & Row.

Schlögel, Karl. 1998. *Berlin Ostbahnhof Europas: Russen und Deutsche in ihrem Jahrhundert*. Berlin: Siedler Verlag.

Schlozman, Kay Lehman, and Sidney Verba. 1979. *Injury to Insult: Unemployment, Class, and Political Response*. Cambridge, MA: Harvard University Press.

Schmidley, A. Dianne, and J. Gregory Robinson. 1998. "How Well Does the Current Population Survey Measure the Foreign Born Population in the United States?" Population Division Working Paper no. 22. Washington, DC: U.S. Bureau of the Census.

Schor, Ralph. 1985. *L'opinion française et les étrangers en France 1919–1939*. Paris: Publications de la Sorbonne.

1996. *Histoire de l'immigration en France de la fin du XIXᵉ siècle à nos jours*. Paris: Armand Colin.

Sears, David O., Richard R. Lau, Tom R. Tyler, and Harris M. Allen Jr. 1980. "Self-Interest vs. Symbolic Politics in Policy Attitudes and Presidential Voting." *American Political Science Review* 74 (3):670–684.

Semmingsen, Ingrid. 1978. *Norway to America: A History of the Migration* Einar Haugen, trans. Minneapolis: University of Minnesota Press.

Şen, Faruk. 1993. "1961 bis 1993: Eine kurze Geschichte der Türken in

Deutschland." Pp. 17–36 in Claus Leggewie and Zafer Şenocak, eds., *Deutsche Türken: Das Ende der Geduld / Türk Almanlar: Sabrın sonu.* Reinbek bei Hamburg: Rowohlt.

Shirer, William. 1960. *The Rise and Fall of the Third Reich: A History of Nazi Germany.* New York: Simon and Schuster.

Sigelman, Lee, James W. Shockey, and Carol K. Sigelman. 1993. "Ethnic Stereotyping: A Black-White Comparison." Pp. 104–126 in Paul M. Sniderman, Philip E. Tetlock, and Edward G. Carmines, eds., *Prejudice, Politics, and the American Dilemma.* Stanford: Stanford University Press.

Siméant, Johanna. 1998. *La cause des sans-papiers.* Paris: Presses de Sciences Po.

Simmons, Harvey G. 1996. *The French National Front: The Extremist Challenge to Democracy.* Boulder, CO: Westview.

Simon, Julian L. 1989. *The Economic Consequences of Immigration.* Cambridge: Basil Blackwell and the Cato Institute.

Simon, Rita J. 1987. "Immigration and American Attitudes." *Public Opinion* 10 (2):47–50.

——— 1997. *In the Golden Land: A Century of Russian and Soviet Jewish Immigration in America.* Westport, CT: Praeger.

Simon, Rita J., and Susan H. Alexander. 1993. *The Ambivalent Welcome: Print Media, Public Opinion and Immigration.* Westport, CT: Praeger.

Simpson, J. A., and E. S. C. Weiner, eds. 1989. *The Oxford English Dictionary.* Vol. 10, *Moul–Ovum.* 2d ed. Oxford: Clarendon Press.

Skerry, Peter. 1993. *Mexican Americans: The Ambivalent Minority.* New York: Free Press.

Slater, Courtenay. 1996. *Business Statistics of the United States.* 1995 ed. Lanham, MD: Bernan Press.

Slater, Courtenay M., and George E. Hall. 1993. *1993 County and City Extra: Annual Metro, City and County Data Book.* Lanham, MD: Bernan Press.

Smith, Howard R. 1955. *Economic History of the United States.* New York: Ronald Press.

Smith, Rogers M. 1997. *Civic Ideals: Conflicting Visions of Citizenship in U.S. History.* New Haven: Yale University Press.

SOFRES. 1989. *L'état de l'opinion: Clés pour 1989.* Paris: Éditions du Seuil.

Soper, J. Christopher, and Joel S. Fetzer. In press. "Religion and Politics in a Secular Europe: Cutting against the Grain." In Clyde Wilcox and Ted G. Jelen, eds., *The One, the Few, and the Many: Religion and Politics in Comparative Perspective.* Cambridge: Cambridge University Press.

Sorin, Gerald. 1992. *A Time for Building: The Third Migration, 1880–1920.* Baltimore: Johns Hopkins University Press.

Soule, Suzanne R. 1997. "Affect or the Economy? Public Opinion and Anti-Immigrant Sentiment." Paper presented at the annual meeting of the American Political Science Association, Washington, DC.

Soysal, Yasemin Nuhoğlu. 1994. *Limits of Citizenship: Migrants and Postnational Membership in Europe.* Chicago: University of Chicago Press.

Der Spiegel. 1993. "Weder Heimat noch Freunde." *Der Spiegel* 23:16–29.

Statistics Directorate. 1997. *Main Economic Indicators, October 1997.* Paris: Organization for Economic Co-operation and Development.
1998. *Main Economic Indicators, March 1998.* Paris: Organization for Economic Co-operation and Development.
Statistisches Bundesamt. 1956. *Statistisches Jahrbuch für die Bundesrepublik Deutschland 1957.* Stuttgart: Verlag W. Kohlhammer.
1965. *Statistisches Jahrbuch für die Bundesrepublik Deutschland 1964.* Stuttgart: Verlag W. Kohlhammer.
1967. *Statistisches Jahrbuch für die Bundesrepublik Deutschland 1966.* Stuttgart: Verlag W. Kohlhammer.
1972. *Bevölkerung und Wirtschaft 1872–1972.* Stuttgart: Verlag W. Kohlhammer.
1981. *Statistisches Jahrbuch für die Bundesrepublik Deutschland 1980.* Stuttgart: Verlag W. Kohlhammer.
1988. *Statistisches Jahrbuch für die Bundesrepublik Deutschland.* Stuttgart: Verlag W. Kohlhammer.
1989. *Statistisches Jahrbuch für die Bundesrepublik Deutschland.* Stuttgart: Metzler-Poeschel.
1990. *Wirtschaft und Statistik.* 1/1990. Wiesbaden: Statistisches Bundesamt.
1991. *Wirtschaft und Statistik.* 1/1991. Wiesbaden: Statistisches Bundesamt.
1992a. *Wirtschaft und Statistik.* 1/1992. Wiesbaden: Statistisches Bundesamt.
1992b. *Statistisches Jahrbuch 1992 für die Bundesrepublik Deutschland.* Stuttgart: Metzler-Poeschel.
1993a. *Wirtschaft und Statistik.* 1/1993. Wiesbaden: Statistisches Bundesamt.
1993b. *Wirtschaft und Statistik.* 12/1993. Wiesbaden: Statistisches Bundesamt.
1994a. *Bevölkerung und Erwerbstätigkeit.* Technical ser. 1, subpart 2, *Ausländer, 1993.* Stuttgart: Metzler-Poeschel.
1994b. *Statistisches Jahrbuch 1994 für die Bundesrepublik Deutschland.* Stuttgart: Verlag W. Kohlhammer.
1994c. *Volkswirtschaftliche Gesamtrechnungen.* Technical ser. 18, subpart 1.3, *Konten und Standardtabellen, 1993 Hauptbericht.* Wiesbaden: Statistisches Bundesamt.
1995a. *Wirtschaft und Statistik.* 1/1995. Wiesbaden: Statistisches Bundesamt.
1995b. Telefax to author, February 16. Unpublished data based on Bevölkerungsfortschreibung.
1996. *Statistisches Jahrbuch 1996 für die Bundesrepublik Deutschland.* Stuttgart: Metzler-Poeschel.
1998a. *Statistisches Jahrbuch 1998 für die Bundesrepublik Deutschland.* Stuttgart: Metzler-Poeschel.
1998b. Telefax to author, July 31. Unpublished data based on Bevölkerungsfortschreibung.

Statistisches Reichsamt. 1922. *Statistisches Jahrbuch für das Deutsche Reich 1921/22.* Berlin: Verlag für Politik und Wirtshaft.

1926. *Statistisches Jahrbuch für das Deutsche Reich 1926.* Berlin: Verlag von Reimar Hobbing.

1933. *Statistisches Jahrbuch für das Deutsche Reich 1933.* Berlin: Verlag von Reimar Hobbing.

1942. *Statistisches Jahrbuch für das Deutsche Reich 1941/42.* Berlin: Statistisches Reichsamt.

Stonequist, Everett V. 1961. *The Marginal Man: A Study in Personality and Culture Conflict.* New York: Russell & Russell.

Svoray, Yaron, and Nick Taylor. 1994. *In Hitler's Shadow: An Israeli's Amazing Journey inside Germany's Neo-Nazi Movement.* New York: Nan A. Talese.

Tajfel, Henri. 1970. "Experiments in Intergroup Discrimination." *Scientific American* 233:96–102.

Takaki, Ronald. 1989. *Strangers from a Different Shore: A History of Asian Americans.* New York: Penguin.

Tapinos, Georges. 1975. *L'immigration étrangère en France 1946–1973.* Institut national d'études démographiques, Travaux et Documents, Cahier no. 71. Paris: Presses Universitaires de France.

Tec, Nechama. 1986. *When Light Pierced the Darkness: Christian Rescue of Jews in Nazi-Occupied Poland.* Oxford: Oxford University Press.

1997a. Telephone conversation with author, October 23.

1997b. "Foreword." Pp. vii-xiii in Michael Phayer and Eva Fleischner, *Cries in the Night: Women Who Challenged the Holocaust.* Kansas City, MO: Sheed & Ward.

Thomas, Gordon, and Max Morgan-Witts. 1974. *Voyage of the Damned.* London: Hodder and Stoughton.

Thorwald, Jürgen. 1995. *Es begann an der Weichsel: Flucht und Vertreibung der Deutschen aus dem Osten.* Munich: Knaur.

Thränhardt, Dietrich. 1994. "Integration in Germany." Universität Münster. Unpublished manuscript.

Tincq, Henri. 1992. "Le Front National vingt ans après: La résistance des Églises." *Le Monde,* February 5, section "politique."

Tobin, James. 1958. "Estimation of Relationships for Limited Dependent Variables." *Econometrica* 26:24–36.

Töppen, Max. 1969. *Geschichte Masurens: Ein Beitrag zur preußischen Landes- und Kulturgeschichte.* Reprint of 1870 Danzig ed. Aalen: Scientia.

Tribalat, Michèle. 1991. *Cent ans d'immigration, étrangers d'hier Français d'aujourd'hui: Apport démographique, dynamique familiale et économique de l'immigration étrangère.* Paris: Presses Universitaires de France and Institut National d'Études Démographiques.

1995. *Faire France: Une enquête sur les immigrés et leurs enfants.* Paris: Éditions La Découverte.

Troeltsch, Ernst. 1960. *The Social Teaching of the Christian Churches.* Vol. 1. Olive Wyon, trans. New York: Harper & Brothers.

Tucker, Robert C., ed. 1978. *The Marx-Engels Reader.* 2d ed. New York: Norton.

Tufte, Edward R. 1978. *Political Control of the Economy.* Princeton: Princeton University Press.

Valdés, Dennis Nodín. 1988. "Mexican Revolutionary Nationalism and Repatriation during the Great Depression." *Mexican Studies/Estudios mexicanos* 4:1–23.

van Braght, Thieleman J. [1660] 1972. *The Bloody Theater, or, Martyrs' Mirror of the Defenseless Christians, Who Baptized Only Upon Confession of Faith, and Who Suffered and Died for the Testimony of Jesus, Their Saviour, From the Time of Christ to the Year A.D. 1660.* Joseph F. Sohm, trans. Scottsdale, PA: Herald Press.

Varennes, Harvey. 1993. "The Question of European Nationalism." Pp. 223–240 in Thomas M. Wilson and M. Estellie Smith, eds., *Cultural Change and the New Europe: Perspectives on the European Community.* Boulder, CO: Westview.

Veen, Hans-Joachim, Norbert Lepszy, and Peter Mnich. 1993. *The Republikaner Party in Germany: Right-Wing Menace or Protest Catchall?* Westport, CT: Praeger.

Vega, Bernardo. 1984. *Memoirs of Bernardo Vega: A Contribution to the History of the Puerto Rican Community in New York.* César Andreu Iglesias, ed.; Juan Flores, trans. New York: *Monthly Review* Press.

Vertone, Teodosio. 1977. "Antécédents et causes des événements d'Aigues-Mortes." *Affari sociali internazionali* 3–4 (fall–winter):105–138.

Villa, Pierre. 1993. *Une analyse macroéconomique de la France au XXe siècle.* Paris: CNRS éditions.

Wald, Kenneth D. 1992. *Religion and Politics in the United States.* 2d ed. Washington, DC: Congressional Quarterly.

Wallraff, Günter. 1985. *Ganz unten.* Cologne: Kiepenheuer & Witsch.

Watts, Meredith W. 1997. *Xenophobia in United Germany: Generations, Modernizations, and Ideology.* New York: St. Martin's.

Weber, Reinhold. 1983. *Masuren: Geschichte – Land und Leute.* Leer: Verlag Gerhard Rautenberg.

Weil, Patrick. 1991. *La France et ses étrangers: L'aventure d'une politique de l'immigration de 1938 à nos jours.* Paris: Gallimard/Éditions Calmann-Lévy.

———. 1995. "Racisme et discrimination dans la politique française de l'immigration, 1938–1945/1974–1995." *Vingtième siècle: Revue d'histoire*, no. 67 (July–September), pp. 77–102.

———. 1998. "The Transformation of Immigration Policies. Immigration Control and Nationality Laws in Europe: A Comparative Approach." EUI Working Paper EUF no. 98/5. Florence: European University Institute.

Wertheimer, Jack. 1987. *Unwelcome Strangers: East European Jews in Imperial Germany.* New York: Oxford University Press.

White, Michael J., and Afaf Omer. 1997. "Segregation by Ethnicity and Immigrant Status in New Jersey." Pp. 375–394 in Thomas J.

Espenshade, ed., *Keys to Successful Immigration: Implications of the New Jersey Experience.* Washington, DC: Urban Institute Press.

Widdis, Randy William. 1998. *With Scarcely a Ripple: Anglo-Canadian Migration into the United States and Western Canada, 1880–1920.* Montreal: McGill-Queen's University Press.

Wihtol de Wenden, Catherine. 1988. *Les immigrés et la politique: Cent cinquante ans d'évolution.* Paris: Presses de la Fondation nationale des sciences politiques.

——— 1994. "Citoyenneté et nationalité: Le cas français." Pp. 41–59 in Bernard Falga, Catherine Wihtol de Wenden, and Claus Leggewie, eds., *De l'immigration à l'intégration en France et en Allemagne.* Paris: Éditions du cerf.

Willems, Helmut. 1995. "Right-Wing Extremism, Racism or Youth Violence?: Explaining Violence against Foreigners in Germany." *New Community* 21 (4):501–523.

Williams, Robin M., Jr. 1947. *The Reduction of Intergroup Tensions: A Survey of Research on Problems of Ethnic, Racial, and Religious Group Relations.* Bulletin 57. New York: Social Science Research Council.

Williamson, Chilton, Jr. 1996. *The Immigration Mystique: America's False Conscience.* New York: Basic Books.

Wirth, Louis. 1945. "The Problem of Minority Groups." Pp. 347–372 in Ralph Linton, ed., *The Science of Man in the World Crisis.* New York: Columbia University Press.

Womack, Anita. 1995. "'Common Threat' Galvanizes Black and Hispanic Working Coalitions." *Black Issues in Higher Education* 12 (15):17–19.

Wyman, Davis S. 1968. *Paper Walls: America and the Refugee Crisis, 1938–1941.* Amherst, MA: University of Massachusetts Press.

——— 1984. *The Abandonment of the Jews: America and the Holocaust, 1941–1945.* New York: Pantheon.

Zaller, John R. 1992. *The Nature and Origins of Mass Opinion.* Cambridge: Cambridge University Press.

Zhu, Liping. 1997. *A Chinaman's Chance: The Chinese on the Rocky Mountain Mining Frontier.* Niwot: University Press of Colorado.

Index

INDEX